Economics:
The User's
Guide

HA-JOON CHANG

Economics: The User's Guide

BLOOMSBURY PUBLISHING

NEW YORK · LONDON · OXFORD · NEW DELHI · SYDNEY

BLOOMSBURY PUBLISHING
Bloomsbury Publishing Inc.
1385 Broadway, New York, NY 10018, USA

BLOOMSBURY, BLOOMSBURY PUBLISHING, and the Diana logo are
trademarks of Bloomsbury Publishing Plc

First published in the United States 2014
This paperback edition published 2015

ISBN: HB: 978-1-62040-812-4; PB: 978-1-62040-814-8; eBook: 978-1-62040-813-1

Library of Congress Cataloging-in-Publication Data is available.

8   10   9   7

Typeset by Hewer Text UK Ltd, Edinburgh
Printed and bound in the U.S.A. by Sheridan Books Inc., Chelsea, Michigan

To find out more about our authors and books visit www.bloomsbury.com
and sign up for our newsletters.

Bloomsbury books may be purchased for business or promotional use.
For information on bulk purchases please contact Macmillan Corporate
and Premium Sales Department at specialmarkets@macmillan.com.

To my parents

Contents

ACKNOWLEDGEMENTS

The idea of writing an introduction to economics that is accessible to the broadest possible audience was first raised by Penguin through my then editor, Will Goodlad, in the autumn of 2011. Will has since then moved on to other things, but he provided helpful inputs into the shaping and the writing of the book, even while he was going through an intense phase of establishing a new venture.

The book could not have been written without Laura Stickney, my editor. It must have been difficult for her, as she had to put up with periods of silence and numerous rewrites of the earlier chapters. However, she put her faith in me and saw me through the process, with only the gentlest prodding and with an enormous amount of excellent advice, both substantive and editorial. I cannot thank her more.

Ivan Mulcahy, my literary agent, as usual, provided very important input. In particular, his suggestions on some of an earlier incomplete draft breathed life back into the book, when the writing process was in danger of losing its momentum, and I was in danger of losing my faith in the book myself.

Peter Ginna, my US editor, also gave me a lot of important input, especially in the final phase of the book.

Numerous friends provided me with help and encouragement, but three individuals deserve a special mention. Duncan Green, William Milberg and Deepak Nayyar read all the chapters (some of them in more than one version) and gave me extremely helpful comments. They also gave me moral support through difficult phases of the project, of which there were many.

Felix Martin provided very important inputs into the shaping of the book from the stage when it was a mere plan. He also read several chapters of the book and given me very helpful comments. Milford Bateman read almost all the chapters of the book and offered very useful comments. Finlay Green also read most of the chapters and suggested many ways in which I could improve the accessibility of my writing.

I would also like to thank many people who read various versions of the book plan or chapters of the book and gave me useful comments. They are, in alphabetical order, Jonathan Aldred, Antonio Andreoni, John Ashton, Roger Backhouse, Stephanie Blankenberg, Aditya Chakrabortty, Hasok Chang, Victoria Chick, Michele Clara, Gary Dymski, Ilene Grabel, Geoffrey Hodgson, Adriana Kocornik-Mina, David Kucera, Costas Lapavitsas, Sangheon Lee, Carlos Lopez-Gomez, Tiago Mata, Gay Meeks, Seumas Milne, Dimitris Milonakis, Brett Scott, Jeff Sommers, Daniel Tudor, Bhaskar Vira and Yuan Yang.

My PhD student and research assistant, Ming Leong Kuan, provided me with extremely efficient and creative help in securing and processing the necessary data for the book. Given the importance that I am attaching to 'real-life numbers' in this book, Ming Leong's assistance was essential in making the book what it is.

During the two years in which I was writing the book, Hee-Jeong, my wife, Yuna, my daughter, and Jin-Gyu, my son, suffered a lot but gave me a huge amount of love and support. Hee-Jeong and Yuna also read many of the chapters and gave me a lot of very helpful comments. Jin-Gyu kept reminding me that there are more important things in life than economics, such as Dr Who, Hercule Poirot and Harry Potter.

My little family in England would not have had the solidity it has without the love of our extended family back in Korea. My parents-in-law have showered us with a lot of loving support. My own parents have been a continuous source of love and encouragement for us. Above all, I would not be what I am today without their sacrifice and nurturing. I dedicate the book to them.

Why Bother?

WHY DO YOU NEED TO LEARN ECONOMICS?

Why Are People Not Very Interested in Economics?

Since you have picked up this book, you probably have at least a passing interest in economics. Even so, you may be reading this with some trepidation. Economics is supposed to be difficult – perhaps not physics-difficult but demanding enough. Some of you may remember hearing an economist on the radio making an argument that sounded questionable but accepting it because, after all, he is the expert, and you haven't even read a proper book on economics.

But is economics really that difficult? It doesn't need to be – if it is explained in plain terms. In my previous book, *23 Things They Don't Tell You about Capitalism*, I even stuck my neck out and said that 95 per cent of economics is common sense – made to look difficult, with the use of jargons and mathematics.

Economics is not alone in appearing to be more difficult to outsiders than it really is. In any profession that involves some technical competence – be it economics, plumbing or medicine – jargons that facilitate communication within the profession make its communication with outsiders more difficult. A little more cynically, all technical professions have an incentive to make themselves look more complicated than they really are so that they can justify the high fees their members charge for their services.

Even considering all this, economics has been uniquely successful in making the general public reluctant to engage with its territory. People express strong opinions on all sorts of things despite not having the appropriate expertise: climate change, gay marriage, the Iraq War, nuclear power stations. But when it comes to economic issues, many people are not even interested, not to speak of not having a strong opinion about them. When was the last time you had a debate on the future of the Euro, inequality in China or the future of the American manufacturing industry? These issues can have a huge impact on your life, wherever you live, by affecting, positively or negatively, your job prospects, your wage and eventually your pension, but you probably haven't thought about them seriously.

This curious state of affairs is only partly explained by the fact that economic issues lack the visceral appeals that things like love, dislocation, death and war have. It exists mainly because, especially in the last few decades, people have been led to believe that, like physics or chemistry, economics is a 'science', in which there is only one correct answer to everything; thus non-experts should simply accept the 'professional consensus' and stop thinking about it. Gregory Mankiw, the Harvard economics professor and the author of one of the most popular economics textbooks, says: 'Economists like to strike the pose of a scientist. I know, because I often do it myself. When I teach undergraduates, I very consciously describe the field of economics as a science, so no student would start the course thinking he was embarking on some squishy academic endeavor.'[1]

As it will become clearer throughout the book, however, economics can never be a science in the sense that physics or chemistry is. There are many different types of economic theory, each emphasizing different aspects of complex reality, making different moral and political value judgements and drawing different conclusions. Moreover, economic theories constantly fail to predict real-world developments even in areas on which they focus, not least because human beings have their own free will, unlike chemical molecules or physical objects.[2]

If there is no one right answer in economics, then we cannot leave it to the experts alone. This means that every responsible citizen needs to learn some economics. By this I don't mean picking up a thick textbook and absorbing one particular economic point of view. What is needed is to learn economics in such a way that one becomes aware of different types of economic arguments and develops the critical faculty to judge which argument makes most sense in a given economic circumstance and in light of which moral values and political goals (note that I am not saying 'which argument is correct'). This requires a book that discusses economics in a way that has not been tried, which I believe this book does.

How Is This Book Different?

How is this book different from other introductory books to economics?

One difference is that I take my readers seriously. And I mean it. This book will not be a digested version of some complicated eternal truth. I introduce my readers to many different ways of analysing the economy in the belief that they are perfectly capable of judging between different approaches. I do not eschew discussing the most fundamental methodological issues in economics, such as whether it can be a science or what role moral values do (and should) play in economics. Whenever possible, I try to reveal the assumptions underlying different economic theories so that readers can make their own judgements about their realism and plausibility. I also tell my readers how numbers in economics are defined and put together, urging them not to take them as something as objective as, say, the weight of an elephant or the temperature of a pot of water.* In short, I try to explain to my reader how to think, rather than what to think.

Engaging the reader at the deepest level of analysis, however, does not mean that the book is going to be difficult. There is nothing in this book that the reader cannot understand, as far as he or she has had a secondary education. All I ask of my readers is the curiosity to find out what is really going on and the patience to read through a few paragraphs at the same time.

Another critical difference with other economics books is that my book contains a lot of information on the real world. And when I say 'world', I mean it. This book provides information on many different countries. This is not to say that all countries get equal attention. But, unlike most other books in economics, the information will not be confined to one or two countries or to one type of country (say, rich countries or poor countries). Much of the information provided will be numbers: how large the world economy is, how much of it is produced by the US or Brazil, what proportions of their outputs China or the Democratic Republic of Congo invest, how long people work in Greece or Germany. But this will be complemented by qualitative information on institutional arrangements, historical

---

* But then scientists will tell you that even those numbers are not totally objective, if you asked them.

backgrounds, typical policy and the like. The hope is that at the end of this book the reader can say that he or she has some feel about the way in which the economy actually works in the real world.

'And now for something completely different . . .'*

---

* As they used to say on *Monty Python's Flying Circus*.

How to Read This Book

I realize that not all readers are ready to spend a lot of time on this book, at least to begin with. Therefore, I suggest several different ways of reading this book, depending on how much time you think you can afford.

If you have ten minutes: Read the chapter titles and the first page of each chapter. If I am lucky, at the end of those ten minutes, you may suddenly find that you have a couple of hours to spare.

If you have a couple of hours: Read Chapters 1 and 2 and then the Epilogue. Flick through the rest.

If you have half a day: Read only the headlines – section titles and the summaries in italics that occur every few paragraphs. If you are a fast reader, you may also cram in the introductory section and the concluding remarks in each chapter.

If you have the time and the patience to read through: Please do. That will be the most effective way. And you will make me very happy. But even then you can skip bits that don't interest you much and read only the headlines in those bits.

PART ONE

Getting
Used to It

CHAPTER 1

Life, the Universe and Everything

WHAT IS ECONOMICS?

What is economics?

A reader who is not familiar with the subject might reckon that it is the study of the economy. After all, chemistry is the study of chemicals, biology is the study of living things, and sociology is the study of society, so economics must be the study of the economy.

But according to some of the most popular economics books of our time, economics is much more than that. According to them, economics is about the Ultimate Question – of 'Life, the Universe and Everything' – as in *The Hitchhiker's Guide to the Galaxy*, the cult comedy science fiction by Douglas Adams, which was made into a movie in 2005, with Martin 'The Hobbit' Freeman in the leading role.

According to Tim Harford, the *Financial Times* journalist and the author of the successful book *The Undercover Economist*, economics is about Life – he has named his second book *The Logic of Life*.

No economist has yet claimed that economics can explain the Universe. The Universe remains, for now, the turf of physicists, whom most economists have for centuries been looking up to as their role models, in their desire to make their subject a true science.* But some economists have come close – they have claimed that economics is about 'the world'. For example, the subtitle of the second volume in Robert Frank's popular *Economic Naturalist* series is *How Economics Helps You Make Sense of Your World*.

Then there is the Everything bit. The subtitle of *Logic of Life* is *Uncovering the New Economics of Everything*. According to its subtitle, *Freakonomics* by Steven Levitt and Stephen Dubner – probably the best-known economics

---

* This is known as a case of physics envy.

book of our time – is an exploration of the *Hidden Side of Everything*. Robert Frank agrees, even though he is far more modest in his claim. In the subtitle of his first *Economic Naturalist* book, he only said *Why Economics Explains Almost Everything* (emphasis added).

So, there we go. Economics is (almost) about Life, the Universe and Everything.*

When you think about it, this is some claim coming from a subject that has spectacularly failed in what most non-economists think is its main job – that is, explaining the economy.

In the run-up to the 2008 financial crisis, the majority of the economics profession was preaching to the world that markets are rarely wrong and that modern economics has found ways to iron out those few wrinkles that markets may have; Robert Lucas, the 1995 winner of the Nobel Prize in Economics,† had declared in 2003 that the 'problem of depression prevention has been solved'.[1] So most economists were caught completely by surprise by the 2008 global financial crisis.‡ Not only that, they have not been able to come up with decent solutions to the ongoing aftermaths of that crisis.

Given all this, economics seems to suffer from a serious case of megalomania – how can a subject that cannot even manage to explain its own area very well claim to explain (almost) everything?

Economics Is the Study of Rational Human Choice . . .

You may think I am being unfair. Aren't all these books aimed at the mass market, where competition for readership is fierce, and therefore publishers and authors are tempted to hype things up? Surely, you would think, serious

---

*   Incidentally, this should make economists' jobs really easy, because we already know the answer to that Ultimate Question: it is 42. But let's leave that subject aside for the moment.

†   The Nobel Prize in Economics is not a real Nobel prize. Unlike the original Nobel Prizes (Physics, Chemistry, Physiology, Medicine, Literature and Peace), established by the Swedish industrialist Alfred Nobel at the end of the nineteenth century, the economics prize was established by the Swedish central bank (Sveriges Riksbank) in 1968 and is thus officially called the Sveriges Riksbank Prize in Economic Sciences in Memory of Alfred Nobel.

‡   But then this would not have surprised the late John Kenneth Galbraith (1908–2006), who once deadpanned that 'the only function of economic forecasting is to make astrology respectable'.

academic discourses would not make such a grand claim that the subject is about 'everything'.

These titles *are* hyped up. But the point is that they are hyped up in a particular way. The hypes could have been something along the line of 'how economics explains everything about the economy', but they are instead along the lines of 'how economics can explain not just the economy but everything else as well'.

The hypes are of this particular variety because of the way in which the currently dominant school of economics, that is, the so-called Neoclassical school, defines economics. The standard Neoclassical definition of economics, the variants of which are still used, is given in the 1932 book by Lionel Robbins, *An Essay on the Nature and Significance of Economic Science*. In the book, Robbins defined economics as 'the science which studies human behaviour as a relationship between ends and scarce means which have alternative uses'.

In this view, economics is defined by its theoretical approach, rather than its subject matter. Economics is a study of **rational choice**, that is, choice made on the basis of deliberate, systematic calculation of the maximum extent to which the ends can be met by using the inevitably scarce means. The subject matter of the calculation can be anything – marriage, having children, crime or drug addiction, as Gary Becker, the famous Chicago economist and the winner of 1992 Nobel Prize in Economics, has written about – and not just 'economic' issues, as non-economists would define them, such as jobs, money or international trade. When Becker titled his 1976 book *The Economic Approach to Human Behaviour*, he was really declaring without the hype that economics *is* about everything.

This trend of applying the so-called economic approach to everything, called by its critics 'economics imperialism', has reached its apex recently in books like *Freakonomics*. Little of *Freakonomics* is actually about economic issues as most people would define them. It talks about Japanese sumo wrestlers, American schoolteachers, Chicago drug gangs, participants in the TV quiz show *The Weakest Link*, real estate agents and the Ku Klux Klan.

Most people would think (and the authors also admit) that none of these people, except real estate agents and drug gangs, have anything to do with economics. But, from the point of view of most economists today, how Japanese sumo wrestlers collude to help each other out or how American schoolteachers fabricate their pupils' marks to get better job assessments are as legitimate subjects of economics as whether Greece should stay in the Eurozone, how Samsung and Apple fight it out in the smartphone market or how we can reduce youth unemployment in Spain (which is over 55 per cent at the time of writing). To those economists, those 'economic' issues do not have privileged status in economics, they are just some of many things (oh, I forgot, some of everything) that economics can explain, because they define their subject in terms of its theoretical approach, rather than its subject matter.

. . . or Is It the Study of the Economy?

An obvious alternative definition of economics, which I have been implying, is that it is the study of the economy. But what *is* the economy?

The economy is about money – or is it?

The most intuitive answer to most readers may be that the economy is anything to do with money – not having it, earning it, spending it, running out of it, saving it, borrowing it and repaying it. This is not quite right, but it is a good starting point for thinking about the economy – and economics.

Now, when we talk of the economy being about money, we are not really talking about physical money. Physical money – be it a banknote, a gold coin or the huge, virtually immovable stones that were used as money in some Pacific islands – is only a symbol. **Money** is a symbol of what others in your society owe you, or your claim on particular amounts of the society's resources.[2]

How money and other financial claims – such as company shares, derivatives and many complex financial products, which I will explain in later chapters – are created, sold and bought is one huge area of economics, called financial economics. These days, given the dominance of the financial industry in many countries, a lot of people equate economics with financial economics, but it is actually only a small part of economics.

Your money – or the claims you have over resources – may be generated in a number of different ways. And a lot of economics is (or should be) about those.

The most common way to get money is to have a job

The most common way to get money – unless you have been born into it – is to have a job (including being your own boss) and earn money from it. So, a lot of economics is about **jobs**. We can reflect on jobs from different perspectives.

Jobs can be understood from the point of view of the individual worker. Whether you get a job and how much you are paid for it depends on the skills you have and how many demands there are for them. You may get very high wages because you have very rare skills, like Cristiano Ronaldo, the football player. You may lose your job (or become unemployed) because someone invents a machine that can do what you do 100 times faster – as happened to Mr Bucket, Charlie's father, a toothpaste cap-screwer, in the 2005 movie version of Roald Dahl's *Charlie and the Chocolate Factory*.* Or you have to accept lower wages or worse working conditions because your company is losing money thanks to cheaper imports from, say, China. And so on. So, in order to understand jobs even at the individual level, we need to know about skills, technological innovation and international trade.

Wages and working conditions are also deeply affected by 'political' decisions to change the very scope and the characteristics of the labour market (I have put 'political' in quotation marks, as in the end the boundary between economics and politics is blurry, but that is a topic for later – see Chapter 11). The accession of the Eastern European countries to the European Union has had huge impacts on the wages and behaviours of Western European workers, by suddenly expanding the supply of workers in their labour markets. The restriction on child labour in the late nineteenth century and early twentieth centuries had the opposite effect of shrinking the boundary of the labour market – suddenly a large proportion of the potential employees were shut out of the labour market. Regulations on working hours, working conditions and minimum wages are examples of less dramatic 'political' decisions that affect our jobs.

---

* In the original novel, Mr Bucket lost his job because his factory went bust rather than because it bought a machine to replace him.

There are also a lot of transfers of money going on in the economy

In addition to holding down a job, you can get money through **transfers** – that is, by simply being given it. This can be either in the form of cash or 'in kind', that is, direct provision of particular goods (e.g., food) or services (e.g., primary education). Whether in cash or in kind, these transfers can be made in a number of different ways.

There are transfers made by 'people you know'. Examples include parental support for children, people taking care of elderly family members, gifts from local community members, say, for your daughter's wedding.

Then there is charitable giving, that is, transfer voluntarily made to strangers. People – sometimes individually sometimes collectively (e.g., through corporations or voluntary associations) – give to charities that help others.

In terms of its quantity, charitable giving is overshadowed in many multiples by transfers made through governments, which tax some people to subsidize others. So a lot of economics is naturally about these things – or the areas of economics known as public economics.

Even in very poor countries, there are some government schemes to give cash or goods in kind (e.g., free grains) to those who are in the worst positions (e.g., the aged, the disabled, the starving). But the richer societies, especially those in Europe, have transfer schemes that are much more comprehensive in scope and generous in amounts. This is known as the **welfare state** and is based on **progressive taxation** (those who earn more paying proportionally larger shares of their incomes in taxes) and **universal benefits** (where everyone, not just the poorest or the disabled, is entitled to a minimum income and to basic services, such as health care and education).

Resources earned or transferred get consumed in goods or services

Once you gain access to resources, whether through jobs or transfers, you consume them. As physical beings, we need to consume some minimum amount of food, clothes, energy, housing, and other **goods** to fulfil our basic needs. And then we consume other goods for 'higher' mental wants – books, musical instruments, exercise equipment, TV, computers and so on. We also buy and consume **services** – a bus ride, a haircut, a dinner at a restaurant or even a holiday abroad.[3]

So a lot of economics is devoted to the study of **consumption** – how people allocate money between different types of goods and services, how they make choices between competing varieties of the same product, how they are manipulated and/or informed by advertisements, how companies spend money to build their 'brand images' and so on.

Ultimately goods and services have to be produced

In order to be consumed, these goods and services have to be produced in the first place – goods in farms and factories and services in offices and shops. This is the realm of **production** – an area of economics that has been rather neglected since the Neoclassical school, which puts emphasis on exchange and consumption, became dominant in the 1960s.

In standard economics textbooks, production appears as a 'black box', in which somehow quantities of **labour** (work by humans) and **capital** (machines and tools) are combined to produce the goods and services. There is little recognition that production is a lot more than combining some abstract quanta called labour and capital and involves getting many 'nitty-gritty' things right. And these are things that most readers may not normally have associated with economics, despite their crucial importance for the economy: how the factory is physically organized, how to control the workers or deal with trade unions, how to systematically improve the technologies used through research.

Most economists are very happy to leave the study of these things to 'other people' – engineers and business managers. But, when you think about it, production is the ultimate foundation of any economy. Indeed, the changes in the sphere of production usually have been the most powerful sources of social change. Our modern world has been made by the series of changes in technologies and institutions relating to the sphere of production that have been made since the Industrial Revolution. The economics profession, and the rest of us whose views of the economy are informed by it, need to pay far more attention to production than currently.

Concluding Remarks: Economics as the Study of the Economy

My belief is that economics should be defined not in terms of its methodology, or theoretical approach, but in terms of its subject matter, as is the case with all other disciplines. The subject matter of economics should be the economy – which involves money, work, technology, international trade, taxes and other things that have to do with the ways in which we produce goods and services, distribute the incomes generated in the process and consume the things thus produced – rather than 'Life, the Universe and Everything' (or 'almost everything'), as many economists think.

Defining economics in this way makes this book unlike most other economics books in one fundamental way.

As they define economics in terms of its methodology, most economics books assume that there is only one right way of 'doing economics' – that is, the Neoclassical approach. The worst examples won't even tell you that there are other schools of economics than the Neoclassical one.

By defining economics in terms of the subject matter, this book highlights the fact that there are many different ways of doing economics, each with its emphases, blind spots, strengths and weaknesses. After all, what we want from economics is the best possible explanation of various economic phenomena rather than a constant 'proof' that a particular economic theory can explain not just the economy but everything.

Further Reading

R. BACKHOUSE
The Puzzle of Modern Economics: Science or Ideology? (Cambridge: Cambridge University Press, 2012).

B. FINE AND D. MILONAKIS
From Economics Imperialism to Freakonomics: The Shifting Boundaries between Economics and the Other Social Sciences (London: Routledge, 2009).

CHAPTER 2

From Pin
to PIN

CAPITALISM 1776 AND 2014

From Pin to PIN

What is the first ever thing written about in economics? Gold? Land? Banking? Or international trade?

The answer is the pin.

Not the one that you use for your credit cards. But that little metal thing that most of you do *not* use – that is, unless you have long hair and like to keep it tidy or make your own clothes.

The making of the pin is the subject of the very first chapter of what is commonly (albeit mistakenly)[1] considered to be the first economics book, namely, *An Inquiry into the Nature and Causes of the Wealth of Nations*, by Adam Smith (1723–90).

Smith starts his book by arguing that the ultimate source of increase in wealth lies in the increase in productivity through greater **division of labour**, which refers to the division of production processes into smaller, specialized parts. He argued that this increases productivity in three ways. First, by repeating the same one or two tasks, workers become good at what they do more quickly ('practice makes perfect'). Second, by specializing, workers do not have to spend time moving – physically and mentally – between different tasks (reduction in 'transition costs'). Last, but not least, a finer breakdown of the process makes each step easier to be automated and thus be performed at superhuman speed (mechanization).

And to illustrate this point, Smith discusses how ten people dividing up the production process of making a pin and specializing in one or two of the sub-processes can produce 48,000 pins (or 4,800 pins per person) a day. Compare this to the at most 20 pins each of them can produce a day, Smith pointed out, if each individual worker performed the whole process alone.

Smith called the pin manufacture a 'trifling' example and later went on to note how more complicated the divisions of labour for other products are, but there is no denying that he lived in a time when ten people working together to make a pin was still considered cool – well, at least cool enough to front someone's would-be *magnum opus* in what then was a cutting-edge subject.

The next two and a half centuries have seen dramatic developments in technology, driven by mechanization and the use of chemical processes, not least in the pin industry. Two generations after Smith, the output per worker had nearly doubled. Following Smith's example, Charles Babbage, the nineteenth-century mathematician who is known as the conceptual father of the computer, studied pin factories in 1832.* He found that they were producing about 8,000 pins per worker a day. 150 more years of technological progress increased productivity by yet another 100 times, to 800,000 pins per worker per day, according to the 1980 study by the late Clifford Pratten, a Cambridge economist.[2]

The increase in the productivity of making the same thing, such as the pin, is only one part of the story. Today, we produce so many things that people living in Smith's time could only dream about, such as the flying machine, or could not even imagine, such as the microchip, the computer, the fibre-optic cable and numerous other technologies that we need in order to use our pin – sorry, PIN.

All Change: How the Actors and the Institutions of Capitalism Have Changed

It is not only production technologies – or how things are made – that have changed between Adam Smith's time and ours. **Economic actors** – or those who engage in economic activities – and **economic institutions** – or the rules regarding how production and other economic activities are organized – have also gone through fundamental transformations.

The British economy in Smith's time, which he called the 'commercial society', shared some fundamental similarities with those that we find

---

* Babbage's first computer was called the difference engine, which provided the title for one of the classic 'steam punk' sci-fi novels by William Gibson and Bruce Sterling.

in most of today's economies. Otherwise his work would be irrelevant. Unlike most other economies of the time (the other exceptions being the Netherlands, Belgium and parts of Italy), it was already 'capitalist'.

So what is the capitalist economy, or **capitalism**? It is an economy in which production is organized in pursuit of profit, rather than for own consumption (as in **subsistence farming**, where you grow your own food) or for political obligations (as in feudal societies or in socialist economies, where political authorities, respectively aristocrats and the central planning authority, tell you what to produce).

Profit is the difference between what you earn by selling something in the market (this is known as the sales revenue, or simply **revenue**) and the **costs** of all the inputs that have gone into the production of it. In the case of the pin factory, its profit would be the difference between the revenue from selling the pins and the costs that it has incurred in making them – the steel wire that has been turned into pins, the wages for its workers, the rent for the factory building and so on.

Capitalism is organized by capitalists, or those who own **capital goods**. Capital goods are also known as the **means of production** and refer to durable inputs into the production process (for example, machines, but not, say, raw materials). In everyday usage, we also use the term 'capital' for the money invested in a business venture.*

Capitalists own the means of production either directly or, more commonly these days, indirectly by owning **shares** (or **stocks**) in a company – that is, proportional claims on the total value of the company – that owns those means of production. Capitalists hire other people on a commercial basis to operate these means of production. These people are known as **wage labourers**, or simply workers. Capitalists make profits by producing things and selling them to other people through the **market**, which is where goods and services are bought and sold. Smith believed that **competition** among sellers in the market will ensure that profit-seeking producers will produce at the lowest possible costs, thereby benefiting everyone.

However, the similarities between Smith's capitalism and today's capitalism do not stretch much beyond those basic aspects. There are huge

---

* In economics theory, this is known as finance capital or money capital.

differences between the two eras in terms of how these essential characteristics – private ownership of means of production, profit-seeking, wage
employment and market exchange – are actually translated into realities.

Capitalists are different

In Adam Smith's day, most factories (and farms) were owned and run by
single individual capitalists or by partnerships made up of a small number of
individuals who knew and understood each other. These capitalists were usually personally involved in production – often physically on the factory floor,
ordering their workers about, swearing at them and even beating them up.

Today, most factories are owned and operated by 'unnatural' persons,
namely, corporations. These corporations are 'persons' only in the legal
sense. They are in turn owned by a multitude of individuals, who buy shares
in them and part-own them. But being a shareholder does not make you a
capitalist in the classical sense. Owning 300 of Volkswagen's 300 million
shares does not entitle you to fly to its factory in, say, Wolfsburg, Germany
and order 'your' workers about in 'your' factory for one-millionth of their
working time. Ownership of the enterprise and control of its operations are
largely separated in the largest enterprises.

Today's owners in most large corporations have only **limited liabilities**.
In a limited liability company (LLC) or a public limited company (PLC), if
something goes wrong with the company, shareholders only lose the money
invested in their shares and that is that. In Smith's time, most company
owners had unlimited liabilities, which meant that when the business failed,
they had to sell their own personal assets to pay back the debts, failing
which they ended up in a debtors' prison.* Smith was against the principle
of limited liability. He argued that those who manage limited liability companies without owning them are playing with 'other people's money' (his
phrase, and the title of a famous play and then 1991 movie, starring Danny
DeVito) and thus won't be as vigilant in their management as those who
have to risk everything they have.

Companies are organized very differently from in Smith's days too, whatever the ownership form. In Smith's day, most companies were small with

---

* A small number of companies engaged in risky ventures of national significance, such as colonial
expansion (the East India Companies of Britain and of the Netherlands) or large-scale banking, were
allowed to be based on limited liabilities.

one production site under a simple command structure made up of a few foremen and ordinary workers, and perhaps a 'caretaker' (which is what the hired manager was called then). Today, many companies are huge, often employing tens of thousands of workers or even millions of them all over the world. Walmart employs 2.1 million people, while McDonald's, including franchises,* employs around 1.8 million people. They have complicated internal structures, variously made up of divisions, profit centres, semi-autonomous units and what not, hiring people with complicated job specifications and pay grades within a complex, bureaucratic command structure.

Workers are different too

In Smith's time, most people did *not* work for capitalists as wage labourers. The majority of people still worked in agriculture even in Western Europe, where capitalism was then most advanced.[3] A small minority of them worked as wage labourers for agricultural capitalists, but most of them were either small subsistence farmers or **tenants** (those who rent land and pay a proportion of their output in return) of aristocratic **landlords**.

During this era, even many of those who worked for capitalists were not wage labourers. There were still slaves around. Like tractors or traction animals, slaves were means of production owned by capitalists, especially the plantation owners in the American South, the Caribbean, Brazil and elsewhere. It was two generations after the publication of *The Wealth of Nations* (henceforth *TWON*) that slavery was abolished in Britain (1833). It was nearly a century after *TWON* and after a bloody civil war that slavery was abolished in the US (1862). Brazil abolished it only in 1888.

While a large proportion of people who worked for capitalists were not wage labourers, many wage labourers were people who wouldn't be allowed to become wage labourers today. They were children. Few thought that there was anything wrong with hiring children. In his 1724 book *A Tour Through the Whole Island of Great Britain*, Daniel Defoe, the author of *Robinson Crusoe*, expressed his delight at the fact that in Norwich, then a centre for cotton textiles, 'the very children after 4 or 5 years of age could everyone earn their own bread', thanks to the 1700 ban on the import of calicoes,

---

* Franchises are independent companies using a bigger company's brand and supplies, rather than branches operated directly by the bigger company.

the then prized Indian cotton textile.[4] Child labour subsequently became restricted and then banned, but that was generations after Adam Smith's death in 1790.

Today, in Britain and other rich countries, the picture is completely different.* Children are not allowed to work, except for limited hours for a limited range of things, such as paper rounds. There are no legal slaves. Of the adult workers, around 10 per cent are **self-employed** – that is, they work for themselves – 15–25 per cent work for the government, and the rest are wage labourers working for capitalists.[5]

Markets have changed

In Smith's time, markets were largely local or at most national in scope, except in key commodities that were traded internationally (e.g., sugar, slaves or spices) or a limited range of manufactured goods (e.g., silk, cotton and woollen clothes). These markets were served by numerous small-scale firms, resulting in the state that economists these days call **perfect competition**, in which no single seller can influence the price. For people from Smith's time, it would have been impossible even to imagine companies hiring over twice the then size of London's population (0.8 million in 1800) operating in territories that outnumber the then British colonial territories (around twenty) by a factor of six (McDonald's operates in over 120 countries).[6]

Today, most markets are populated, and often manipulated, by large companies. Some of them are the only supplier (**monopoly**) or, more typically, one of the few suppliers (**oligopoly**) – not just at the national level but increasingly at the global level. For example, Boeing and Airbus supply close to 90 per cent of world civilian aircrafts. Companies may also be the sole buyer (**monopsony**) or one of the few buyers (**oligopsony**).

Unlike the small companies in Adam Smith's world, monopolistic or oligopolistic firms can influence market outcomes – they have what economists call **market power**. A monopolistic firm may deliberately restrict its output to raise its prices to the point that its profit is maximized (I explain the

---

* In most developing countries, in which capitalism is still underdeveloped, the situation is still not too dissimilar from that found in Western Europe in Smith's time. In the poorest ones, child labour is still prevalent, while a lot of people are still tenants of semi-feudal landlords. Anything between 30 per cent and 90 per cent of the workforce in these countries may be self-employed, many of whom are engaged in subsistence farming.

technical points in Chapter 11 – feel free to ignore them now). Oligopolistic firms cannot manipulate their markets as much as a monopolistic firm can, but they may deliberately collude to maximize their profits by not undercutting each other's prices – this is known as a **cartel**. As a result, most countries now have a **competition law** (sometimes called an **anti-trust law**) in order to counter such **anti-competitive behaviours** – breaking up monopolies (for example, the US government broke up AT&T, the telephone company, in 1984) and banning collusion among oligopolistic firms.

Monopsonistic and oligopsonistic firms were considered to be theoretical curiosities even a few decades ago. Today, some of them are even more important than monopolistic and oligopolistic firms in shaping our economy. Exercising their powers as one of the few buyers of certain products, sometimes on a global scale, companies like Walmart, Amazon, Tesco and Carrefour exercise great – sometimes even defining – influence on what gets produced where, who gets how big a slice of profit and what consumers buy.

Money – the financial system – has also changed[7]

We now take it for granted that countries have only one bank that issues its notes (and coins) – that is, the **central bank**, such as the US Federal Reserve Board or the Bank of Japan. In Europe in Adam Smith's day, most banks (and even some big merchants) issued their own notes.

These notes (or bills, if you are in the US) were not notes in the modern sense. Each note was issued to a particular person, had a unique value and was signed by the cashier issuing it.[8] It was only in 1759 that the Bank of England started issuing fixed-denomination notes (the £10 note in this case – the £5 note came only in 1793, three years after Adam Smith died). And it wasn't until two generations after Smith (in 1853) that fully printed notes, with no name of the payee and no signature by issuing cashiers, were issued. But even these fixed-denomination notes were not notes in the modern sense, as their values were explicitly linked to precious metals like gold or silver that the issuing bank possessed. This is known as the **Gold** (or Silver or other) **Standard**.

The Gold (Silver) Standard is a monetary system in which the paper money issued by the central bank is freely exchangeable with a specified weight of gold (or silver). This did not mean that the central bank had to have in reserve an amount of gold equal to the value of the currency that it had issued; however, the **convertibility** of paper money into gold made it necessary for it to hold a very large gold reserve – for example, the US Federal Reserve Board kept gold equivalent to 40 per cent of the value of currency it issued. The result was that the central bank had little discretion in deciding how much paper money it could issue. The Gold Standard was first adopted by Britain in 1717 – by Isaac Newton,* the then head of the Royal Mint – and adopted by the other European countries in the 1870s. This system played a very important role in the evolution of capitalism in the next two generations, but that is a subject for later: see Chapter 3.

Use of banknotes is one thing, but saving with and borrowing from banks – namely, **banking** – is another. This was even less developed. Only a small minority had access to banking. Three-quarters of the French population did not have access to banks until the 1860s – nearly a century after *TWON*. Even in Britain, whose banking industry was far more developed than that of France, banking was highly fragmented, with the interest rates being different in different parts of the country well into the twentieth century.

Stock markets, where company shares (stocks) are bought and sold, had been in existence for a couple of centuries or so by Smith's time. But, given that few companies issued shares (as mentioned above, there was only a small number of limited liability companies), the stock market remained a sideshow to the unfolding capitalist drama. Worse, many people considered stock markets to be little more than gambling dens (some would say they still are). Stock market regulation was minimal and hardly enforced; stockbrokers were not obliged to reveal much information about the companies whose shares they were selling.

Other financial markets were even more primitive. The market for **government bonds**, that is, IOUs that can be transferred to anyone, issued by a government borrowing money (the very market that is at the centre of the Euro crisis that has shaken the world since 2009), existed only in a few countries, such as Britain, France and the Netherlands. The market for **corporate bonds** (IOUs issued by companies) was not very developed even in Britain.

Today, we have a highly developed – some would say over-developed –

---

* Yes, that's the scientist, who also doubled as an alchemist and a stock market speculator.

financial industry. This is made up of not just the banking sector, the stock market and bond markets, but increasingly the markets for financial derivatives (futures, options, swaps) and the alphabet soup of composite financial products like MBS, CDO and CDS (don't worry, I will explain what all these are in Chapter 8). The system is ultimately backed by the central bank, which acts as the **lender of last resort** and lends without limits during financial crises, when no one else wants to lend. Indeed, the absence of a central bank made the management of financial panic very difficult back in Smith's time.

Unlike in Smith's time, today there are a lot of rules on what actors in the financial market can do – how many multiples of their equity capital they can lend, what kind of information about themselves companies selling shares need to reveal, what kinds of assets different financial institutions are allowed to hold (e.g., pension funds are not allowed to hold risky assets). Despite this, the multiplicity and complexity of financial markets have made their regulation difficult – as we have learned since the 2008 global financial crisis.

Concluding Remarks: Real-world Changes and Economic Theories

As these contrasts show, capitalism has undergone enormous changes in the last two and a half centuries. While some of Smith's basic principles remain valid, they do so only at very general levels.

For example, competition among profit-seeking firms may still be the key driving force of capitalism, as in Smith's scheme. But it is not between small, anonymous firms which, accepting consumer tastes, fight it out by increasing the efficiency in the use of given technology. Today, competition is among huge multinational companies, with the ability not only to influence prices but to redefine technologies in a short span of time (think about the battle between Apple and Samsung) and to manipulate consumer tastes through brand-image building and advertising.

However great an economic theory may be, it is specific to its time and space. To apply it fruitfully, therefore, we require a good knowledge of the technological and institutional forces that characterize the particular markets, industries and countries that we are trying to analyse with the help of the theory. This is why, if we are to understand different economic theories in their right contexts, we need to know how capitalism has evolved. This is the task we turn to in the next chapter.

Further Reading

H.-J. CHANG
Kicking Away the Ladder: Development Strategy in Historical Perspective (London: Anthem, 2002).

R. HEILBRONER AND W. MILBERG
The Making of Economic Society, 13th edition (Boston: Pearson, 2012).

G. THERBORN
The World: A Beginner's Guide (Cambridge: Polity, 2011).

CHAPTER 3

How Have We Got Here?

A BRIEF HISTORY OF CAPITALISM

'*Mrs Lintott*: Now. How do you define history, Mr Rudge?

Rudge: Can I speak freely, Miss? Without being hit?

Mrs Lintott: I will protect you.

Rudge: How do I define history? It's just one fucking thing after another.'

ALAN BENNETT, *THE HISTORY BOYS*

One Fucking Thing after Another:
What Use Is History?

Many readers probably feel the same way about history as young Rudge in *The History Boys* – Alan Bennett's hit play and 2006 film about a bunch of bright but underprivileged Sheffield boys trying to gain admission to Oxford to study history.

Many people consider **economic history**, or the history of how our economies have evolved, especially pointless. Do we really need to know what happened two, three centuries ago in order to know that free trade promotes economic growth, that high taxes discourage wealth creation or that cutting red tape encourages business activities? Aren't these and other economic wisdoms of our time all propositions derived from logically airtight theories and checked against a vast amount of contemporary statistical evidence?

The majority of economists agree. Economic history used to be a compulsory subject in graduate economics training in most American universities until the 1980s, but many of them don't even offer courses in economic history any more. Among the more theoretically oriented economists, there is even a tendency to consider economic history at best as a harmless distraction, like trainspotting, and at worst as a refuge for the intellectually challenged who cannot handle 'hard' stuff like mathematics and statistics.

However, I present my readers with a brief (well, not so brief) history of capitalism because having some knowledge of that history is vital to fully understanding contemporary economic phenomena.

Life is stranger than fiction: why history matters

History affects the present – not simply because it is what came before the present but also because it (or, rather, what people think they know about it) informs people's decisions. A lot of policy recommendations are backed up by historical examples because nothing is as effective as spectacular real-life cases – successful or otherwise – in persuading people. For example, those who promote free trade always point out that Britain and then the US became the world's economic superpowers through free trade. If they realized that their version of history is incorrect (as I will show below), they might not have such conviction in their policy recommendations. They would also find it harder to persuade others.

History also forces us to question some assumptions that are taken for granted. Once you know that lots of things that cannot be bought and sold today – human beings (slaves), child labour, government offices – used to be perfectly marketable, you will stop thinking that the boundary of the 'free market' is drawn by some timeless law of science and begin to see that it can be redrawn. When you learn that the advanced capitalist economies grew the fastest in history between the 1950s and the 1970s, when there were a lot of regulations and high taxes, you will immediately become sceptical of the view that promoting growth requires cuts in taxes and red tape.

History is useful in highlighting the limits of economic theory. Life is often stranger than fiction, and history provides many successful economic experiences (at all levels – nations, companies, individuals) that cannot be tidily explained by any single economic theory. For example, if you only read things like *The Economist* or the *Wall Street Journal*, you would only hear about Singapore's free trade policy and its welcoming attitudes towards foreign investment. This may make you conclude that Singapore's economic success proves that free trade and the free market are the best for economic development – until you also learn that almost all the land in Singapore is owned by the government, 85 per cent of housing is supplied by the government-owned housing agency (the Housing Development Board) and 22 per cent of national output is produced by state-owned enterprises (the international average is around 10 per cent). There is no single type of economic theory – Neoclassical, Marxist, Keynesian, you name it – that can explain the success of this combination of free market and socialism. Examples like this should make you both more sceptical about the power of economic theory and more cautious in drawing policy conclusions from it.

Last but not least, we need to look at history because we have the moral duty to avoid 'live experiments' with people as much as possible. From the central planning in the former socialist bloc (and their 'Big Bang' transition back to capitalism), through to the disasters of 'austerity' policies in most European countries following the Great Depression, down to the failures of 'trickle-down economics' in the US and the UK during the 1980s and the 1990s, history is littered with radical policy experiments that have destroyed the lives of millions, or even tens of millions, of people. Studying history won't allow us to completely avoid mistakes in the present, but we should do our best to extract lessons from history before we formulate a policy that will affect lives.

If you have been persuaded by any of the above points, please read through the rest of the chapter, in which a lot of the historical 'facts' that you thought you knew may be challenged and thus the way you understand capitalism hopefully transformed at least a little bit.

Tortoise vs. Snails: the World Economy before Capitalism

Western Europe grew really slowly . . .

Capitalism started in Western Europe, especially in Britain and the Low Countries (what are Belgium and the Netherlands today) around the sixteenth and the seventeenth centuries. Why it started there – rather than, say, China or India, which had been comparable to Western Europe in their levels of economic development until then – is a subject of intense and long-running debate. Everything from the Chinese elite's disdain for practical pursuits (like commerce and industry) to the discovery of the Americas and the pattern of Britain's coal deposits has been identified as the explanation. This debate need not detain us here. The fact is that capitalism developed first in Western Europe.

Before the rise of capitalism, the Western European societies, like all the other pre-capitalist societies, changed very slowly. The society was basically organized around farming, which used virtually the same technologies for centuries, with a limited degree of commerce and handicraft industries.

Between 1000 and 1500, the medieval era, **income per capita**, namely, income per person, in Western Europe grew at 0.12 per cent per year.[1] This means that income in 1500 was only 82 per cent higher than that in 1000. To put it into perspective, this is a growth that China, growing at 11 per cent a year, experienced in just six years between 2002 and 2008. This means that, in terms of material progress, one year in China today is equivalent to eighty-three years in medieval Western Europe (which were equivalent to three-and-a-half medieval lifetimes, as the average life expectancy at the time was only twenty-four years).

. . . but its growth was still faster than elsewhere in the world

Having said all this, growth in Western Europe was still a sprint compared to those in Asia and Eastern Europe (including Russia), which are estimated to have grown at one-third the rate (0.04 per cent). This means that their incomes were only 22 per cent higher after half a millennium. Western Europe may have been moving like a tortoise, but other parts of the world were like snails.

The Dawn of Capitalism: 1500–1820

Capitalism is born – in slow motion

In the sixteenth century, capitalism was born. But its birth was so slow that we cannot easily detect it from the numbers. During 1500–1820, the growth rate of per capita income in Western Europe was still only 0.14 per cent – basically the same to all intents and purposes as the one for 1000–1500 (0.12 per cent).

In Britain and the Netherlands, there was visible growth acceleration by the late eighteenth century, especially in sectors such as cotton textiles and iron.[2] As a result, during 1500–1820, Britain and the Netherlands achieved per capita economic growth rates of 0.27 per cent and 0.28 per cent per year, respectively. These are very low by modern standards, but they were still double the Western European average. Behind this lay a number of changes.

Emergence of new sciences, technologies and institutions

First came the cultural shift towards more 'rational' approaches to understanding the world, which promoted the rise of modern mathematics and sciences. Many of these ideas were initially borrowed from the Arab world and Asia,[3] but in the sixteenth and seventeenth centuries, the Western Europeans started adding their own innovations. The founding fathers of modern science and mathematics – such as Copernicus, Galileo, Fermat, Newton and Leibniz – are from this era. This development of science did not immediately affect the broader economy, but it later enabled the systemization of knowledge that made technological innovations less dependent on individuals and thus more easily transferable, which encouraged the diffusion of new technologies and thus economic growth.

The eighteenth century saw the emergence of several new technologies that heralded the advent of a mechanized production system, especially in textiles, steel-making and chemicals.* As in Adam Smith's pin factory, a finer division of labour was developing, with the use of continuous assembly lines spreading from the early nineteenth century. In the emergence of these new production technologies, a key driver was the desire to increase output in order to be able to sell more and thus make more profit – in other words, the spread of the capitalist mode of production. As Smith argued in his theory of division of labour, the increase in output made a finer division of labour possible, which then increased productivity and consequently output, setting off a 'virtuous cycle' between output growth and productivity growth.

New economic institutions emerged to accommodate the new realities of capitalist production. With the spread of market transactions, banks evolved to facilitate them. Emergence of investment projects requiring capital beyond the wealth of even the richest individuals prompted the invention of the *corporation*, or limited liability company, and thus the stock market.

Colonial expansion starts

The Western European countries started to expand rapidly outwards from the early fifteenth century. Euphemistically known as the 'Age of Discovery', this expansion involved expropriating land, resources and people for labour from the native populations through colonialism.

---

* These included the flying shuttle (1733) and spinning jenny (1764) in the textile industry, coke-smelting (1709) in steel-making and various processes for large-scale sulphuric-acid manufacture (the 1730s and the 1740s) in the chemical industry.

Beginning with Portugal in Asia and Spain in the Americas from the late fifteenth century, the Western European nations ruthlessly moved out. By the middle of the eighteenth century, North America was divided up between Britain, France and Spain. Most Latin American countries were ruled by Spain and Portugal until the 1810s and the 1820s. Parts of India were ruled by the British (mainly Bengal and Bihar), the French (the southeastern coast) and the Portuguese (various coastal areas, especially Goa). Australia was beginning to be settled around this time (the first penal colony was established in 1788). Not much of Africa was affected yet, with small colonies along the coasts settled by the Portuguese (the formerly uninhabited islands of Cape Verde and Sao Tome and Principe) and the Dutch (Cape Town in the seventeenth century).

Colonialism was run on capitalist principles. Symbolically, until 1858, British rule in India was actually administered by a corporation (the East India Company), not by the government. These colonies brought new resources to Europe. The early expansions were motivated by the quest for precious metals to use as money (gold and silver) and spices (especially black pepper). Over time, plantations using slaves, mostly captives from Africa, were established in the new colonies – especially the US, Brazil and the Caribbean – to grow and bring back to Europe new crops such as (cane) sugar, rubber, cotton and tobacco. Some of the New World crops were grown in Europe and beyond and became basic food items. It stretches the imagination to think of the days when the British did not have their chips, the Italians lacked tomatoes and polenta (made with maize, or sweetcorn) and the Indians, the Thais and the Koreans did not eat any chillies.

Colonialism leaves big scars

There is a long-running debate on whether capitalism could have developed without the colonial resources of the sixteenth–eighteenth centuries – precious metal to be used as money, extra food sources such as potato and sugar and industrial inputs such as cotton.[4] While there is no question that the colonizers greatly benefited from those resources, those countries would probably have developed capitalism even without them. There is no question, however, that colonialism devastated colonized societies.

Native populations were exterminated or driven on to the margins. Their land, and the resources over and under it, was taken away. Marginalization of the indigenous population has been so extensive that Evo Morales, the current president of Bolivia, elected in 2006, is only the second head of state from the indigenous population in the Americas since the Europeans arrived in 1492 (the first was Benito Juarez, the Mexican president between 1858 and 1872).

Millions of Africans – 12 million is a common estimate – were captured and shipped out as slaves by both the Europeans and the Arabs. This was not only a tragedy for those who became slaves (if they survived the atrocious journey) but it also depleted many African societies of workers and destroyed their social fabric. Countries were created out of thin air, with arbitrary boundaries, affecting the internal and the international politics of those countries to this day. The fact that so many borders in Africa are straight is a testimony to that; natural borders are never straight because they are usually formed along rivers, mountain ranges and other geographical features.

Colonialism often meant the deliberate destruction of existing productive activities in the economically more advanced regions. Most importantly, in 1700, Britain banned the import of Indian cotton textiles ('calicoes') – we encountered the event in Chapter 2 – in order to promote its own cotton textile industry, dealing a heavy blow to the Indian cotton textile industry. The industry was finished off in the mid-nineteenth century by the influx of exports from the then mechanized British cotton textile industry. As a colony, India could not use tariffs and other policy measures to protect its own producers against British imports. In 1835, Lord Bentinck, the Governor-General of the East India Company, famously reported that 'the bones of the cotton weavers are bleaching the plains of India'.[5]

1820–1870: The Industrial Revolution

The turbo-charged drive: the Industrial Revolution starts

Capitalism really took off around 1820, with a visible acceleration of economic growth all around Western Europe and then in the 'Western offshoots' in North America and Oceania. The growth acceleration was so dramatic that the half-century following 1820 is typically referred to as the Industrial Revolution.[6]

In those fifty years, per capita income in Western Europe grew at 1 per cent, a poor growth rate these days (Japan grew at that rate during the so-called 'lost decade' of the 1990s), but compared to the 0.14 per cent growth rate between 1500 and 1820, it was a turbo-charged drive.

Expect to live for seventeen years and work eighty hours a week: misery increases for some

This acceleration of growth in per capita income, however, was initially accompanied by a fall in living standards for many. Some with old skills – such as textile artisans – lost their jobs, having been replaced by machines operated by cheaper, unskilled workers, including many children. Some machines were even designed with the small sizes of children in mind. Those who were hired to work in factories, or in the small workshops that supplied inputs for them, worked long hours – seventy to eighty hours per week was the norm, and some worked more than 100 hours a week with usually only half of Sunday free.

Working conditions were extremely hazardous. Many British cotton textile workers died of lung diseases from the dust generated in the production process. The urban working class lived in crowded conditions, sometimes fifteen to twenty people in a room. It was typical that hundreds of people shared one toilet. They died off like flies. In poor areas of Manchester, life expectancy was seventeen years[7] – 30 per cent *lower* than what it had been for the whole of Britain before the Norman Conquest, back in 1000 (then twenty-four years).

The rise of anti-capitalist movements

Given the misery that capitalism was creating, it is no wonder that various forms of anti-capitalist movements arose. Some of them merely tried to turn the clock back. The Luddites – textile artisans of England who lost their jobs to mechanized production in the 1810s – turned to destroying the machines, the immediate cause of their unemployment and the most obvious symbol of capitalist progress. Others sought to build a better, more egalitarian society through voluntary associations. Robert Owen, the Welsh businessman, tried to build a society based on communal working and living among the like-minded – rather like the Israeli kibbutz.

The most important anti-capitalist visionary was, however, Karl Marx (1818–83), the German economist and revolutionary, who spent most of his time exiled in England – his grave is in Highgate Cemetery in London. Marx labelled Owen and others like him as 'utopian socialists' for believing that a post-capitalist society can be based on idyllic communal living. Calling his own approach 'scientific socialism', he argued that the new society should build on, rather than reject, the achievements of capitalism. A socialist society should abolish private ownership in the means of production but it should preserve the large production units created by capitalism so that it can take full advantage of their high productivities. Moreover, Marx proposed that a socialist society should be run like a capitalist firm in one important respect – it should plan its economic affairs centrally, in the same way in which a capitalist firm plans all its operations centrally. This is known as **central planning**.

Marx and many of his followers – including Vladimir Lenin, the leader of the Russian Revolution – believed that a socialist society could only be created through a revolution, led by workers, given that the capitalists would not voluntarily give up what they had. However, some of his followers, known as the 'revisionists' or social democrats, such as Eduard Bernstein and Karl Kautsky, thought that the problems of capitalism could be alleviated through the reform, rather than abolition, of capitalism through parliamentary democracy. They advocated measures like regulation of working hours and working conditions as well as the development of the welfare state.

With hindsight, it is easy to see that those reformists read the historical trend the best, as the system they advocated is what all the advanced capitalist economies have today. At the time, however, it was not obvious that workers could be made better off under capitalism, not least because there was fierce resistance to reform from most capitalists.

From around 1870, there were palpable improvements in the conditions of the working class. Wages went up. At least in Britain, the average adult wage was finally high enough to allow the workers to buy more than the bare necessities, and some workers were now working less than sixty hours a week. Life expectancy was up from thirty-six years in 1800 to forty-one years in 1860.[8] At the end of this period, there were even the beginnings of the welfare state, which started in Germany with the 1871 industrial accident insurance scheme, introduced by Otto von Bismarck, the Chancellor of the newly united Germany.

The myth of free market and free trade: How capitalism really developed

The advancement of capitalism in the Western European countries and their offshoots in the nineteenth century is often attributed to the spread of **free trade** and **free market**. It is only because the government in these countries, it is argued, did not tax or restrict international trade (free trade) and, more generally, did not interfere in the workings of the market (free market) that these countries could develop capitalism. Britain and the US are said to have forged ahead of other countries because they were the first ones to adopt the free market and, especially, free trade.

This could not be further from the truth. The government played a leading role in the early development of capitalism both in Britain and the US, as well as in other Western European countries.[9]

Britain as the pioneer of protectionism

Starting with Henry VII (1485–1509), the Tudor monarchs promoted the woollen textile industry – Europe's then hi-tech industry, led by the Low Countries, especially Flanders – through government intervention. **Tariffs** (taxes on imports) protected the British producers from the superior Low Country producers. The British government even sponsored the poaching of skilled textile artisans, mainly from Flanders, to gain access to advanced technologies. British or American people with names like Flanders, Fleming and Flemyng are descendants of those artisans: without those policies, there wouldn't be 007 (Ian Fleming) or penicillin (Alexander Fleming); and somehow I don't think *The Simpsons* would have been as fun as it is if Ned Flanders were called Ned Lancashire. These policies continued after the Tudors, and by the eighteenth century woollen textile goods accounted for around half of Britain's export revenue. Without those export revenues, Britain would not have been able to import the food and the raw materials that it needed for the Industrial Revolution.

British government intervention was stepped up in 1721, when Robert Walpole, Britain's first prime minister,[10] launched an ambitious and wide-ranging industrial development programme. It provided tariff protection and subsidies (especially to encourage export) to 'strategic' industries. Partly thanks to Walpole's programme, Britain started to forge ahead in the second half of the eighteenth century. By the 1770s, Britain was so obviously ahead of other countries that Adam Smith saw no need for protectionism and other forms of government intervention to help British producers. However, it was only nearly a century after Smith's *TWON* – in 1860 – that Britain fully switched to free trade, when its industrial supremacy was unquestioned. At the time, Britain accounted for 20 per cent of world manufacturing output (as of 1860) and 46 per cent of world trade in manufactured goods (as of 1870), despite having only 2.5 per cent of the world population; these numbers can be put into perspective by noting that the corresponding figures for China today are 15 per cent and 14 per cent, despite its having 19 per cent of the world population.

The US as the champion of protectionism

The US case is yet more interesting. Under British colonial rule, its development of manufacturing was deliberately suppressed. It is reported that, upon hearing about the first attempts by the American colonists to engage in manufacturing, William Pitt the Elder, the British prime minister (1766–8), said that they should 'not be permitted to manufacture so much as a horseshoe nail'.

After gaining independence, many Americans argued that their country should industrialize if it was to rub shoulders with the likes of Britain and France. Leading this camp was no less than the first ever minister in charge of the US economy, Alexander Hamilton, the treasury secretary (that's the one you see on the $10 bill). In his 1791 report to the Congress, *Report on the Subject of Manufactures*, Hamilton argued that the government of an economically backward nation, such as the US, needs to protect and nurture 'industries in their infancy' against superior foreign competitors until they grow up; this is known as the **infant industry argument**. Hamilton proposed the use of tariffs and other measures to help the infant industries; subsidies, public investments in infrastructure (especially canals), a patent law to encourage new inventions and measures to develop the banking system.

In the beginning, the slave-owning landlords from the South, who then dominated US politics, thwarted Hamilton's plan; they didn't see why they should buy inferior 'Yankee'-manufactured products when they could import better and cheaper things from Europe. But, following the Anglo-American War (1812–16) – the first and so far the only time that the US mainland was invaded – many Americans came around to Hamilton's view that a strong country needed a strong manufacturing sector, which was not going to happen without tariffs and other government interventions. The only pity was that Hamilton was not around to see his vision realized. He had been shot dead in a pistol duel in 1804 by a certain Aaron Burr – the serving vice president of the country at the time (yes, those were wild days – a serving vice president shoots a former finance minister dead, and no one goes to prison).

After the shift of direction in 1816, the US trade policy became increasingly protectionist. By the 1830s, the country was boasting the highest average industrial tariff in the world – a status that it would keep for (almost all of) the next hundred years, until the Second World War. During that century, tariffs were much lower in states such as Germany, France and Japan – states that people these days normally associate with protectionism.

In the first half of this protectionist century, together with slavery and federalism, protectionism remained a constant bone of contention between the industrial North and the agrarian South. The issue was finally settled by the Civil War (1861–5), which the North won. The victory was no accident. The North won exactly because it had developed manufacturing industry in the previous half a century behind the wall of protectionism. In Margaret Mitchell's classic novel *Gone with the Wind*, Rhett Butler, the leading male character, tells his Southern compatriots that the Yankees would win the war because they had 'the factories, the foundries, the shipyards, the iron and coal mines – all the things we [the Southerners] haven't got'.

Free trade spreads – mostly through unfree means

Free trade was *not* responsible for the rise of capitalism, but it *did* spread throughout the nineteenth century. Some of it happened in the heartland of capitalism in the 1860s – Britain's adoption of free trade and the signing of a series of bilateral **free-trade agreements** (or FTAs), in which two countries abolish import restrictions and tariffs on each other's exports, among the Western European countries. But much of the spread happened on the periphery of capitalism, in Latin America and Asia.

This was the result of something that you would not normally associate with the word 'free' – that is, force, or at least the threat of using it. Colonization was the obvious route to 'unfree free trade', but even many countries that were not colonized were also forced to adopt free trade. Through 'gunboat diplomacy', they were forced to sign **unequal treaties** that deprived them of, among other things, **tariff autonomy** (the right to set their own tariffs).[11] They were allowed to use only a low uniform tariff rate (3–5 per cent) – enough to raise some government revenue but not enough for infant industry protection.

The most infamous unequal treaty is the Nanking Treaty, which China was forced to sign in 1842, following its defeat in the Opium War. But the unequal treaties had started with the Latin American countries, upon their independence in the 1810s and the 1820s. Between the 1820s and the 1850s, a string of other countries were forced to sign them – the Ottoman Empire (Turkey's predecessor), Persia (Iran today) and Siam (today's Thailand), and even Japan. The Latin American unequal treaties expired in the 1870s and the 1880s, but the Asian ones lasted well into the twentieth century.

The inability to protect and promote their infant industries, whether due to direct colonial rule or to unequal treaties, was a huge contributing factor to the economic retrogression in Asia and Latin America during this period, when they saw *negative* per capita income growths (at the rates of -0.1 and -0.04 per cent per year, respectively).

1870–1913: High Noon

Capitalism gets into a higher gear: the rise of mass production

The development of capitalism began to accelerate around 1870. Clusters of new technological innovations emerged between the 1860s and the 1910s, resulting in the rise of the so-called heavy and chemical industries: electrical machinery, internal combustion engines, synthetic dyes, artificial fertilizers, and so on. Unlike the technologies of the Industrial Revolution, which had been invented by practical men with good intuition, these new technologies were developed through the systematic application of scientific and engineering principles. This meant that, once something was invented, it could be replicated and improved upon very quickly.

In addition, organization of the production process was revolutionized in many industries by the invention of the **mass production system**. The use of a *moving* assembly line (conveyor belt) and interchangeable parts dramatically lowered production costs. This system of production is the backbone (if not the entirety) of our production system today, despite frequent talks of its demise since the 1980s.

New economic institutions emerge to deal with growing
production scale, risk, and instability

During its 'high noon', capitalism acquired the basic institutional shape that it has today – the limited liability company, bankruptcy law, the central bank, the welfare state, labour laws and so on. These institutional shifts came about basically because of the changes in underlying technologies and politics.

Recognizing the growing need for large-scale investments, limited liability, hitherto reserved only for privileged firms, was 'generalized' – that is, granted to any firm that met some minimum conditions. Enabling unprecedented scales of investment, the limited liability company became the most powerful vehicle for capitalist development – Karl Marx, spotting its enormous potential before any self-appointed cheerleader of capitalism, called it 'capitalist production in its highest development'.

Before the 1849 British reform, the bankruptcy law focused on punishing the bankrupt businessman, with a debtors' prison in the worst case. New bankruptcy laws, introduced in the second half of the nineteenth century, gave failed businessmen a second chance by allowing them not to pay interest to creditors while they were reorganizing their business (as in Chapter 11 of the US Federal Bankruptcy Act, introduced in 1898) and by forcing the creditors to write off parts of their debts. Being a businessman became far less risky.

With larger companies came larger banks. The risk was then heightened that the failure of one bank could destabilise the whole financial system, so central banks were set up to deal with such problems by acting as the lender of last resort, starting with the Bank of England in 1844.

With increasing socialist agitation and reformist pressures in relation to the condition of the working class, a raft of welfare and labour legislations were implemented from the 1870s: industrial accident insurance, health insurance, old age pensions and unemployment insurance. Many countries also banned the employment of younger children (typically, those under ten to twelve) and restricted the working hours of older children (initially only to twelve hours!). They also regulated the working conditions and hours of women. Unfortunately, this was done not out of chivalry but out of contempt for women. Unlike men, it was believed, women lacked full mental faculties and therefore could sign a labour contract that was disadvantageous to them – they needed to be protected from themselves. This welfare and labour legislation took the roughest edges off capitalism and made a lot of poor people's lives better – if only slightly at the beginning.

These institutional changes promoted economic growth. Limited liability and debtor-friendly bankruptcy laws reduced risk involved in business activities, thereby encouraging wealth creation. Central banking, on the one hand, and labour and welfare legislations, on the other, also helped growth by enhancing, respectively, economic and political stability, which increased investment and thus growth. The growth rate of per capita income in Western Europe accelerated during this 'high noon' from 1 per cent during 1820–70 to 1.3 per cent during 1870–1913.

How the 'liberal' golden age was not so liberal

The 'high noon' of capitalism is often described as the first age of **globalization**, that is, the first time in which the whole world economy was integrated into one system of production and exchange. Many commentators attribute this outcome to the **liberal** economic policies adopted during this period, when there were few policy restrictions on cross-border movements of goods, capital and people. This liberalism on the international front was matched by the **laissez-faire** approach to domestic economic policy (see the box below for definitions of these terms). Allowance of maximum freedom for business, pursuit of a **balanced budget** (that is, the government spending exactly as much as it collects in taxes) and the adoption of the Gold Standard were the key ingredients, they say. Things were, however, far more complicated.

'LIBERAL': THE MOST CONFUSING TERM IN THE WORLD?

Few words have generated more confusion than the word 'liberal'. Although the term was not explicitly used until the nineteenth century, the ideas behind **liberalism** can be traced back to at least the seventeenth century, starting with thinkers like Thomas Hobbes and John Locke. The classical meaning of the term describes a position that gives priority to freedom of the individual. In economic terms, this means protecting the right of the individual to use his property as he pleases, especially to make money. In this view, the ideal government is the one that provides only the minimum conditions that are conducive to the exercise of such a right, such as law and order. Such a government (state) is known as the **minimal state**. The famous slogan among the liberals of the time was 'laissez faire' (let things be), so liberalism is also known as the laissez-faire doctrine.

Today, liberalism is usually equated with the advocacy of democracy, given its emphasis on individual political rights, including the freedom of speech. However, until the mid-twentieth century, most liberals were *not* democrats. They did reject the conservative view that tradition and social hierarchy should have priority over individual rights. But they also believed that not everyone was worthy of such rights. They thought women lacked full mental faculties and thus did not deserve the right to vote. They also insisted that poor people should not be given the right to vote, since they believed the poor would vote in politicians who would confiscate private properties. Adam Smith openly admitted that the government 'is in reality instituted for the defence of the rich against the poor, or of those who have some property against those who have none at all'.[12]

What makes it even more confusing is that, in the US, the term 'liberal' is used to describe a view that is the left-of-centre. American 'liberals', such as Ted Kennedy or Paul Krugman, would be called social democrats in Europe. In Europe, the term is reserved for people like the supporters of the German Free Democratic Party (FDP), who would be called **libertarians** in the US.

Then there is **neo-liberalism**, which has been the dominant economic view since the 1980s (see below). It is very close to, but not quite the same as, classical liberalism. Economically, it advocates the classical minimal state but with some modifications – most importantly, it accepts the central bank with note issue monopoly, while the classical liberals thought that there should be competition in the production of money too. In political terms, neo-liberals do not openly oppose democracy, as the classical liberals did. But many of them are willing to sacrifice democracy for the sake of private property and the free market.

Neo-liberalism is also known, especially in developing countries, as the **Washington Consensus** view, referring to the fact that it is strongly advocated by the three most powerful economic organizations in the world, all based in Washington, DC, namely, the US Treasury, the International Monetary Fund (IMF) and the World Bank.

The 1870–1913 period did *not* actually see universal liberalism on the international front. In the heartland of capitalism, in Western Europe and the US, trade protectionism actually increased, not decreased.

The US became even more protectionist than before following the conclusion of the Civil War in 1865. Most Western European countries that had signed FTAs in the 1860s and the 1870s did not renew them and significantly increased tariffs after their expiry (they usually had a twenty-year lifetime). This was partly to protect agriculture, which was struggling with new cheap imports from the New World (especially the US and Argentina) and Eastern Europe (Russia and Ukraine) but also to protect and promote the new heavy and chemical industries. Germany and Sweden were the best examples of this 'new protectionism' – famously called the 'marriage of iron and rye' in Germany.

When the unequal treaties they had signed upon independence expired in the 1870s and the 1880s, the Latin American countries introduced rather high protective tariffs (30–40 per cent). However, elsewhere in the 'periphery', the forced free trade we talked about earlier spread much further. European powers competed for parts of the African continent in the 'scramble for Africa', while many Asian countries were also taken as colonies (Malaysia, Singapore and Myanmar by Britain; Cambodia, Vietnam and Laos by France). The British Empire expanded enormously, backed up by its industrial might, leading to the famous saying: 'The sun never sets on the British Empire.' Countries like Germany, Belgium, the US and Japan, which had not so far engaged in much colonialism, also joined in.[13] Not for nothing is this period also known as the 'Age of Imperialism'.

The domestic front also saw a marked increase, not a decrease, in government intervention in the core capitalist countries. There was, indeed, a strong adherence to free-market doctrines in relation to fiscal policy (the balanced budget doctrine) and monetary policy (the Gold Standard). However, this period also saw an enormous increase in the role of the government: labour regulations, social welfare schemes, public investments in infrastructure (especially railways but also canals) and in education (especially the US and Germany).

The liberal golden age of 1870–1913 was thus not as liberal as we think. It was getting less liberal in the core capitalist countries, in terms of both domestic and international policies. Liberalization happened mostly in the weaker countries, but out of compulsion rather than choice – through colonialism and unequal treaties. In the only peripheral region that experienced rapid growth during this period, namely, Latin America, there was a vast increase in protectionism following the expiry of the unequal treaties.[14]

1914–45: The Turmoil

Capitalism trips up: the First World War and the end of the liberal golden age

The outbreak of the First World War in 1914 signalled the end of an era for capitalism. Until then, despite constant threats of revolt by the poor (the 1848 revolutions across Europe, the 1871 Paris commune, etc.) and economic problems (the Long Depression of 1873–96), the only way for capitalism had seemed to be up – and outwards.

This view was rudely shaken by the First World War (1914–18), which totally discredited the then popular view that the thickening web of commerce, which capitalism was building across the globe, would make wars between nations thus intertwined highly unlikely, if not totally impossible.

At one level, the outbreak of the First World War should not have been surprising, given that the globalization of the 'high noon' had been in large part driven by imperialism, rather than market forces. This meant that the international rivalry between the leading capitalist countries had a high chance of escalating into violent conflicts. Some went even further and argued that capitalism had reached a stage in which it could not be sustained without continuous outward expansion, which has to come to an end sooner or later, marking the end of capitalism.

Capitalism gets a rival: the Russian Revolution and the rise of socialism

This was the view most famously expounded in *Imperialism: The Highest Stage of Capitalism* by Vladimir Lenin, the leader of the Russian Revolution in 1917. The Russian Revolution was an even bigger shock to the defenders of capitalism than the First World War, as it led to the creation of an economic system that claims to undermine all the cornerstones of capitalism.

In the decade following the Russian Revolution, private property in the means of production (machines, factory buildings, land, etc.) was abolished. The big break came with the agricultural collectivization in 1928, in which the lands of large farmers, or kulaks, were confiscated and turned into state farms (*sovkhoz*) and small farmers were forced to join agricultural coopera-tives (*kolkhoz*), which were state farms in all but name. Markets were even-tually abolished and replaced by full-blown central planning by 1928, when the first Five Year Plan started. By 1928, the Soviet Union had an economic system that was definitively not capitalist. It ran without private ownership of means of production, profit motives and markets.

As for the other cornerstone of capitalism, wage labour, the picture was more complicated. Yes, in theory the Soviet workers were not wage labour-ers because they owned all the means of production – through state own-ership or cooperatives. In practice they were indistinguishable from wage labourers in a capitalist economy, since they had little control over the way in which their enterprises and the wider economy operated, and their daily work experience was still subject to the same hierarchical relationship.

Soviet socialism was a huge economic (and social) experiment. Until then, no economy had been centrally planned. Karl Marx had left the details rather vague, and the Soviet Union had to make things up as it went along this untrodden path. Even many Marxists, especially Karl Kautsky, were sceptical about its prospects – socialism was, according to Marx himself, supposed to emerge from the most developed capitalist economies. Those economies were only a step away from a fully planned economy, it was argued, because their economic activities were already planned to a high degree by large enterprises and cartels of those enterprises. The Soviet Union – even its more developed European part – was a very backward economy in which capitalism had been hardly developed, where socialism really had no business emerging.

To everyone's surprise, the early Soviet industrialization was a big success, most graphically proven by its ability to repel the Nazi advance on the Eastern Front during the Second World War. Income per capita is estimated to have grown at 5 per cent per year between 1928 and 1938 – an astonishingly rapid rate in a world in which income typically grew at 1–2 per cent per year.[15]

This growth came at the cost of millions of deaths – from political repression and the 1932 famine.* However, the scale of the famine was not

---

* To simplify the story, the 1932 famine happened because too much food was shipped out of the rural areas, following the 1928 agricultural collectivization. The rapidly rising urban population had to be fed, and grains had to be exported to earn foreign exchanges with which to import advanced machinery that the Soviet Union needed for industrialization.

known at the time, and many were impressed by Soviet economic performance, especially given that capitalism was then on its knees, following the Great Depression of 1929.

Capitalism gets depressed: the Great Depression of 1929

The Great Depression was an even more traumatic event for the believers in capitalism than the rise of socialism. This was especially the case in the US, where the Depression started (with the infamous 1929 Wall Street crash) and which was the hardest hit by the experience. Between 1929 and 1932, US output fell by 30 per cent and unemployment increased eightfold, from 3 per cent to 24 per cent.[16] It was not until 1937 that US output regained its 1929 level. Germany and France also suffered badly, with their outputs falling by 16 per cent and 15 per cent respectively.

One influential view, propagated by neo-liberal economists, is that this large but totally manageable financial crisis was turned into a Great Depression because of the collapse in world trade caused by the 'trade war', prompted by the adoption of protectionism by the US through the 1930 Smoot-Hawley Tariffs. This story does not stand up to scrutiny. The tariff increase by Smoot-Hawley was not dramatic – it raised the average US industrial tariff from 37 per cent to 48 per cent. Nor did it cause a massive tariff war. Except for a few economically weak countries such as Italy and Spain, trade protectionism did not increase very much following Smoot–Hawley. Most importantly, studies show that the main reason for the collapse in international trade after 1929 was not tariff increases but the downward spiral in international demand, caused by the adherence by the governments of the core capitalist economies to the doctrine of balanced budget.[17]

After a big financial crisis like the 1929 Wall Street crash or the 2008 global financial crisis, private-sector spending falls. Debts go unpaid, which forces banks to reduce their lending. Being unable to borrow, firms and individuals cut their spending. This, in turn, reduces demands for other firms and individuals that used to sell to them (e.g., firms selling to consumers, firms selling machinery to other firms, workers selling labour services to firms). The demand level in the economy spirals down.

In this environment, the government is the only economic actor that can maintain the level of demand in the economy by spending more than it earns, that is, by running a budget deficit. However, in the days of the Great

Depression, the strong belief in the doctrine of the balanced budget prevented such a course of action. As tax revenues were falling due to reduced levels of economic activity, the only way for them to balance their budgets was to cut their spending, leaving nothing to arrest the downward demand spiral.[18] To make things worse, the Gold Standard meant that their central banks could not increase the supply of money for fear of compromising the value of their currencies. With restricted money supply, credit became scarce, restricting private-sector activities and thus reducing demand even further.

Reform begins: the US and Sweden lead the way

The Great Depression left a lasting mark on capitalism. With it came widespread rejection of the laissez-faire doctrine and serious attempts to reform capitalism.

The reforms were particularly widespread and far-reaching in the US, where the Depression was the greatest and lasted the longest. The so-called First New Deal programme (1933–4) under the new president, Franklin Delano Roosevelt, separated the commercial and investment arms of banks (the 1933 Glass-Steagall Act), set up the bank deposit insurance system to protect small savers against bank failures, tightened stock market regulation (the 1933 Federal Securities Act), expanded and strengthened the farm credit system, provided a minimum farm price guarantee and developed infrastructure (such as the Hoover Dam – that's the one you see in the 1978 *Superman* movie, starring the late Christopher Reeve), and so on. There were even more reforms under the so-called Second New Deal (1935–8), including the Social Security Act (1935), which introduced old age pensions and unemployment insurance, and the Wagner Act (1935), which strengthened trade unions.

Sweden was another country where significant reforms were introduced. Riding on the back of the public discontent with liberal economic policies, which left unemployment at 25 per cent, the Social Democratic Party came to power in 1932. Income tax was introduced – surprisingly belatedly for a country that is today considered the bastion of income tax (Britain introduced income tax in 1842 and even the famously anti-tax US in 1913). The revenues were used for expanding the welfare state (unemployment insurance was introduced in 1934, and the old-age pension was raised) and for helping small farmers (farm credits were expanded, and minimum prices were guaranteed). In 1938, the centralized trade union and the centralized employers' association signed the Saltsjöbaden Agreement, establishing industrial peace.

Other countries did not go as far as the US and Sweden in reforming capitalism, but their reforms presaged the shape of the things to come after the Second World War.

Capitalism falters: growth slows down and socialism outperforms capitalism

The turmoil of the 1914-45 period reached its peak with the outbreak of the Second World War, which killed tens of millions of people, both soldiers and civilians (higher estimates put the death toll at 60 million). The war resulted in the first reversal in the acceleration in economic growth since the early nineteenth century.[19]

1945-73: The Golden Age of Capitalism

Capitalism performs well on all fronts:
growth, employment and stability

The period between 1945, the end of the Second World War, and 1973, the first Oil Shock, is often called the 'Golden Age of capitalism'. The period really deserves the name, as it achieved the highest growth rate ever. Between 1950 and 1973, per capita income in Western Europe grew at an astonishing rate of 4.1 per cent per year. The US grew more slowly, but at an unprecedented rate of 2.5 per cent. West Germany grew at 5.0 per cent, earning the title of the 'Miracle on the Rhine', while Japan grew even faster at 8.1 per cent, starting off the chain of 'economic miracles' in East Asia in the next half a century.

High growth was not the only economic achievement of the Golden Age. Unemployment, the bane of the working class, was virtually eliminated in the advanced capitalist countries (henceforth ACCs) of Western Europe, Japan and the US (see Chapter 10). These economies were also remarkably stable on a number of accounts – output (and thus employment), prices and finance. Outputs fluctuated much less than in the previous periods, not least thanks to Keynesian fiscal policy, which increased government spending during downturns and reduced it during booms.[20] The rate of *inflation*, that is, the rate at which the general price level rises, was relatively low.[21] And there was a very high degree of financial stability. During the Golden Age, virtually no country was in banking crisis. In contrast, since 1975, anything between 5 and 35 per cent of countries in any given year have been in banking crisis, except for a few years in the mid-2000s.[22]

So in every measure the Golden Age was a remarkable period. When Harold Macmillan, the British prime minister, said, 'You've never had it so good,' he wasn't exaggerating. Exactly what lay behind this sterling economic performance, which was unprecedented and has since been unparalleled, is a matter of an ongoing dispute.

Factors behind the Golden Age

Some point out that, after the Second World War, there was an unusually large pool of new technologies that were waiting to be exploited, which gave an impetus to growth in the Golden Age. Many new technologies that had been developed during the war for military purposes had civilian uses – computers, electronics, radar, jet engines, synthetic rubber, microwave (applied from radar technology) and much more. With the end of the war, a lot of new investments that use these technologies were made, first for post-war reconstruction and then for the meeting of consumer demands pent up during wartime austerity.

There were also some important changes in the international economic system that facilitated economic development during the Golden Age.

The 1944 meeting of the Allies in the Second World War in the New Hampshire resort of Bretton Woods established two key institutions of the post-war international financial system, which are thus dubbed the Bretton Woods Institutions (BWIs) – the International Monetary Fund (IMF) and the International Bank for Reconstruction and Development (IBRD), more commonly known as the World Bank.[23]

The IMF was established to provide short-term funding to countries in **balance of payments** crises (balance of payments is the statement of a country's position in economic transactions with the rest of the world – see Chapter 12 for full details). A balance of payments crisis happens when a country is paying other countries (e.g., when it imports goods or services) so much more than it gets from them that no one is willing to lend money to it any more. The typical result is a financial panic, followed by a deep recession. By providing emergency loans to countries in such a situation, the IMF allowed them to tide over such crises with fewer negative consequences.

The World Bank was established to provide loans for 'project lending' (that is, money that is given to particular investment projects, such as building a dam). By providing loans of longer maturities and/or lower interest rates than are offered by the private-sector banks, the World Bank enabled its client countries to invest more aggressively than otherwise possible.

Making up the third leg of the post-war world economic system was the GATT (General Agreement on Trade and Tariffs), which was signed in 1947. Between 1947 and 1967, the GATT organized six series of negotiations (called 'rounds') that resulted in cuts in tariffs (mostly) among the rich countries. Being between countries at similar levels of development, these cuts brought about positive outcomes by expanding markets and stimulating productivity growth through greater competition.

In Europe, a new experiment in international integration with far-reaching consequences was conducted. It started with the creation of the European Coal and Steel Community (ECSC) in 1951 by six countries (West Germany, France, Italy, the Netherlands, Belgium and Luxembourg) and culminated in the creation of the European Economic Community (EEC) – a free-trade agreement – through the Treaty of Rome (1957).[24] In 1973, the UK, Ireland and Denmark joined the group, which was by then called the EC (European Communities). By bringing peace to a region riven with wars and rivalries and by integrating markets, the EEC contributed to the economic development in the member countries.

The most influential explanation of the Golden Age is, however, that it was mainly the result of reforms in economic policies and institutions that gave birth to the **mixed economy** – mixing positive features of capitalism and socialism.

Following the Great Depression, the limits of laissez-faire capitalism came to be widely accepted. It was agreed that the government should take an active role to deal with the failings of unregulated markets. At the same time, the success in wartime planning during the Second World War diminished scepticism about the feasibility of government intervention. Electoral successes by parties of the left in many European countries, thanks to their key roles in fighting fascism, led to the expansion of the welfare state and greater labour rights.

These changes in policies and institutions are seen to have contributed to the making of the Golden Age in a number of ways – creating social peace, encouraging investment, increasing social mobility and promoting technological innovations. Let me elaborate a little, as this is an important point.

Capitalism Remixed: pro-worker policies and institutions

Soon after the Second World War, many European countries took private enterprises into public ownership or set up new **public enterprises**, or **state-owned enterprises** (SOEs), in key industries, such as steel, railways, banking and energy (coal, nuclear and electricity). These were reflective of the European socialist movements' belief in public control over the means of production as a key element of social democracy, as embodied in the famous Clause IV of the British Labour Party (abolished in 1995 under Tony Blair's 'New Labour' make-over). In countries such as France, Finland, Norway and Austria, SOEs are deemed to have played a key role in generating high growth during the Golden Age by aggressively moving into high-technology industries that the private sector firms found too risky.

Welfare measures, first introduced in the late nineteenth century, were vastly strengthened, with the provision of some basic services nationalized in some countries (e.g., Britain's National Health Service). These were funded by a large increase in taxes (as a proportion of national income). Better welfare measures increased social mobility, increasing the legitimacy of the capitalist system. The resulting social peace encouraged more long-term-oriented investments and thus growth.

Managed capitalism: governments regulate and shape markets – in a variety of ways

Learning the lessons of the Great Depression, governments in all ACCs started to deploy deliberately **counter-cyclical macroeconomic policies**, also known as Keynesian policies (see Chapter 4), expanding government spending and money supply from the central bank during economic downturns and reducing them during upturns.

In recognition of the potential dangers of unregulated financial markets, as manifested in the Great Depression, financial regulations were strengthened. Few countries went as far as the US in separating investment banking from commercial banking, but they all had restrictions on what banks and financial investors can do. This was an era when bankers were considered to be respectable but boring people, unlike their swashbuckling successors today.*

Many governments practised **selective industrial policy** that deliberately promoted targeted 'strategic' industries through a range of measures, such as trade protection and subsidies. The US government officially had no industrial policy but greatly influenced the country's industrial development by providing massive research funding to advanced industries such as computers (funded by the Pentagon), semi-conductors (US Navy), aircraft (US Air Forces), the internet (the DARPA, Defense Advanced Research Projects Agency), and pharmaceuticals and life sciences (National Institutes of Health).[25] Governments in countries such as France, Japan and South Korea did not stop at promoting particular industries and explicitly coordinated policies across industrial sectors through their Five Year Plans – an exercise known as **indicative planning**, to distinguish it from the 'directive' Soviet central planning.

The new dawn: developing countries finally have a go at economic development

The Golden Age saw widespread decolonization. Starting with Korea in 1945 (which was then divided into North and South in 1948) and India (from which Pakistan separated) in 1947, most colonies gained independence. Independence in many nations involved violent struggles against the colonizers. Independence came later to Sub-Saharan Africa, with Kenya becoming the first independent country in 1957. Around half the Sub-Saharan African countries became independent in the first half of the 1960s. Some nations had to wait much longer (Angola and Mozambique in 1975 from Portugal; Namibia in 1990 from South Africa), and some are still waiting, but the vast majority of former colonial societies – now called developing countries – gained independence by the end of the Golden Age.

Upon independence, most post-colonial nations rejected the free-market and free-trade policies that had been imposed on them under colonialism. Some of them became outright socialist (China, North Korea, North

---

* Paul Krugman wrote in 2009: 'Thirty-plus years ago, when I was a graduate student in economics, only the least ambitious of my classmates sought careers in the financial world. Even then, investment banks paid more than teaching or public service – but not that much more, and anyway, everyone knew that banking was, well, boring' ('Making banking boring', *The New York Times*, 9 April 2009).

Vietnam and Cuba), but most of them pursued state-led industrialization strategies while basically remaining capitalist. The strategy is known as the **import substitution industrialization** (ISI) strategy – so called because you are substituting imported manufactured goods with your own. This was done by protecting domestic producers from superior foreign competition by restricting imports (infant industry protection) or heavily regulating the activities of foreign companies operating within national borders. Governments often subsidized private-sector producers and set up SOEs in industries in which private-sector investors were unwilling to invest due to high risk.

With independence dates stretching from 1945 to 1973 and beyond, it is impossible to talk about the 'economic performance of developing countries during the Golden Age'. The usual compromise timeframe for judging developing country economic performance is 1960–80. According to the World Bank data, during this period, per capita income in the developing countries grew at 3 per cent per year, which meant that they kept pace with the more advanced economies, in which growth was 3.2 per cent. The 'miracle' economies of South Korea, Taiwan, Singapore and Hong Kong grew at 7–8 per cent per year in per capita terms during this period, achieving some of the fastest growth rates in human history (together with Japan before them and China after them).

One thing to note, however, is that even the more slowly growing developing regions saw considerable progress during this period. During 1960–80, with per capita income growth of 1.6 per cent per year, Sub-Saharan Africa was the slowest-growing region in the world – Latin America grew at double that rate (3.1 per cent), and East Asia at more than triple that rate (5.3 per cent). However, this is still not a growth rate to be sniffed at. Recall that during the Industrial Revolution, the growth rate of per capita income in Western Europe was only 1 per cent.

The middle way: capitalism works the best with
appropriate government interventions

During the Golden Age of capitalism, government intervention increased enormously in almost all areas in all countries, with the exception of international trade in the rich countries. Despite this, economic performance both in the rich and in the developing countries was much better than before. It has not been bettered since the 1980s, when state intervention was considerably reduced, as I shall show shortly. The Golden Age shows that capitalism's potential can be maximized when it is properly regulated and stimulated by appropriate government actions.

1973–9: The Interregnum

The Golden Age started to unravel with the suspension of US dollar–gold convertibility in 1971. In the Bretton Woods system, the old Gold Standard was abandoned on the recognition that it made macroeconomic manage-ment too rigid, as seen during the Great Depression. But the system was still ultimately anchored in gold, because the US dollar, which had fixed exchange rates with all the other major currencies, was freely convertible to gold (at $35 per ounce). This, of course, was based on the assumption that the dollar was 'as good as gold' – not an unreasonable assumption when the US was producing about half of the world's output and there was an acute dollar shortage all around the world, as everyone wanted to buy American things.

With the post-war reconstruction and then rapid development of other economies, this assumption was not valid any more. Once people realized that the US dollar was not as good as gold, they had a greater incentive to convert dollars into gold, which reduced the US gold reserve even further and made the dollar look even less reliable. The US official liabilities (dollar bills and Treasury Bills, namely, the US government bonds), which had been only half the size of its gold reserve until 1959, became one and a half times larger by 1967.[26]

In 1971, the US dropped its commitment to convert any dollar claims into gold, which led other countries to abandon the practice of tying their national currencies to the dollar at fixed rates over the next couple of years. This created instability in the world economy, with currency values fluctuat-ing according to market sentiments and becoming increasingly subject to currency speculation (investors betting on currencies moving up or down in value).

The end of the Golden Age was marked by the First Oil Shock in 1973, in which oil prices rose fourfold overnight, thanks to the price collusion of the cartel of the oil-producing countries, OPEC (Organization of Petroleum

Exporting Countries). Inflation had been slowly increasing in many countries since the late 1960s but, following the Oil Shock, it shot up.

More importantly, the next several years were characterized by **stagflation**. This newly coined term referred to the breakdown of the age-long economic regularity that prices fall during a recession (or stagnation) and rise during a boom. Now, the economy was stagnating (albeit not exactly in a prolonged recession, like during the Great Depression) but prices were rising fast, at 10, 15 or even 25 per cent per year.[27]

The Second Oil Shock in 1979 finished off the Golden Age by bringing about another bout of high inflation and helping neo-liberal governments come to power in the key capitalist countries, especially in Britain and the US.

This period is often depicted as one of an unmitigated economic disaster by free-market economists, who are critical of the mixed economy model. This is misleading. Growth in the ACCs may have slowed down compared to the Golden Age, but, at 2 per cent per capita, the income growth rate during 1973–80 was still much higher than any period up to the Second World War (1.2–1.4 per cent) and slightly higher than what followed in the next three decades of neo-liberalism (1.8 per cent for 1980–2010).[28] The unemployment rate, at 4.1 per cent average, was higher than that of the Golden Age (3 per cent), but not by much.[29] Still, the fact remains that there was enough dissatisfaction with economic performance during this period for there to be radical changes in the following years.

1980–Today: The Rise and Fall of Neo-liberalism

The Iron Lady: Margaret Thatcher and
the end of British post-war compromise

A major turning point came with the election of Margaret Thatcher as the British prime minister in 1979. Rejecting the post-Second World War 'wet' Tory compromise with Labour, Thatcher began a radical dismantling of the mixed economy, in the process earning the sobriquet 'The Iron Lady' for her uncompromising attitude.

The Thatcher government lowered higher-rate income taxes, reduced government spending (especially in education, housing and transport), introduced laws reducing union power and abolished **capital control** (restriction on the cross-border movement of money). The most symbolic move was **privatization** – sales of SOEs to private investors. Gas, water, electricity, steel, airline, automobile and parts of public housing were privatized.

Interest rates were raised in order to reduce inflation by dampening economic activities and thus demand. The high interest rate attracted foreign capital, driving up the value of the British pound, thus making British exports uncompetitive. The result was a huge recession, as consumers and companies retrenched, between 1979 and 1983. Unemployment soared to 3.3 million people – this under a government that came to power by criticizing James Callaghan's Labour government's record on unemployment, which went over the 1 million mark, with the famous slogan 'Labour isn't working', invented by the advertising agency Saatchi & Saatchi.

During the recession, a huge chunk of British manufacturing industry, which had already been suffering from declining competitiveness, was destroyed. Many traditional industrial centres (such as Manchester, Liverpool and Sheffield) and mining areas (North England and Wales) were devastated, as depicted in movies such as *Brassed Off* (about coal miners in Grimley, a thinly disguised version of Yorkshire coal town Grimethorpe).

The actor: Ronald Reagan and the re-making
of the US economy

Ronald Reagan, the former actor and a former governor of California, became the US president in 1981 and outdid Margaret Thatcher. The Reagan government aggressively cut the higher income tax rates, explaining that these cuts would give the rich greater incentives to invest and create wealth, as they could keep more of the fruits of their investments. Once they created more wealth, it was argued, the rich would spend more, creating more jobs and incomes for everyone else; this is known as the **trickle-down theory**. At the same time, subsidies to the poor (especially in housing) were cut and the minimum wage frozen so that they had a greater incentive to work harder. When you think about it, this was a curious logic – why do we need to make the rich richer to make them work harder but make the poor poorer for the same purpose? Curious or not, this logic, known as **supply-side economics**, became the foundational belief of economic policy for the next three decades in the US – and beyond.

As in the UK, interest rates were jacked up in an attempt to reduce inflation. Between 1979 and 1981, interest rates more than doubled from around 10 per cent to over 20 per cent per year. A significant portion of the US manufacturing industry, which had already been losing ground to Japanese and other foreign competition, could not withstand such an increase in financial costs. The traditional industrial heartland in the Midwest was turned into 'the Rust Belt'.

Financial deregulation in the US at this time laid the foundation for the financial system we have today. The rapid increase in **hostile takeovers**, in which a company is taken over against the will of the existing management, changed the whole corporate culture in the US. Many of those taking over were 'corporate raiders' only interested in **asset stripping** (namely, the sales of valuable assets, regardless of the impact on the long-term viability of the company), immortalized by Gordon 'Greed-is-good' Gekko in the 1987 movie *Wall Street*. To avoid such a fate, firms had to deliver profits faster than before. Otherwise impatient shareholders would sell up, reducing the share prices and thus exposing the firm to greater danger of hostile takeover. The easiest way for companies to deliver quick profit was through **downsizing** – reducing the workforce and minimizing investments beyond what is necessary for immediate results, even though these actions diminish the prospect of the company in the longer run.

The Third World debt crisis and the end of the Third World Industrial Revolution

The most lasting legacy of the high interest rate policy in the US in the late 1970s and the early 1980s – sometimes called the Volcker Shock, named after the then chairman of the US central bank (the Federal Reserve Board) – was *not* in the US but in the developing countries.

Most developing countries had borrowed heavily in the 1970s and the early 1980s, partly to finance their industrialization and partly to pay for the more expensive oil, following the Oil Shocks. When the US interest rates doubled, so did international interest rates, and this led to a widespread default on foreign debts by developing nations, starting with the default of Mexico in 1982. This is known as the **Third World Debt Crisis**, thus known because the developing world was then called the Third World, after the First World (the advanced capitalist world) and the Second World (the socialist world).

Facing economic crises, developing countries had to resort to the Bretton Woods Institutions (the IMF and the World Bank, just to remind you). The BWIs made it a condition that borrowing countries implement the **structural adjustment programme** (SAP), which required shrinking the role of the government in the economy by cutting its budget, privatizing SOEs and reducing regulations, especially on international trade.

The results of the SAP were extremely disappointing, to say the least. Despite making all the necessary 'structural' reforms, most countries experienced dramatic growth slowdown in the 1980s and the 1990s. Per capita income growth rates in Latin America (including the Caribbean) collapsed from 3.1 per cent in 1960–80 to 0.3 per cent in 1980–2000. In Sub-Saharan Africa (SSA), per capita income fell during this period; in 2000, it was 13 per cent lower than in 1980. The result was an effective arresting of the Third World Industrial Revolution, which is the name that Ajit Singh, the Cambridge economist, used in order to describe the economic development experience of developing countries in the first few decades following decolonization.

Only Chile did well out of neo-liberal policies of the 1980s and the 1990s, but at considerable human cost under the Pinochet dictatorship (1974–90).[30] All the other success stories of this period were economies that used state intervention extensively and liberalized only gradually. The best examples of this were Japan, the 'tiger' (or 'dragon', depending on your animal preference) economies of East Asia (South Korea, Taiwan and Singapore) and, increasingly, China.

The wall comes crashing down: the collapse of socialism

Then, in 1989, a momentous change happened. That year, the Soviet Union started to unravel, and the Berlin Wall was torn down. Germany was reunited (1990), and most Eastern European countries abandoned communism. By 1991, the Soviet Union itself was dismembered. With China gradually but surely opening up and liberalizing since 1978 and with Vietnam (unified under the Communist rule in 1975) also adopting its 'open door' policy (Doi Moi) in 1986, the socialist bloc was reduced to a few die-hard states, notably North Korea and Cuba.

The problems with the socialist economies were already well known: the difficulty of planning an increasingly diverse economy, incentive problems arising from weak links between performance and reward and widespread politically determined inequality in an ostensibly equal society (see Chapter 9). But few, including the most anti-socialist commentators, had thought that the bloc would implode so quickly.

The ultimate problem was that the Soviet bloc economies had tried to build an alternative economic system based on essentially second-rate technologies. There were, of course, areas like space and arms technologies where they were leading the world (after all, in 1957 the Soviet Union put the first ever man in space), thanks to the disproportionate amount of resources poured into them. However, when it became evident that it could only offer its citizens second-rate consumer products – as symbolized by Trabant, the East German car with plastic body, which quickly became a museum piece after the fall of the Berlin Wall – the citizens revolted.

In the next decade or so, the socialist countries in Eastern Europe made a headlong dash to transform themselves (back) into capitalist ones. Many thought that the 'transition' *could be* made quickly. Surely, it was just a matter of privatizing SOEs and reintroducing the market system, which is after all one of the most 'natural' human institutions? Others added that the transition *had to be* made quickly, in order not to give time to the old ruling elite to regroup itself and resist change. Most countries adopted 'Big Bang' reforms, trying to bring capitalism back overnight.

The result was nothing short of a disaster in most countries. Yugoslavia disintegrated and descended into wars and ethnic cleansing. Many former republics of the Soviet Union experienced deep depressions. In Russia, the economic collapse and the resulting unemployment and economic insecurity caused so much mental stress, alcoholism and other health problems that it is estimated that millions more people died than would have been the case if the pre-transition trends had continued.[31] In many countries, the old elite simply 'changed their suits' and transformed themselves from party *apparatchiks* into businessmen, enriching themselves hugely by acquiring state assets at knock-down prices through corrupt practices and 'insider dealings' in the privatization process. The Central European countries – Poland, Hungary, the Czech Republic and Slovakia – fared better, especially after they joined the European Union in 2004, thanks to being more gradualist in their reform and to their better skill bases. But even in the case of these countries, it is difficult to hail the transition experience as a great success.

The fall of the socialist bloc ushered in a period of 'free-market triumphalism'. Some, such as the American (then) neo-con thinker Francis Fukuyama, pronounced the 'end of history' (no, not the end of the world) on the grounds that we had finally conclusively identified the best economic system in the form of capitalism. The fact that capitalism comes in many varieties, each with particular strengths and weaknesses, was blissfully ignored in the euphoric mood of the day.

One world, ready or not: globalization and the new world economic order

By the mid-1990s, neo-liberalism had spread throughout the world. Most of the old socialist world had been absorbed into the capitalist world economy, either through the 'Big Bang' reforms or, as in the case of China and Vietnam, through gradual but constant opening up and deregulation. By this time, market opening and liberalization had also progressed considerably in most developing countries. In most countries, this happened rapidly due to the SAP, but there were some others where it happened more gradually through voluntary policy changes, such as in India.

Around this time, some important international agreements were signed that signalled a new era of global integration. In 1994, the NAFTA (North American Free Trade Agreement) was signed between the US, Canada and Mexico. It was the first major free-trade agreement between developed countries and a developing country. In 1995, the Uruguay Round of the GATT talks was concluded, resulting in the expansion of the GATT into the WTO (World Trade Organization). The WTO covers many more areas (e.g., intellectual property rights, such as patents and trademarks, and trade in services) and has more sanctioning power than the GATT did. Economic integration progressed further in the EU, with the completion of the 'Single Market' project (with the so-called 'four freedoms of movement' – of goods, services, people and money) in 1993 and with the 1995 accession of Sweden, Finland and Austria.* The combined result was the creation of an interna-

---

* Being 'neutral' countries in the Cold War, these countries had kept their distance from the EU, despite being in Western Europe.

tional trading system that was much more geared towards freer (although not entirely free) trade.

Also the idea of globalization emerged as the defining concept of the time. International economic integration of course had been going on since the sixteenth century, but according to the new globalization narrative, this process has reached an entirely new stage. This was thanks to the technological revolutions in communications (the internet) and transportation (air travel, container shipping), which were leading to the 'death of distance'. According to the globalizers, countries now had no choice but to embrace this new reality and fully open up to international trade and investments, while liberalizing their domestic economies. Those who resisted this inevitability were derided as the 'modern Luddites', who think they can bring back a bygone world by reversing technological progress (see above). Book titles like *The Borderless World*, *The World Is Flat* and *One World, Ready or Not* summed up the essence of this new discourse.

The beginning of the end: the Asian financial crisis

The euphoria of the late 1980s and the early 1990s didn't last. The first sign that not everything was fine with the 'brave new world' came with the financial crisis in Mexico in 1995. Too many people had invested in Mexican financial assets with the unrealistic expectation that, having fully embraced free-market policies and having signed the NAFTA, the country was going to be the next miracle economy. Mexico was bailed out by the US and the Canadian governments (who didn't want a collapse in their new free-trade partner) as well as by the IMF.

In 1997, a bigger shock came about with the Asian financial crisis. A number of hitherto successful Asian economies – the so-called 'MIT economies' (Malaysia, Indonesia and Thailand) and South Korea – got into financial troubles. The culprit was the bursting of the **asset bubbles** (asset prices rising well above their realistic levels, based on unrealistic expectations).

While they had been more cautious than other developing regions in opening up their economies, these countries opened up their financial markets quite radically in the late 1980s and the early 1990s. Now facing fewer restrictions, their banks borrowed aggressively from the rich countries, which had lower interest rates. In their turn, the rich-country banks saw little risk in lending to countries with decades-long excellent economic records. As more foreign capital flowed in, asset prices went up, which enabled firms and households in the Asian countries to borrow even more, using their now more valuable assets as collateral. Soon the process became a self-fulfilling prophecy, as the expectation of ever-rising asset prices justified further borrowing and lending (sounds familiar?). When it later became clear that those asset prices were unsustainable, money was pulled out, and financial crises ensued.

The Asian crisis left a huge scar in the afflicted economies. In economies where 5 per cent growth (in per capita terms) was considered a 'recession', output *fell* in 1998 by 16 per cent in Indonesia and 6–7 per cent in the other economies. Tens of millions of people were thrown out of work in societies where unemployment means penury, given the small size of the welfare state.

In return for the bail-out money from the IMF and the rich countries, the crisis-stricken Asian countries had to accept a lot of policy changes – all in the direction of liberalizing their markets, especially their financial markets. While it pushed the Asian economies themselves on in a more market-oriented direction, the Asian crisis – and the Brazilian and the Russian crises that immediately followed it – actually planted the first seed of scepticism about post-Cold War free-market triumphalism. There were serious discussions about the need to reform the global financial system, much of them along the same lines as the ones that we have seen following the 2008 global financial crisis. Even many leading advocates of globalization – like the *Financial Times* columnist Martin Wolf and the free-trade economist Jagdish Bhagwati – started questioning the wisdom of allowing free international capital flows. All was not well with the new global economy.

The false dawn: from the dot.com boom to
the Great Moderation

When these crises were brought under control, talk of global financial reform receded. In the US, a major push in the other direction came in the form of the 1999 repeal of the iconic New Deal legislation, the 1933 Glass-Steagall Act, which structurally separated commercial banking from investment banking.

There was another moment of panic in 2000, when the so-called dot.com bubble – in which internet-based companies with no prospect of generating any profit in the foreseeable future had their shares valued at absurdly high levels – burst in the US. The panic soon receded, as the US Federal Reserve intervened and cut interest rates aggressively and the central banks of other rich economies followed suit.

From then on, the early years of the millennium seemed to be going swimmingly well in the rich countries, especially in the US. Growth was robust, if not exactly spectacular. Asset prices (prices of real estate, company shares and so on) seemed to be going up forever. Inflation remained low. Economists – including Ben Bernanke, the chairman of the Federal Reserve Board between February 2006 and January 2014 – talked of the 'Great Moderation', in which the science of economics had finally conquered **boom and bust** (or the economy going up and down by large margins). Alan Greenspan, the chairman of the Federal Reserve Board between August 1987 and January 2006, was revered as the 'Maestro' (as immortalized in the title of his biography by Bob Woodward of Watergate fame) who had a near-alchemical skill in managing a permanent economic boom without stoking inflation or courting financial trouble.

During the middle years of the 2000s, the rest of the world finally started to feel the 'miracle' growth of China of the preceding two decades. In 1978, at the beginning of its economic reform, the Chinese economy accounted for only 2.5 per cent of the world economy.[32] It had minimal impact on the rest of the world – its share of world merchandise (goods) export was a mere 0.8 per cent.[33] By 2007, the corresponding numbers had risen to 6 per cent and 8.7 per cent.[34] Being relatively poorly endowed with natural resources and growing at breakneck speed, it started sucking in food, minerals and fuel from the rest of the world, and the effect of its growing weight was felt more and more strongly.

This gave a boost to the raw-material exporters of Africa and Latin America, finally allowing these economies to make up some of the ground they had lost in the 1980s and the 1990s. China also became a major lender and investor in some African countries, giving the latter some leverage in negotiating with the BWIs and the traditional aid donors, such as the US and the European countries. In the case of the Latin American countries, this period also saw a departure from the neo-liberal policies that had served them so poorly in several countries. Brazil (Lula), Bolivia (Morales),

Venezuela (Chavez), Argentina (Kirchner), Ecuador (Correa) and Uruguay (Vasquez) were the most prominent examples.

A crack in the wall: the 2008 global financial crisis

In early 2007, alarm bells were rung by those who were worried about the (non-)repayment of mortgage loans that are euphemistically called 'sub-prime' (read 'having high chance of default'), made by US financial firms in the preceding housing boom. People with no stable income and chequered credit histories were lent more money than they could afford to pay back, on the assumption that house prices would keep going up. They would be able to repay their loans, it was reckoned, by selling their houses, if worse came to worst. On top of that, thousands or even hundreds of thousands of these high-risk mortgage loans were combined into 'composite' financial products, such as the MBS and the CDO (no need to know what they were at this stage – I will explain them in detail in Chapter 8) and sold as low-risk assets, on the assumption that the chance of a large number of borrowers simultaneously getting into trouble must be much lower than that for individual borrowers.

Initially, the problem mortgage loans in the US were estimated to be $50–100 billion – not a small amount but an amount that can be easily absorbed by the system (or so many claimed at the time). However, the crisis erupted properly in the summer of 2008, with the bankruptcy of the investment banks Bear Stearns and then Lehmann Brothers. A huge financial panic swept the world. It was revealed that even some of the most venerable names in the financial industry were in big trouble, having generated and bought huge numbers of dubious composite financial products.

The 'Keynesian spring' and the return of the
free-market orthodoxy – with a vengeance

The initial responses of the major economies were very different from those following the Great Depression. Macroeconomic policies were Keynesian in the sense that they let huge budget deficits develop – at least not by cutting spending in line with falling tax revenues and in some cases by increasing government spending (China did this most aggressively). Major financial institutions (e.g., the UK's Royal Bank of Scotland) and industrial firms (e.g., GM and Chrysler in the US) were bailed out with public money. Central banks brought interest rates down to historical lows – for example, the Bank of England cut its interest rate to the lowest level since its foundation in 1694. When they could not cut their interest rates any more, they engaged in what is known as **quantitative easing** (QE) – basically, the central bank creating money out of thin air and releasing it into the economy, mainly by buying government bonds.

Soon, however, free-market orthodoxy came back with a vengeance. May 2010 was the turning point. The election of the Conservative-led coalition government in the UK and the imposition of the Eurozone bail-out programme for Greece in that month signalled the comeback of the old balanced budget doctrine. **Austerity** budgets, in which spending is cut radically, have been imposed in the UK and in the so-called PIIGS economies (Portugal, Italy, Ireland, Greece and Spain). The success of the Republicans in pushing the Obama government in the US to accept a huge spending cut programme in 2011 and the reaffirmation of the anti-deficit bias of the core European countries in the form of the European Fiscal Compact, signed in 2012, pushed things even further in that direction. In all these countries, but especially the UK, the political right are even using the argument for balancing the budget as an excuse to severely prune back the welfare state, which they have always wanted to reduce.

The consequences: the lost decade?

The 2008 crisis has had devastating consequences, and its end is nowhere in sight. Four years after the crisis, at the end of 2012, per capita output remained lower than in 2007 in twenty-two of the thirty-four member countries of the OECD (Organization for Economic Cooperation and Development), the Paris-based club of rich countries (with a handful of developing country members).* GDP per capita in 2012, when filtering out the effect of price inflation, was 26 per cent below the 2007 level in Greece, 12 per cent below in Ireland, 7 per cent below in Spain and 6 per cent below in the UK. Even in the US, which is said to have recovered better than other

---

* The OECD was founded in 1961, and comprises most Western European countries, Turkey, the US and Canada. By the mid-1970s, Japan, Finland, Australia and New Zealand were added. Since the mid-1990s, several former socialist countries (e.g., Hungary and Estonia) and some richer developing countries (Mexico and Chile) have joined it.

countries from the crisis, per capita income in 2012 was still 1.4 per cent below the 2007 level.*

With the austerity budget, the prospect for economic recovery in many of these countries is dim. The problem is that a radical cut in government spending in a stagnating (or even shrinking) economy holds back recovery. We have already seen this during the Great Depression. As a result, it may take a good part of the decade before many of these countries can get back to what they used to be in 2007. They could well be in the middle of a 'lost decade', as was experienced in Japan (the 1990s) and in Latin America (the 1980s).

It is estimated that, at its depth, the crisis created 80 million extra unemployed people worldwide. In Spain and Greece, unemployment shot up from around 8 per cent before the crisis to 26 per cent and 28 per cent respectively in the summer of 2013. Youth unemployment is well over 55 per cent. Even in countries experiencing 'milder' unemployment problems, such as the US and the UK, official unemployment rates reached 8–10 per cent at their heights.

Too little too late?: prospects for reform

Despite the scale of the crisis, policy reforms have been slow in coming. Despite the fact that the cause of the crisis lay in excessive liberalization in the financial market, financial reforms have been rather mild and are being introduced very slowly (over several years, when the US banks had a year to comply with the much tougher New Deal financial reforms). There are areas of finance, such as the trading in overly complex financial products, in which even mild and slow reforms are not being introduced.

Of course, this trend could be reversed. After all, in both the post-Depression US and Sweden, the reforms came only after a few years of economic downturn and hardship. Indeed, the electorate in the Netherlands, France and Greece voted out pro-austerity parties in the spring of 2012; Italian voters did likewise in 2013. The EU has introduced some financial regulations that are tougher than what many people had imagined likely (e.g., financial transaction tax, cap on financial sector bonuses). Switzerland,

---

* At the time of writing (early January 2014), the figures for 2013 were not out, but, on a provisional estimate made on the basis of the OECD data, in the third quarter of 2013 per capita output remained lower than in 2007 in nineteen out of the thirty-four OECD member countries.

frequently considered the haven of the super-rich, passed a law in 2013 preventing high rewards for top managers with mediocre performances. While there remains a lot more to be done in relation to financial reform, these are actually developments that would have been considered impossible before the crisis.

Further Reading

P. BAIROCH
Economics and World History: Myths and Paradoxes (New York and London: Harvester Wheatsheaf, 1993).

H.-J. CHANG
Kicking Away the Ladder: Development Strategy in Historical Perspective (London: Anthem, 2002).

B. EICHENGREEN
The European Economy since 1945: Coordinated Capitalism and Beyond (Princeton, NJ: Princeton University Press, 2007).

A. GLYN
Capitalism Unleashed (Oxford: Oxford University Press, 2007).

D. LANDES
The Unbound Prometheus (Cambridge: Cambridge University Press, 2003).

A. MADDISON
Contours of the World Economy, 1-2030 AD (Oxford: Oxford University Press, 2007).

S. MARGLIN AND J. SCHOR (EDS.)
The Golden Age of Capitalism (Oxford: Clarendon, 1990).

D. NAYYAR
Catch Up: Developing Countries in the World Economy (Oxford: Oxford University Press, 2013).

CHAPTER 4

Let a Hundred Flowers Bloom

HOW TO 'DO' ECONOMICS

'Any customer can have a car painted any colour that he wants so long as it is black.'
HENRY FORD

'Let a hundred flowers bloom, let a hundred schools of thought contend.'
MAO ZEDONG

The One Ring to Rule Them All?: The Diversity of Approaches to Economics

Contrary to what most economists would have you believe, there isn't just one kind of economics – Neoclassical economics. In this chapter, I introduce no less than nine different kinds, or schools, as they are often known.*

These schools are not irreconcilable enemies, however; the boundaries between schools are actually fuzzy.[1] But it is important to recognize that there are distinctive ways of conceptualizing and explaining the economy, or 'doing' economics, if you like. And none of these schools can claim superiority over others and still less a monopoly over truth.

One reason is the nature of theory itself. All theories, including natural sciences like physics, necessarily involve abstraction and thus cannot capture every aspect of the complexity of the real world.[2] This means that no theory is good at explaining everything. Each theory possesses particular strengths and weaknesses, depending on what it highlights and ignores, how it conceptualizes things and how it analyses relationships between them. There is no such thing as one theory that can explain everything better than others – or the 'one ring to rule them all',[3] if you are a fan of *The Lord of the Rings*.

Added to this is the fact that, unlike things that are studied by natural scientists, human beings have their own free will and imagination. They do not simply respond to external conditions. They try – and often succeed – to

---

* There are even more, if we include smaller schools (e.g., the Neo-Ricardian school, the Latin American Structuralist school, feminist economics, ecological economics). The number would be increased if we made sub-schools of some of the schools independent (e.g., different strands listed under the Developmentalist tradition).

change those very conditions by imagining a utopia, persuading others and organizing society differently; as Karl Marx once eloquently put it, '[m]en make their own history'.* Any subject studying human beings, including economics, has to be humble about its predictive power.

Moreover, unlike the natural sciences, economics involves value judgements, even though many Neoclassical economists would tell you that what they do is *value-free* science. As I will show in the following chapters, behind technical concepts and dry numbers lie all sorts of value judgements: what is the good life; how minority views should be treated; how social improvements should be defined; and what are morally acceptable ways of achieving the 'greater good', however it is defined.[4] Even if one theory is more 'correct' from some political or ethical points of view, it may not be so from another.

Cocktails or the Whole Drinks Cabinet?: How to Read This Chapter

While there is a good reason for the reader to learn about different schools of economics, I accept that being suddenly asked to taste nine different flavours of ice cream when you had thought that there is only plain vanilla can be quite overwhelming.

Even though I simplify things a lot, readers may still find the discussion too complicated. In order to help them, I preface my presentation of each school with a one-sentence summary. These summaries are, of course, far too simplistic, but at least they will help you overcome the initial fear that you are about to walk into a new city without a map, or, rather, a smart phone.

Now, even those who are willing to learn about more than one school may feel that nine schools is six or seven too many. I agree. For them, I offer in the box below a number of 'cocktails' made up of two to four different schools, each of which covers particular issues well. Some of these cocktails, such as CMSI or CK, will be like Bloody Mary with a lot of Tabasco sauce, given the disagreements present. Some others, such as MDKI or CMDS, may taste like a Planter's Punch, with different flavours complementing each other.

---

* He then immediately added that 'they do not make it under circumstances chosen by themselves', emphasizing that we change our environment but are also its products.

My hope is that tasting one or two of those cocktails may even make you want to taste the whole drinks cabinet. Even if you don't want to go the whole length, tasting one or two of them will still have shown you that there is more than one way to 'do' economics.

ECONOMICS COCKTAILS

Ingredients: A, B, C, D, I, K, M, N and S
or
Austrian, Behaviouralist, Classical,
Developmentalist, Institutionalist, Keynesian,
Marxist, Neoclassical and Schumpeterian.

On diverging views of the vitality and the viability of capitalism, take CMSI.

If you want to know why we sometimes need government intervention, take NDK.

To discover different ways of conceptualizing the individual, take NAB.

In order to learn that there is a lot more to the economy than markets, take MIB.

If you want to see how groups, especially classes, are theorized, take CMKI.

To study how technologies develop and productivities rise, take CMDS.

To understand economic systems, rather than just their components, take MDKI.

If you want to find out why corporations exist and how they work, take SIB.

If exploring how individuals and society interact is your thing, take ANIB.

For debates surrounding unemployment and recession, take CK.

For various ways of defending the free market, take CAN.

Health warning: On no account drink only one ingredient – liable to lead to tunnel vision, arrogance and possibly brain death.

The Classical School

One-sentence summary: *The market keeps all producers alert through competition, so leave it alone.*

Today, the Neoclassical school dominates. As you will have guessed, there was Classical economics before Neoclassical economics, of which the latter is the supposed heir (although the Marxist school has an equally good claim to be its heir, as I shall explain).

The Classical school of economics – or, rather the Classical school of **political economy**, as the subject was then called – emerged in the late eighteenth century and dominated the subject until the late nineteenth century. Its founder is Adam Smith (1723–90), who we have discussed already. Smith's ideas were further developed in the early nineteenth century by three near-contemporaries – David Ricardo (1772–1823), Jean-Baptiste Say (1767–1832), and Robert Malthus (1766–1834).

The invisible hand, Say's Law and free trade: the key arguments of the Classical school

According to the Classical school, the pursuit of self-interests by individual economic actors produces a socially beneficial outcome, in the form of maximum national wealth. This paradoxical outcome is made possible by the power of competition in the market. In their attempts to make profits, producers strive to supply cheaper and better things, ultimately producing their products at the minimum possible costs, thus maximizing national output. This idea is known as the **invisible hand** and has become arguably the most influential metaphor in economics, although Smith himself used it only once in *The Wealth of Nations* (*TWON*) and did not accord it a prominent role in his theory.*

Most Classical economists believed in the so-called Say's Law, which states that supply creates its own demand. The reasoning was that every economic activity generates incomes (wages, profits, etc.) equivalent to the

---

* Smith, unlike most other Classical economists, was aware that people have motives besides self-seeking, such as sympathy, passion and adherence to social norms. These motives were the main subjects of *The Theory of Moral Sentiments*, the companion volume to *TWON*.

value of its output. Therefore, it was argued, there can be no such thing as a recession due to a shortfall in demand. Any recession had to be due to exogenous factors, such as a war or the failure of a major bank. Since the market was incapable of naturally generating a recession, any government attempt to counter it, say, through deliberate deficit spending, was condemned as disturbing the natural order. This meant that recessions that could have been cut short or made milder became prolonged in the days of Classical economics.

The Classical school rejected any attempt by the government to restrict the free market, say, through protectionism or regulation. Ricardo developed a new theory of international trade, known as the theory of **comparative advantage**, further strengthening the argument for free trade. His theory showed that, under certain assumptions, even when a country cannot produce any product more cheaply than another country can, free trade between them will allow both to maximize their outputs. They can achieve this by specializing in, and exporting, products in which they have *comparative* advantage – those with the largest relative cost advantages in the case of the more efficient country and those with the smallest relative cost disadvantages in the case of the less efficient country.*

The Classical school viewed the capitalist economy as being made up of 'three classes of the community', in Ricardo's words – that is, capitalists, workers and landlords. The school, especially Ricardo, emphasized that it is in the long-term interest of everyone that the greatest share of national income go to the capitalist class (that is, profits), because it is the only class that invests and generates economic growth; the working class was too poor to save and invest, while the landlord class was using its income (rents) on 'unproductive' luxury consumption, such as the employment of servants. According to Ricardo and his followers, the growing population in Britain was forcing the cultivation of increasingly lower-quality land, constantly raising the rents for existing (higher-quality) land. This meant that the share of profit was gradually falling, threatening investment and growth. His recommendation was to abolish the protection for grain producers (called the

---

* So, *comparative* in comparative advantage refers to comparison between the products that a country can potentially produce. The possibility that one country is more efficient than another in producing the same product is already reflected in the term *advantage*. For a more detailed exposition of the theory, see Chapter 3, 'My Six Year Old Son Should Get a Job', in my book *Bad Samaritans*.

Corn Laws in Britain at the time) and import cheaper food from countries where good-quality land was still available, so that the share going to profits, and thus the ability of the economy to invest and grow, could be raised.

Class analysis and comparative advantage: the
Classical school's relevance for today

Despite being an old school with few current practitioners, the Classical school is still relevant for our time.

The notion of the economy as being made up of classes, rather than individuals, allows us to see how an individual's behaviour is strongly affected by her place in the system of production. The fact that marketing companies still use class categories in devising their strategies suggests that class is still a very relevant category, even though most academic economists may not use the concept or even actively deny its existence.

Ricardo's theory of comparative advantage, while having clear limitations as a static theory that takes a country's technologies as given, is still one of the best theories of international trade. It is more realistic than the Neoclassical version, known as the Heckscher-Ohlin-Samuelson theory (henceforth HOS), which is today the dominant version.* In HOS, it is assumed that all countries are technologically and organizationally capable of producing everything. They choose to specialize in different products only because different products use different combinations of capital and labour, whose relative endowments differ across countries. This assumption leads to unrealistic conclusions: if Guatemala isn't producing things like BMWs, it is not because it cannot but because it is not economical to do so, given that their production uses a lot of capital and little labour, when Guatemala has a lot of labour and little capital.

Sometimes wrong, sometimes outdated: limitations of the Classical school

Some of the theories of the Classical school were simply wrong. The school's adherence to Say's Law made it incapable of dealing with **macroeconomic** problems (namely, problems that are to do with the overall

---

* The theory is named after Eli Heckscher and Bertil Ohlin, the two Swedish economists who developed the idea, and Paul Samuelson, the American economist (and the author of the most famous economics textbook in the twentieth century), who perfected it.

state of the economy, such as recession or unemployment). Its theory of the market at the **microeconomic** level (namely, the level of individual economic actors) was also severely limited. It did not have the theoretical tools to explain why unrestrained competition in the market might not produce socially desirable outcomes.

Some Classical theories, even if not wrong in the logical sense, have limited applicability today because they were designed for a world very different from ours. A lot of 'iron laws' of Classical economics turned out to be no such things. For example, the Classical economists thought that population pressure would raise agricultural rents and squeeze industrial profits to such an extent that investment might cease, because they did not – and could not – know how much the technologies for food production and birth control would develop.

The Neoclassical School

One-sentence summary: *Individuals know what they are doing, so leave them alone – except when markets malfunction.*

The Neoclassical school arose in the 1870s, from the works of William Jevons (1835–82) and Leon Walras (1834–1910). It was firmly established with the publication of Alfred Marshall's *Principles of Economics* in 1890.

Around Marshall's time, Neoclassical economists also succeeded in changing the name of the discipline from the traditional 'political economy' to 'economics'. The change signalled that the Neoclassical school wanted its analysis to become a pure science, shorn of political (and thus ethical) dimensions that involve subjective value judgements.

Demand factors, individuals and exchanges:
differences with the Classical school
The Neoclassical school claimed to be the intellectual heir of the Classical school but felt itself to be sufficiently different to attach the prefix 'Neo'. The key differences are as follows.

It emphasized the role of demand conditions (derived from the subjective valuation of products by consumers) in the determination of the value of a good. Classical economists believed that the value of a product is determined by supply conditions, that is, the costs of its production. They measured the costs by the labour time expended in producing it – this is known as the **labour theory of value**. Neoclassical economists emphasized that the value (which they called the price) of a product also depends on how much the product is valued by potential consumers; the fact that something is difficult to produce does not mean that it is more valuable. Marshall refined this idea by arguing that demand conditions matter more in determining prices in the short run, when supply cannot be changed, while supply conditions matter more in the long run, when more investments (disinvestments) can be made in facilities to produce more (less) of what is demanded more (less).

The school conceptualized the economy as a collection of rational and selfish individuals, rather than as a collection of distinct classes, as the Classical school did. The individual as envisaged in Neoclassical economics is a rather one-dimensional being – a 'pleasure machine', as he was called, devoted to the maximization of pleasure (**utility**) and the minimization of pain (**disutility**), usually in narrowly defined material terms. As I shall discuss in Chapter 5, this severely limits the explanatory power of Neoclassical economics.[5]

The Neoclassical school shifted the focus of economics from production to consumption and exchange. For the Classical school, especially Adam Smith, production was at the heart of the economic system. As we saw in Chapter 2, Smith was deeply interested in how the changes in the organization of production were transforming the economy. He had a view of history in which societies develop in stages according to the dominant form of production – hunting, pastoralism, agriculture and commerce (this idea was further developed by Karl Marx, as I shall discuss below). In contrast, in Neoclassical economics, the economic system is essentially envisaged as a web of exchanges, ultimately driven by choices made by 'sovereign' consumers. There is little discussion of how actual processes of production are organized and changed.

Self-interested individuals and self-equilibrating
markets: similarities with the Classical school

Despite these differences, the Neoclassical school inherited and developed two central ideas of the Classical school. The first is the idea that economic actors are driven by self-interest but that the competition in the market ensures that their actions collectively produce a socially benign outcome. The other is the idea that markets are self-equilibrating. The conclusion is, as in Classical economics, that capitalism – or, rather, the market economy, as the school prefers to call it – is a system that is best left alone, as it has a tendency to revert to the equilibrium.

This laissez-faire conclusion of the Neoclassical school was further intensified by a critical theoretical development in the early twentieth century, intended to allow us to judge social improvements in an objective way. Vilfredo Pareto (1848–1923) argued that, if we respect the rights of every sovereign individual, we should consider a social change an improvement only when it makes some people better off without making anyone worse off. There should be no more individual sacrifices in the name of the 'greater good'. This is known as the **Pareto criterion** and forms the basis for all judgements on social improvements in Neoclassical economics today.[6] In real life, unfortunately, there are few changes that hurt no one; thus the Pareto criterion effectively becomes a recipe to stick to the status quo and let things be – laissez faire. Its adoption thus imparted a huge conservative bias to the Neoclassical school.

The anti-free-market revolution: the market failure approach

Two theoretical developments in the 1920s and the 1930s severed the apparently unbreakable link between Neoclassical economics and the advocacy of free-market policies. After these developments, it has become impossible to equate Neoclassical economics with free-market economics, as some people still mistakenly do.

The more fundamental of these was the birth of welfare economics, or the **market failure approach**, developed by Cambridge professor Arthur Pigou in the 1920s. Pigou argued that there are occasions when market prices fail to reflect the true social costs and benefits. For example, a factory may pollute air and water because air and water have no market prices and thus it can treat them as free goods. But as a result of such 'over-production' of pollution, the environment is destroyed, and the society suffers.

The problem is that the effects of some economic activities are not priced in the market and thus not reflected in economic decisions – this is known as an **externality**. In this case, it would be justified for the government to make the factory, which is said to create a **negative externality**, pollute less through pollution taxes or regulations (e.g., a fine on excessive release of effluents). Conversely, there may be activities that have a **positive externality**. An example may be research and development (or R&D) activities by a company. By generating new knowledge that can be used by others, R&D creates more value than what accrues to the company conducting it. On this occasion, the government would be justified to pay subsidies to anyone who does R&D so that there would be more of it. Subsequently, other types of market failure were added to Pigou's externality, as I will discuss in Chapter 11.

A more minor yet important modification came in the 1930s, in the form of the **compensation principle**. The principle proposes that a change may be deemed a social improvement even when it violates the Pareto criterion (in the sense of there being some losers), if the total gains for the gainers are large enough to compensate all the losers and still leave something behind. By allowing them to endorse a change that may hurt some people (but can fully compensate for their damages), the compensation principle has allowed Neoclassical economists to avoid the ultra-conservative bias of the Pareto criterion. Of course, the trouble is that the compensation is rarely made in reality.*

The counter-revolution: the renaissance of the free-market view

With these modifications, there was no reason for the Neoclassical school to remain committed to free-market policies any more. Indeed, between the 1930s and the 1970s, many Neoclassical economists were *not* free-market economists. The current state of affairs in which the predominant majority of Neoclassical economists are of free-market leaning is actually due more to the shift in political ideology since the 1980s than to the absence or the poor quality of theories within Neoclassical economics identifying the limits of the free market. If anything, the arsenal for Neoclassical economists who reject free-market policies has been expanded since the 1980s by the development of **information economics**, led by

---

* Despite the fact that it was going to hurt US workers in industries like automobile and textiles, many Neoclassical economists advocated the NAFTA, the free-trade agreement with Mexico and Canada, on the ground that the national gains from increased trade are more than enough to compensate those (and other) losers. Unfortunately, the losers have not been fully compensated, so the outcome could not be called a Pareto improvement.

Joseph Stiglitz, George Akerlof and Michael Spence. Information economics explains why **asymmetric information** – the situation in which one party to a market exchange knows something that the other does not – makes markets malfunction or even cease to exist.[7]

However, since the 1980s, many Neoclassical economists have also developed theories that go so far as to deny the possibility of market failures, such as the 'rational expectation' theory in macroeconomics or the 'efficient market hypothesis' in financial economics, basically arguing that people know what they are doing and therefore the government should leave them alone – or, in technical terms, economic agents are rational and therefore market outcomes efficient. At the same time, the **government failure** argument was advanced, to argue that market failure in itself cannot justify government intervention because governments may fail even more than markets do (more on this in Chapter 11).

Precision and versatility: the strengths of the Neoclassical school

The Neoclassical school has some unique strengths. Its insistence on breaking phenomena down to the individual level gives it a high degree of precision and logical clarity. It is also versatile. It may be very difficult for someone to be a 'right-wing' Marxist or a 'left-wing' Austrian, but there are many 'left-wing' Neoclassical economists, such as Joseph Stiglitz and Paul Krugman, as well as very 'right-wing' ones, like James Buchanan and Gary Becker. To exaggerate only slightly, if you are clever enough, you can justify any government policy, any corporate strategy, or any individual action with the help of Neoclassical economics.

Unrealistic individuals, over-acceptance of the status quo and neglect of production: limitations of the Neoclassical school

The Neoclassical school has been criticized for assuming too strongly that people are selfish and rational. From soldiers selflessly taking bullets for their comrades to highly educated bankers and economists believing in the fairy tale of never-ending financial boom (until 2008), there is simply too much evidence against this assumption (see Chapter 5 for details).

Neoclassical economics is too accepting of the status quo. In analysing individual choices, it accepts as given the underlying social structure – the distribution of money and power, if you will. This makes it look at only choices that are possible without fundamental social changes. For example, many Neoclassical economists, even the 'liberal' Paul Krugman, argue that we should not criticize low-wage factory jobs in poor countries because the alternative may be no job at all. This is true, *if* we take the underlying socio-economic structure as given. However, once we are willing to change the structure itself, there are a lot of alternatives to those low-wage jobs. With new labour laws that strengthen worker rights, land reform that reduces the supply of cheap labour to factories (as more people stay in the countryside) or industrial policies that create high-skilled jobs, the choice for workers can be between low-wage jobs and higher-wage ones, rather than between low-wage jobs and no jobs.

The Neoclassical school's focus on exchange and consumption makes it neglect the sphere of production, which is a large – and the most important, according to many other schools of economics – part of our economy. Commenting on this deficiency, Ronald Coase, the Institutionalist economist, in his 1992 Nobel Economics Prize lecture, disparagingly described Neoclassical economics as a theory fit only for the analysis of 'lone individuals exchanging nuts and berries on the edge of the forest'.

The Marxist School

One-sentence summary: *Capitalism is a powerful vehicle for economic progress, but it will collapse, as private property ownership becomes an obstacle to further progress.*

The Marxist school of economics emerged from the works of Karl Marx, produced between the 1840s and the 1860s, starting with the publication of *The Communist Manifesto* in 1848 (co-authored with Friedrich Engels (1820–95), his intellectual partner and financial patron) and culminating in the publication of the first volume of *Capital* in 1867.[8] It was further developed in Germany and Austria and then in the Soviet Union in the late nineteenth and the early twentieth centuries.* More recently, it was elaborated in the US and Europe during the 1960s and the 1970s.

---

* Before the Russian Revolution, the leading Marxist economists were Karl Kautsky (1854–1938), Rosa Luxemburg (1871–1919) and Rudolf Hilferding (1877–1941). The key Soviet Marxist theorists were Vladimir Lenin (1870–1924), Yevgeni Preobrazhensky (1886–1937) and Nikolai Bukharin (1888–1938).

Labour theory of value, classes, and production: The Marxist
school as the truer heir of the Classical school

As I mentioned earlier, the Marxist school inherited many elements from the Classical school. In many ways, it is *truer* to the Classical doctrine than the latter's self-proclaimed successor, the Neoclassical school. It adopted the labour theory of value, which was explicitly rejected by the Neoclassical school. It also focused on production, whereas consumption and exchange were the keys for the Neoclassical school. It envisioned an economy comprised of classes rather than individuals – another key idea of the Classical school rejected by the Neoclassical school.

Developing the Classical school, Marx and his followers came up with a type of economics very different from that offered by its half-brother, the Neoclassical school.

Production at the centre of economics

Taking the Classical school's production-based view of the economy further, the Marxist school argued that 'production is . . . the basis of social order', in the words of Engels. Every society is seen as being built on an economic **base**, or the **mode of production.** This base is made up of the **forces of production** (technologies, machines, human skills) and the **relations of production** (property rights, employment relationship, division of labour). Upon this base is the **superstructure,** which comprises culture, politics and other aspects of human life, which in turn affect the way the economy is run. In this sense, Marx was probably the first economist to systematically explore the role of institutions in the economy, presaging the Institutionalist school.

Further developing Adam Smith's 'stages of development' theory, the Marxist school saw societies as evolving through a series of historical stages, defined in terms of their mode of production: primitive communism ('tribal' societies); antiquarian mode of production (based on slavery, as in Greece and Rome); feudalism (based on landlords commanding semi-slaves, or serfs, tied to their lands); capitalism; communism.* Capitalism is seen as but

---

* In some formulations, communism is divided into two phases. The first phase is also called socialism and is run through central planning. The second, or 'higher', phase is called 'pure communism', in which the state will have withered away. In this book, I use the terms communism and socialism interchangeably.

one stage of human development before we reach the ultimate stage of communism. This recognition of the historical nature of economic problems is a great contrast to the Neoclassical school, which considers the 'economic' problem of utility maximization universal – for Robinson Crusoe in a desert island, for participants in a weekly market of medieval Europe, for subsistence farmers in Tanzania and for an affluent German consumer in the twenty-first century, you name it.

Class struggle and the systemic collapse of capitalism

The Marxist school took the class-based view of society of the Classical school to another level. It viewed **class conflicts** as the central force of history – summarized in the declaration in *The Communist Manifesto*: 'The history of hitherto existing society is the history of class struggles.' Moreover, the school refused to see the working class as a passive entity, as did the Classical school, and accorded it an active role in history.

Classical economists viewed workers as simple souls unable to even control their biological urges. As soon as the economy expands and the demand for labour grows and higher wages are paid, workers have more children. This means more workers, bringing the wages again down to subsistence level. Only a life of misery lay ahead of them, those economists believed, unless they learned to exercise restraint and stop producing so many children – a highly unlikely prospect, those economists surmised, given their base nature.

Marx had a totally different view. For him, workers were not the powerless 'huddled mass' in Classical economics but active agents of social change – the 'grave digger of capitalism' in his words – whose organizational skills and discipline were being forged in the harsh hierarchy within factories of ever-growing size and complexity.

Marx did not believe that workers could start a revolution and topple capitalism at will. The time had to be ripe. This would come only when capitalism has developed sufficiently, leading to a heightened contradiction between the technological requirements of the system (forces of production) and its institutional set-up (relations of production).

With the continuous development of technologies, spurred by the need on the part of capitalists to invest and innovate in order to survive the unrelenting competition, the division of labour becomes increasingly more 'social', making capitalist firms become more dependent on each other as suppliers and buyers. This makes coordination of activities among those related firms increasingly more necessary, but the persistence of private ownership of the means of production makes such coordination very difficult, if not totally impossible. The result is increasing contradiction in the system, finally leading to its collapse. Capitalism would be replaced by socialism, in which the central planning authority fully coordinates the activities of all the related enterprises, now collectively owned by all workers.

Fatally flawed, but still useful: theories of the firm,
work, and technological progress

The Marxist school has many fatal flaws. Above all, its prediction that capitalism will collapse under its own weight has not come true. Capitalism has proved far more capable of reforming itself than the school had predicted. Insofar as socialism emerged, it did so in countries like Russia and China, where capitalism was hardly developed, rather than in the most advanced capitalist economies, as Marx had predicted. Because it was so intertwined with a political project, along the way, many of its followers developed blind faith in whatever Marx said or, even worse, what the Soviet Union said was the right interpretation of his ideas. The collapse of the socialist bloc has revealed that the Marxist theory of how the alternative to capitalism should be organized was highly inadequate. The list goes on.

Despite these limitations, the Marxist school still offers some very useful insights into the workings of capitalism.

Marx was the first economist to pay attention to the differences between the two key institutions of capitalism – the hierarchical, planned order of the firm and the (formally) free, spontaneous order of the market. He described capitalist firms as islands of rational planning in an anarchic sea of the market. Moreover, he foresaw that large-scale enterprises owned by multitudes of shareholders with limited liability – which were called 'joint stock companies' in his time – would become the leading actors of capitalism, at a time when most free-market economists were still against the very idea of limited liability.

Unlike most other economists, Marx and some of his followers have paid attention to work for its own sake, rather than as a disutility that people have to put up with in order to earn money to pay for their consumption. He believed that work can allow human beings to express their inherent creativity. He criticized the hierarchical capitalist firm for blocking such possibility. He emphasized the dehumanizing and mind-numbing effects of the repetitive work that emanates from increasingly fine divisions of labour. It is interesting to note that, while praising the positive productivity effects of finer divisions of labour, Adam Smith had also worried about the negative impact of fragmented work on individual workers.

Last but not least, Marx was also the first major economist who truly understood the importance of technological innovation in the process of capitalist development, making it the central element in his theory.

The Developmentalist Tradition

One-sentence summary: *Backward economies can't develop if they leave things entirely to the market.*

A neglected tradition
Unbeknownst to most people and rarely mentioned even in books on the history of economic thought, there is a tradition in economics that is even older than the Classical school. It is what I call the Developmentalist tradition, which started in the late sixteenth and the early seventeenth centuries – two centuries or so before the Classical school.

I don't call the Developmentalist tradition a *school*, because the latter term implies that there are identifiable founders and followers, with clear core theories. This tradition is very dispersed, with multiple sources of inspiration and with a complicated intellectual lineage.

This is because policy-makers, who are interested in solving real-world problems, rather than intellectual purity, started the tradition.* They pulled together elements from different sources in a pragmatic, eclectic manner, even though some of them have made important original contributions of their own.

---

* A few, like Jean-Baptiste Colbert (Louis XIV's finance minister between 1665 and 1683), are still remembered for their policies. Most are forgotten altogether. Some, such as Henry VII and Robert Walpole, are still remembered but not for their economic policies.

But the tradition is no less important for that. It is arguably the most important intellectual tradition in economics in terms of its impact on the real world. It is this tradition, rather than the narrow rationalism of Neoclassical economics or the Marxist vision of classless society, that has been behind almost all of the successful economic development experiences in human history, from eighteenth-century Britain, through nineteenth-century America and Germany, down to today's China.[9]

Raising productive capabilities to overcome economic backwardness

The Developmentalist tradition is focused on helping economically backward countries develop their economies and catch up with the more advanced ones. For economists belonging to the tradition, economic development is not simply a matter of increasing income, which could happen due to a resource bonanza, such as striking oil or diamonds. It is a matter of acquiring more sophisticated **productive capabilities**, that is, the abilities to produce by using (and developing new) technologies and organizations.

The tradition argues that some economic activities, such as hi-tech manufacturing industries, are better than others at enabling countries to develop their productive capabilities. However, it argues, these activities do not naturally develop in a backward economy, as they are already conducted by firms in the more advanced economies. In such an economy, unless the government intervenes – with tariffs, subsidies and regulations – to promote such activities, free markets will constantly pull it back to what it is already good at – namely, low-productivity activities, based on natural resources or cheap labour.[10] The tradition emphasizes that desirable activities and appropriate policies depend on time and context. Yesterday's hi-tech industry (e.g., textiles in the eighteenth century) may be today's dead-end industry, while a policy that is good for an advanced economy (e.g., free trade) may be bad for a less developed country.

Early strands in the Developmentalist tradition: Mercantilism, the infant industry argument and the German historical school

Although the policy practice started earlier (for example, under Henry VII, who reigned between 1485 and 1509), theoretical writings in the Developmentalist tradition started in the late sixteenth and the early seventeenth centuries, with Renaissance Italian economists like Giovanni Botero and Antonio Serra, who emphasized the need for promotion of manufacturing activities by the government.

The Developmentalist economists of the seventeenth and eighteenth centuries – known as **Mercantilists** – are these days typically portrayed as having been solely focused on generating trade surplus, that is, the difference between your exports and imports when the former is larger. But many of them were actually more interested in promoting higher-productivity economic activities through policy interventions. At least the more sophisticated of them valued trade surplus as a symptom of economic success (that is, the development of high-productivity activities), rather than as a goal in itself.

From the late eighteenth century, shedding the Mercantilist garb and its interest in trade surplus, the Developmentalist tradition became more clearly focused on production. The critical development came from Alexander Hamilton's invention of the infant industry argument, which we encountered in the last chapter. Hamilton's theory was further developed by the German economist Friedrich List, who is these days often mistakenly known as the father of the infant industry argument.[11] Alongside List, in the mid-nineteenth century, the German Historical school emerged and dominated German economics until the mid-twentieth century. It also heavily influenced American economics.* The school emphasized the importance of understanding the history of how the material production system has changed, both influencing and influenced by law and other social institutions.[12]

The Developmentalist tradition in the modern world: Development Economics
The Developmentalist tradition was advanced in its modern form in the 1950s and the 1960s by economists such as, in alphabetical order, Albert Hirschman (1915–2012), Simon Kuznets (1901–85), Arthur Lewis (1915–91) and Gunnar Myrdal (1899–87) – this time, under the rubric of Development Economics. Writing mostly about the countries on the periphery of capitalism in Asia, Africa and Latin America, they and their followers not only

---

*   The early leaders of the American Economic Association, John Bates Clark (1847–1938) and Richard Ely (1854–1943) studied under economists of the German Historical school, such as Wilhelm Roscher (1817–94) and Karl Knies (1821–98).

refined the earlier Developmentalist theories but also added quite a lot of new theoretical innovations.

The most important innovation came from Hirschman, who pointed out that some industries have particularly dense **linkages** (or connections) with other industries; in other words, they buy from – and sell to – a particularly large number of industries. If the government identified and deliberately promoted these industries (the automobile and the steel industries are common examples), the economy would grow more vigorously than when left to the market.

More recently, some development economists have emphasized the need to complement infant industry protection with investments in building an economy's productive capabilities.[13] Trade protection only creates the space within which a country's firms can raise productivity, they argued. The actual raising of productivity requires deliberate investments in education, training and R&D.

A lot more than meets the eye: assessing the Developmentalist tradition

As I have pointed out earlier, the lack of a coherent, overarching theory is a crucial weakness of the Developmentalist tradition. Given the human tendency to be seduced by a theory that supposedly explains everything, this has put the tradition in seriously lower esteem in most people's eyes than more coherent and self-confident schools, such as the Neoclassical school or the Marxist one.

The tradition is more vulnerable to the government failure argument than other economic schools that advocate an active role for the government. It recommends a particularly wide-ranging set of policies, which is more likely to stretch the administrative capabilities of the government.

Despite these weaknesses, the Developmentalist tradition deserves more attention. Its crucial weakness, namely its eclecticism, can actually be a strength. Given the complexity of the world, a more eclectic theory may be better at explaining it. The success of Singapore's unique combination of free-market policies and socialist policies, which we encountered in Chapter 3, is a case in point. Moreover, its impressive track record in generating real world changes suggests that there is a lot more to it than meets the eye.

The Austrian School

One-sentence summary: *No one knows enough, so leave everyone alone.*

Oranges are not the only fruit: different types of free-market economics
Not all Neoclassical economists are free-market economists. Nor are all free-market economists Neoclassical. The adherents of the Austrian school are even more ardent supporters of the free market than most followers of the Neoclassical school.

The Austrian school was started by Carl Menger (1840–1921) in the late nineteenth century. Ludwig von Mises (1881–1973) and Friedrich von Hayek (1899–1992) extended the school's influence beyond its homeland. It gained international attention during the so-called Calculation Debate in the 1920s and the 1930s, in which it battled the Marxists on the feasibility of central planning.[14] In 1944, Hayek published an extremely influential popular book, *The Road to Serfdom*, which passionately warned against the danger of government intervention leading to the loss of fundamental individual liberty.

The Austrian school is these days in the same laissez-faire camp with the free-market wing (today the majority) of the Neoclassical school, producing similar, if somewhat more extreme, policy conclusions. However, methodologically it is very different from the Neoclassical school. The alliance between the two groups is due more to their politics than economics.

Complexity and limited rationality: the Austrian defence of the free market
While emphasizing the importance of individuals, the Austrian school does *not* believe that individuals are atomistic rational beings, as assumed in Neoclassical economics. It sees human rationality as severely limited. It argues that rational behaviour is only possible because we humans voluntarily, if subconsciously, limit our choices by unquestioningly accepting social norms – 'custom and tradition stand *between* instinct and reason', Hayek intoned. For example, by assuming that most people will respect moral codes, we can devote our mental energy to calculating the costs and the benefits of a potential market transaction, rather than to calculating the odds of being cheated.

The Austrian school also argues that the world is highly complex and uncertain. As its members pointed out in the Calculation Debate, it is impossible for anyone – even the all-powerful central planning authority of a socialist country that can demand any information it wants from anyone – to acquire all the information needed to run a complex economy. It is only through the **spontaneous order** of the competitive market that the diverse and ever-changing plans of numerous economic actors, responding to unpredictable and complex shifts of the world, can be reconciled with each other.

Thus, the Austrians say that the free market is the best economic system not because we are perfectly rational and know everything (or at least can know everything that we need to know), as in Neoclassical theories, but exactly because we are not very rational and because there are so many things in the world that are inherently 'unknowable'. This defence of the free market is a lot more realistic than the Neoclassical one, based on the assumption of absurd degrees of human rationality and on the unrealistic belief in the 'knowability' of the world.

Spontaneous vs. constructed order: limits to the Austrian argument

The Austrian school is absolutely right in saying that we may be better off relying on the spontaneous order of the market because our ability to deliberately create order is limited. But capitalism is full of deliberately 'constructed orders', such as the limited liability company, the central bank or intellectual property laws, which did not exist until the late nineteenth century. The diversity of institutional arrangements – and the resulting differences in economic performances – between different capitalist economies is also in large part the result of deliberate construction, rather than spontaneous emergence, of order.[15]

Moreover, the market itself is a constructed (rather than spontaneous) order. It is based on deliberately designed rules and regulations that prohibit certain things, discourage others and encourage still others. This point can be more clearly seen when we recall that the boundaries of the market have been repeatedly drawn and redrawn through deliberate political decisions – a fact that the Austrian school fails to, or even refuses to, accept. Many once-legal objects of market exchange – slaves, child labour, certain narcotics – have been withdrawn from the market. At the same time, many formerly unmarketable things have become marketable due to political decisions. 'Commons', the grazing lands that were collectively owned by communities and therefore could not be bought and sold, became private land through the Enclosure in Britain between the sixteenth and eighteenth centuries. The market for carbon emission permits was created only in the 1990s.[16] By calling the market a spontaneous order, the Austrians are seriously misrepresenting the nature of the capitalist economy.

The Austrian position against government intervention is too extreme. Their view is that any government intervention other than the provision of law and order, especially protection of private property, will launch the society on to a slippery slope down to socialism – a view most explicitly advanced in Hayek's *The Road to Serfdom*. This is not theoretically convincing; nor has it been borne out by history. There is a huge gradation in the ways market and the state combine across countries and within countries. Chocolate bars in the US are provided in a much more market-oriented way than is primary school education. South Korea may rely more on market solutions than Britain does in the provision of health care, but the case is the reverse in water or railways. If the 'slippery slope' existed, we wouldn't have these kinds of diversity.

The (Neo-)Schumpeterian School

One-sentence summary: *Capitalism is a powerful vehicle of economic progress, but it will atrophy, as firms become larger and more bureaucratic.*

Joseph Schumpeter (1883–1950) is not one of the biggest names in the history of economics. But his thoughts were original enough to have a whole school named after him – the Schumpeterian, or neo-Schumpeterian, school.* (Not even Adam Smith has a school named after him.)

Like the Austrians, Schumpeter worked under the shadow of the Marxist school – so much so that the first four chapters of his magnum opus, *Capitalism, Socialism, and Democracy* (henceforth *CSD*), published in 1942, are devoted to Marx.[17] Joan Robinson, the famous Keynesian economist, once famously quipped that Schumpeter was just 'Marx with the adjectives changed'.

---

* The prefix 'neo' is debatable. The differences between the two are much less than those between, for example, the Classical school and the Neoclassical school.

Gales of creative destruction: Schumpeter's theory of capitalist development

Schumpeter developed Marx's emphasis on the role of technological development as the driving force of capitalism. He argued that capitalism develops through **innovations** by entrepreneurs, namely, the creation of new production technologies, new products and new markets. Innovations give the successful entrepreneurs temporary monopolies in their respective markets, allowing them to earn exceptional profit, which he called the **entrepreneurial profit**. Over time, their competitors imitate the innovations, forcing everyone's profit down to the 'normal' level; just think about the way in which there are now so many products in the tablet computer market, once an almost exclusive domain of the Apple iPad.

This competition driven by technological innovations, in Schumpeter's view, is much more powerful and important than Neoclassical price competition – producers trying to undercut each other with lower prices, by increasing the efficiency with which they use *given* technologies. He argued that competition through innovation is 'as much more effective than [price competition] as a bombardment is in comparison with forcing a door'.

On this, Schumpeter has proven prescient. He argued that no firm, however entrenched it may look, is safe from these 'gales of creative destruction' in the long run. The decline of companies like IBM and General Motors, or the disappearance of Kodak, which at their peaks dominated the world in their respective industries, demonstrates the power of competition through innovation.

Why did Schumpeter predict the atrophy of capitalism and why was he wrong?

Despite being such a believer in the dynamism of capitalism, Schumpeter was not optimistic about its future. In *CSD*, he observed that, with the growing scale of capitalist firms and the application of scientific principles in technological innovation (the emergence of 'corporate labs'), entrepreneurs were making way for professional managers, whom he disparagingly called the 'executive types'. With the bureaucratization of the management of its firms, capitalism would lose its dynamism, which ultimately rests on the vision and the drive of charismatic heroes called entrepreneurs. Capitalism would slowly wither away and morph into socialism, rather than meeting the violent death predicted by Marx.

Schumpeter's prediction has not come true. Capitalism has become actually *more* dynamic since his gloomy foretelling of its death. He made such an incorrect prediction because he had failed to see how entrepreneurship was fast becoming a collective endeavour, involving not just the visionary entrepreneur but also many other actors inside and outside the firm.

Much of technological progress in complex modern industries happens through **incremental innovations** originating from pragmatic attempts to solve problems arising in the production process. This means that even production-line workers are involved in innovation. Indeed, Japanese automobile firms, especially Toyota, have benefited from a production method that maximizes worker inputs into the innovation process. Gone are the days when a genius like James Watt or Thomas Edison could (almost) single-handedly perfect new technologies. That is not all. When they innovate, firms draw on research output and research funding provided by various non-commercial actors – the government, universities and charitable foundations. The whole society is now involved in innovation.

Having failed to appreciate the role of all these 'other guys' in the innovation process, Schumpeter came to the mistaken conclusion that the diminishing room for individual entrepreneurs will make capitalism less dynamic and atrophy.

Fortunately, Schumpeter's intellectual heirs (sometimes called the neo-Schumpeterian school) have overcome this limitation in his theory, especially through the **national system of innovation** approach, which looks at interactions between different actors in the innovation process – firms, universities, governments, and others.* Having said that, the (neo-) Schumpeterian school may be criticized for focusing overly on technology and innovation and relatively neglecting other economic issues, such as labour, finance and macroeconomics. To be fair, other schools too focus on particular issues, but the Schumpeterian school exhibits a narrower focus than most.

---

* Leading members of the school, which is sometimes called evolutionary economics, are, in alphabetical order, Mario Cimoli, Giovanni Dosi, the late Christopher Freeman, Bengt-Åke Lundvall, Richard Nelson and Sidney Winter.

The Keynesian School

One-sentence summary: *What is good for individuals may not be good for the whole economy.*

Born in the same year as Schumpeter and sharing the honour of having a whole school named after him is John Maynard Keynes (1883–1946). In terms of intellectual influence, there is no comparison between the two. Keynes was arguably the most important economist of the twentieth century. He redefined the subject by inventing the field of macroeconomics – the branch of economics that analyses the whole economy as an entity that is different from the sum total of its parts.

Before Keynes, most people agreed with Adam Smith when he said, 'What is prudence in the conduct of every private family can scarce be folly in that of a great kingdom.' And some people still do. David Cameron, the British prime minister, said in October 2011 that all Britons should try to pay off their credit card debts, without realizing that demand in the British economy would collapse if a sufficient number of people actually heeded his advice and reduced spending to pay off their debts. He simply did not understand that one person's spending is another's income – until he was forced by his advisors to withdraw the embarrassing remark.

Rejecting this view, Keynes sought to explain how there could be unemployed workers, idle factories and unsold products for prolonged periods when markets are supposed to equate supply and demand.

Why is there unemployment?: the Keynesian explanation

Keynes started from the obvious observation that an economy doesn't consume all that it produces. The difference – that is, savings – needs to be invested, if everything that has been produced is to be sold and if all productive inputs, including the labour service of workers, are to be employed (this is known as **full employment**).

Unfortunately, there is no guarantee that savings will equal investment, especially when those who invest and those who save are not one and the same, unlike in the early days of capitalism, when capitalists mostly invested out of their own savings and workers could not save, given their low wages. This is because investment, whose returns are not immediate, is dependent on investors' expectations about the future. In turn, these expectations are driven by psychological factors rather than rational calculation because the future is full of **uncertainty**.

Uncertainty is not simply about not knowing exactly what is going to happen in the future. For some things, we can rather accurately calculate the probability of each possible contingency – economists call this **risk**. Indeed, our ability to calculate the risk involved in many aspects of human life – death, fire, car accident and so on – is the very foundation of the insurance industry. However, for many other things, we do not even know all the possible contingencies, not to speak of their respective likelihoods. The best explanation of the concept of uncertainty was given by, perhaps surprisingly, Donald Rumsfeld, the defence secretary in the first government of George W. Bush. In a press briefing regarding the situation in Afghanistan in 2002, Rumsfeld opined: 'There are known knowns. There are things we know that we know. There are known unknowns. That is to say, there are things that we now know we don't know. But there are also unknown unknowns. There are things we do not know we don't know.' The idea of 'unknown unknowns' nicely sums up Keynes' concept of uncertainty.

Active fiscal policy for full employment: the
Keynesian solution

In an uncertain world, investors may suddenly become pessimistic about the future and reduce their investments. In such a situation, there will be more savings than are needed – there will be, in technical terms, a 'savings glut'. The Classical economists thought this glut would be sooner or later eliminated, as the lower demand for savings would drive the interest rate (that is, the price of borrowing, if you like) down, making investments more attractive.

Keynes argued that this does not happen. As investment falls, overall spending falls, which then reduces income, as one person's spending is another's income. A reduction in income in turn reduces savings, as savings are essentially what are left after consumption (which tends not to change much in response to a fall in income, being determined by our survival necessities and habit). In the end, savings will contract to match the now lower investment demand. If excess savings are reduced in this way, there will be no downward pressure on interest rates and thus no extra stimulus for investment.

Keynes thought that investment will be high enough for full employment only when **animal spirits** – 'a spontaneous urge to action rather than inaction', as he defines it – of the potential investors are stimulated by new technologies, financial euphoria and other unusual events. The normal state of affairs, in his view, would be that investment is equated to savings at a level of **effective demand** (the demand that is actually backed up by purchasing power) that is insufficient to support full employment. In order to achieve full employment, Keynes argued, the government therefore has to use its spending actively to prop up the level of demand.[18]

Money gets a real job in economics: the Keynesian theory of finance

The prevalence of uncertainty in Keynesian economics means that money is not simply an accounting unit or merely a convenient medium of exchange, as the Classical (and the Neoclassical) school thought. It is a means to provide **liquidity** (or the means to quickly change one's financial position) in an uncertain world.

Given this, the financial market is not just a means to provide money to invest but also a place to make money by taking advantage of the differences among people's views about returns on the same investment projects – in other words, a place for **speculation**. In this market, the buying and selling of an asset is driven not mainly by the ultimate return that it will deliver but by expectations about the future – and, more importantly, the expectations about what other people expect, or, as Keynes put it, the 'average opinion about the average opinion'. This, according to Keynes, provides the basis for the herd behaviour that is often witnessed in financial markets, making it inherently prone to bouts of financial speculation, boom and ultimately bust.[19]

It is upon this analysis that Keynes famously warned against the danger that the speculation-driven financial system can pose: 'Speculators may do no harm as bubbles on a steady stream of enterprise. But the position is serious when enterprise becomes the bubble on a whirlpool of speculation. When the capital development of a country becomes a by-product of the activities of a casino, the job is likely to be ill-done.' He should know – he was a very successful financial speculator himself, amassing a fortune of over £10 million (or $15 million) in today's money, even after very generous donations to charitable causes.[20]

An economic theory fit for the twentieth century – and beyond?

The Keynesian school built an economic theory that was more fit for the advanced capitalist economy in the twentieth century than that of the Classical or Neoclassical schools.

Keynesian macroeconomic theory is built on the recognition that the structural separation of savers and investors that emerged from the late nineteenth century has made the equalization of savings and investment, and thus the achievement of full employment, more difficult.

Moreover, the Keynesian school rightly highlights the key role that finance plays in modern capitalism. The Classical school did not pay too much attention to finance, as it was developed at a time when the financial market was primitive. The Neoclassical theory was developed in a world which was already quite similar to the one Keynes was living in, but, given its failure to acknowledge uncertainty, money is not essential in it. In contrast, finance plays a key role in Keynesian theories, which is why it has been so useful in helping us understand episodes like the Great Depression of 1929 and the 2008 global financial crisis.

'In the long run we are all dead': shortcomings of the Keynesian school

The Keynesian school can be criticized for paying too much attention to short-term issues – as summarized in the famous quip by Keynes that 'in the long run we are all dead'.

Keynes was absolutely right in emphasizing that we cannot run economic policies on the hope that in the long run the 'fundamental' forces, such as technology and demography, will somehow sort everything out, as the Classical economists used to argue. Nevertheless, its focus on short-run macroeconomic variables has made the Keynesian school rather weak on long-term issues, such as technological progress and institutional changes.[21]

The Institutionalist School – Old and New?

One-sentence summary: *Individuals are products of their society, even though they may change its rules.*

From the late nineteenth century, a group of American economists challenged the then dominant Classical and Neoclassical schools for underplaying, or even ignoring, the social nature of individuals – that is, the fact that they are products of their societies. They argued that we need to analyse the **institutions**, or social rules, that affect, and even shape, individuals. This group of economists are known as the Institutionalist school – or the Old Institutional Economics (OIE), in recognition of the emergence of the so-called New Institutional Economics (NIE) since the 1980s.

Individuals are shaped by society: the rise of the Institutionalist school

The emergence of the Institutionalist school can be traced back to Thorstein Veblen (1857–1929), who made his name for questioning the notion of the rational, self-seeking individual. He argued that humans have layers of motivations behind their behaviours – instinct, habit, belief and, only finally, reason. Veblen also emphasized that human rationality cannot be defined as a timeless thing but is shaped by the social environment, made up of institutions – formal rules (e.g., laws, internal rules of companies) and informal rules (e.g., social customs, conventions in business dealings) – that surround the particular individuals that we are observing. Institutions, Veblen believed, did not just affect the way in which people behaved but actually changed them, and they in turn changed those institutions.[22]

Taking inspiration from Veblen's emphasis on institutions, but also drawing, overtly and covertly, from Marxism and the German Historical school, a new generation of American economists emerged in the early twentieth century to establish a distinctive economic school. The school was officially proclaimed as the Institutionalist school in 1918 with Veblen's blessing, under the leadership of Wesley Mitchell (1874–1948), Veblen's student and the then leader of the group.*

The school's shining moment was the New Deal, in whose design and administration many of its members participated. These days the New Deal is commonly thought of as a Keynesian policy programme. But, when you think about it, *The General Theory of Employment, Interest, and Money*, Keynes's *magnum opus*, did not come out until 1936, which is one year after the second New Deal of 1935 (the first was in 1933). The New Deal was much

---

* The heavyweight John Commons (1862–1945), whose work had affinity with the school, explicitly declared his membership of the school in the mid-1920s. John Maurice Clark (1884–1963), the son of John Bates Clark, was another important, younger, figure.

more about institutions – financial regulation, social security, trade unions and utilities regulation – rather than about macroeconomic policy, as I discussed in Chapter 3. Institutional economists, such as Arthur Burns (chairman of the Council of Economic Advisors to the US President, 1953–6; then chairman of the Federal Reserve Board, 1970–78), played important parts in the making of US economic policy even after the Second World War.

Individuals are not fully determined by society: the decline of the Institutionalist school

After the 1960s, the Institutionalist school went into decline. Part of this was due to the rise of Neoclassical economics in the US in the 1950s. The Neoclassical school's rather narrow view of what economics should be – with its emphasis on individual-based theory, 'universal' assumptions and abstract modelling – made it regard the Institutional school as not just different but intellectually inferior.

But the decline was also because of the weaknesses of the Institutional school itself. The school failed to fully theorize the diverse mechanisms through which institutions themselves emerge, persist and change. They only saw institutions as outcomes of formal collective decisions (e.g., legislation) or as products of history (e.g., cultural norms). However, institutions may come into being in other ways: as a spontaneous order emerging out of interactions of rational individuals (the Austrian school and the New Institutionalist Economics); through attempts by individuals and organizations to develop cognitive devices that will allow them to cope with complexity (the Behaviouralist school); or as a result of an attempt to maintain existing power relationships (the Marxist school).

Another big problem was that some members of the school went overboard in emphasizing the social nature of individuals and effectively adopted a structural determinism. Social institutions and the structure they create were everything; individuals were seen as being totally determined by the society they live in – 'there is no such thing as an individual', infamously declared Clarence Ayres, who dominated the (declining) Institutionalist school in the US in the early post-Second World War period.

Transaction costs and institutions: the rise of the
New Institutional Economics

From the 1980s, a group of economists with Neoclassical and Austrian leanings – led by Douglass North, Ronald Coase and Oliver Williamson – started a new school of institutional economics, known as the New Institutional Economics (NIE).[23]

By calling themselves *institutional* economists, the New Institutionalist economists made it clear that they were not typical Neoclassical economists, who looked at only individuals but not the institutions that affect their behaviour. However, by emphasizing the adjective *new*, this group clearly dissociated itself from the original Institutionalist school – now called the Old Institutional Economics (OIE). The main point of departure from the OIE was that the NIE analysed how institutions emerge out of deliberate choices by individuals.[24]

The key concept in the NIE is that of **transaction cost**. In Neoclassical economics, the only cost is the cost of production (costs of material, wages, etc.). However, the NIE emphasizes that there are also costs of organizing our economic activities. Some define transaction cost rather narrowly as the cost involved in market exchange itself – finding out about alternative products ('shopping around'), spending time and money actually doing the shopping and sometimes bargaining for better prices. Others define it more broadly as the 'cost of running the economic system', which includes the cost of conducting market exchange but also the cost involved in enforcing the contract after the exchange is over. So, in this broader definition, transaction cost includes the cost of policing against thefts, running the court system and even monitoring workers in factories so that they put in the maximum possible amount of labour service specified in their contract.

Institutions are not just constraints: contributions and
limitations of the New Institutional Economics

Deploying the concept of transaction cost, the NIE has developed a wide range of interesting theories and case studies. One prominent example is the question as to why, in a supposedly 'market' economy, so many economic activities are conducted within firms. The (simplified) answer is that market transactions are often very costly due to the high cost of information and contract enforcement. In such cases, it would be much more efficient if things were done through hierarchical commands within the firm. Another example is the analysis of the impacts of the exact nature of **property rights** (the rules on what owners can do with which kinds of property) on patterns of investments, choice of production technologies, and other economic decisions.

Despite these very important contributions, the NIE has a critical limit as an 'institutionalist' theory. It sees institutions basically as constraints – on unfettered self-seeking behaviour. But institutions are not just 'constraining' but can also be 'enabling'. Often institutions limit our individual freedom exactly in order to enable us to do more collectively – traffic rules, for example. Most members of the NIE would not deny the enabling role of institutions, but by not talking about it explicitly and continually referring to institutions as constraints, they convey a negative impression of institutions. More importantly, the NIE fails to see the 'constitutive' role of institutions. Institutions shape the motives of individuals and do not merely constrain their behaviour. Missing out on this critical dimension of what institutions do, the NIE falls short of being a full-blown institutional economics.

The Behaviouralist School

One-sentence summary: *We are not smart enough, so we need to deliberately constrain our own freedom of choice through rules.*

The Behaviouralist school is so called because it tries to model human behaviours as they actually are, rejecting the dominant Neoclassical assumption that human beings always behave in a rational and selfish way. The school extends this approach to the study of economic institutions and organizations – for example, how best to organize a firm or how to design financial regulation. The school thus has a fundamental affinity, and some overlap in membership, with the Institutionalist school.

The Behaviouralist school is the youngest of the schools of economics that we have so far examined, but it is older than most people think. The school has recently come to prominence through the fields of behavioural finance and experimental economics. But it has its origins in the 1940s and the 1950s, especially in the works of Herbert Simon (1916–2001), the 1978 Nobel economics laureate.*

Limits to human rationality and the need for individual and social rules

Simon's central concept is **bounded rationality**. He criticizes the Neoclassical school for assuming that people possess unlimited capabilities to process information, or God-like rationality (he calls it 'Olympian rationality').

Simon did *not* argue that human beings are irrational. His view was that we try to be rational but that our ability to be so is very limited, especially given the complexity of the world – or given the prevalence of uncertainty, if you want to formulate it in the Keynesian way. This means that often the main constraint on our decision-making is not the lack of information but our limited capability to process the information we have.

Given our bounded rationality, Simon argued, we develop mental 'shortcuts' that allow us to economize on our mental capabilities. These are known as **heuristics** (or intuitive thinking) and can take different forms: rule of thumb, common sense or expert judgement. Underlying all these mental devices is the ability to recognize patterns, which allows us to abandon a large range of alternatives and focus on a small, manageable but most promising range of possibilities. Simon often used the chess masters as an example of someone using such a mental approach – their secret lay in their abilities to rapidly eliminate less promising search paths and converge on a sequence of moves that are likely to yield the best outcomes.

Focusing on a subset of possibilities means that the resulting choice may *not* be optimal, but this approach enables us to handle the complexity and the uncertainty of the world with our bounded rationality. Therefore, Simon argues, when they make their choices, human beings **satisfice**, that

---

* Simon was the last Renaissance Man, as I call him in Thing 16 of my book, *23 Things They Don't Tell You about Capitalism*. He made path-breaking contributions not just in economics but across many fields. He was one of the founding fathers of artificial intelligence (AI) and of Operations Research (OR, a branch of business administration). He also wrote one of the classics in the field of public administration (*Administrative Behaviour*, published in 1947) and was a leading scholar in cognitive psychology. So he knew a thing or two about how people think and act.

is, we look for 'good enough' solutions rather than the best ones, as in the Neoclassical theory.[25]

Market economy vs. organization economy

Even though it starts with the study of individual decision-making, the interest of the Behaviouralist school stretches much further. According to the school, it isn't just at the individual level that we build simplifying decision rules that help us operate in a complex world with our bounded rationality.

We build **organization routines** as well as social institutions so that we can compensate for our bounded rationality. Like heuristics at the individual level, these organizational and social rules restrict our freedom of choice but help us make better choices because they also reduce the complexity of the problem. Particularly emphasized is the fact that these rules make it easier for us to predict the behaviour of other related actors, who would follow those rules and behave in particular ways. This is a point that the Austrian school also emphasizes using slightly different language, when they talk about the importance of 'tradition' as the basis for reason.

Adopting the Behaviouralist perspective, we begin to see our economy in a way that is very different from the dominant Neoclassical one. The Neoclassical economists usually describe the modern capitalist economy as the 'market economy'. The Behaviouralists emphasize that the market actually accounts for only a rather small part of it. Herbert Simon, writing in the mid-1990s, reckoned that something like 80 per cent of economic activities in the US happen inside organizations, such as the firm and the government, rather than through the market.[26] He argued that it would be more appropriate to call it the **organization economy**.

Why emotion, loyalty and fairness matter

The Behaviouralist school also provides persuasive reasons as to why human qualities like emotion, loyalty and fairness matter – things that most economists, especially the Neoclassicals and the Marxists, would dismiss as at best irrelevant and at worst as distracting people from rational decisions.

The theory of bounded rationality explains why our emotion is not necessarily the stumbling block to rational decision-making but may be often a useful part of our (bounded) rational decision-making process. According to

Simon, given our bounded rationality, we need to focus our limited mental resources on solving the most important problem at hand. Emotion provides such focus. The Behaviouralists argue that organizational loyalty of their members is essential for organizations to operate well, as an organization full of disloyal members would be overwhelmed by the costs of monitoring and punishing their selfish behaviours. The issue of fairness is very important in this regard, as the members of an organization or a society will not develop loyalty to it, if they think they are being treated unfairly.

Too focused on individuals?: assessing the Behaviouralist school

The Behaviouralist school, despite being the youngest school of economics, has helped us radically rethink our theories about human rationality and motivations. Thanks to it, we have a much more sophisticated understanding of how people think and behave.

The Behaviouralist school's attempt to understand human society from individuals up – actually from a place 'lower' than that, that is, from our thinking process up – is both its strength and its weakness. Focusing too much at this 'micro' level, the school often loses sight of the bigger economic system. This does not have to be; after all, Simon wrote a lot about the economic system. But most members of the school have focused too much on individuals – especially those economists who are engaged in experimental economics (trying to establish whether people are rational and selfish through controlled experiments) or neuroeconomics (trying to establish links between brain activities and particular types of behaviour). It also needs to be added that, given its focus on human cognition and psychology, the Behaviouralist school has few things to say about issues of technology and macroeconomics.

Concluding Remarks: How to Make Economics Better

Preserving intellectual diversity and encouraging
cross-fertilization of ideas

Recognizing that there are different approaches to economics is not enough. This diversity needs to be preserved, or even promoted. Given that different approaches emphasize different aspects and offer different perspectives, knowing a range of schools, and not just one or two of them, allows us to have a fuller, more balanced understanding of the complex entity called the economy. Especially in the longer run, in the same way in which a biological group with a more diverse gene pool is more resilient to shocks, a discipline that contains a variety of theoretical approaches can cope with a changing world better than one characterized by intellectual mono-cropping can. We are actually living through a proof of this – the world economy would have experienced a collapse similar to the 1929 Great Depression, had the key governments not decided to ditch their free-market economics and adopt Keynesian policies in the early days of the 2008 global financial crisis.

I would go one step further and argue that preserving diversity is not enough. We shouldn't just let a hundred flowers bloom. We need to have them cross-fertilized. Different approaches to economics can actually benefit a lot from learning from each other, making our understanding of the economic world richer.

Some schools with obvious intellectual affinities have already been cross-fertilizing. The Developmentalist tradition and the Schumpeterian school have interacted to the benefit of both, the former providing theories to understand the bigger context in which technological development occurs and the latter providing more detailed theories of how technological innovation happens. The Marxist, the Institutionalist and the Behaviouralist schools have long interacted with each other, often in hostile manners, in relation to the understanding of the internal workings of the firm and especially the capitalist–worker relationship in it. The common emphasis on psychological factors by the Keynesian and the Behaviouralist schools has always existed but has recently produced particularly notable cross-fertilization of ideas in the new field of 'behavioural finance'.

However, cross-fertilization can happen between schools that most people think are incompatible with each other. Even if they are spread across the political spectrum, the Classicals (right), the Keynesians (centre) and the Marxists (left) all share a class-based vision of the society. The Austrians and the Keynesians may have locked horns since the 1930s, but they share with each other (as well as with the Behaviouralists and the Institutionalists) the view that the world is a very complex and uncertain place and that our rationality to deal with it is severely limited. The Austrians, the Institutionalists and the Behaviouralists all share a view of human beings as layered entities, made up of – if we use the Institutionalist formulation – instinct, habit, belief and reason, even though some Austrians may think that the others are objectionable left-wingers.

How all of us, not just professional economists, can
play a role in making economics better

Even those readers who have been persuaded by my argument for intellectual diversity and cross-fertilization in economics may still ask, 'What does that have to do with me?' After all, only a very small number of readers will ever have a chance to preserve or increase the diversity of economics as professional economists.

The fact is, we all need to know something about diverse approaches to economics if we are not to become passive victims of someone else's decision. Behind every economic policy and corporate action that affects our lives – the minimum wage, outsourcing, social security, food safety, pensions and what not – lies some economic theory that either has inspired those actions or, more frequently, is providing justification of what those in power want to do anyway.

Only when we know that there are different economic theories will we be able to tell those in power that they are wrong to tell us that 'there is no alternative' (TINA), as Margaret Thatcher once infamously put it in defence of her controversial policies. When we learn how much intellectual common ground there is between supposed 'enemy factions' in economics, we can more effectively resist those who try to polarize the debate by portraying everything in black and white. Once we learn that different economic theories say different things partly because they are based on different ethical and political values, we will have the confidence to discuss economics for what it really is – a political argument – and not a 'science' in which there is clear right and wrong. And only when the general public displays awareness of these issues will professional economists find it impossible to browbeat them by declaring themselves to be custodians of scientific truths.

Knowing different types of economics and knowing their respective strengths and weaknesses, thus seen, is not an esoteric exercise reserved only for professional economists. It is a vital part of learning about economics and also a contribution to our collective effort to make the subject better serve humanity.

Appendix: Comparing Different Schools of Economics

	CLASSICAL	NEOCLASSICAL
The economy is made up of...	classes	individuals
Individuals are...	selfish and rational (but rationality is defined in class terms)	selfish and rational
The world is...	certain ('iron laws')	certain with calculable risk
The most important domain of the economy is...	production	exchange and consumption
Economies change through...	capital accumulation (investment)	individual choices
Policy recommendations	free market	free market or interventionism, depending on the economist's view on market failures and government failures

MARXIST	DEVELOP-MENTALIST	AUSTRIAN
classes	no strong view, but more focused on classes	individuals
selfish and rational, except for workers fighting for socialism	no strong view	selfish but layered (rational only because of an unquestioning acceptance of tradition)
certain ('laws of motion')	uncertain, but no strong view	complex and uncertain
production	production	exchange
class struggle, capital accumulation and technological progress	developments in productive capabilities	individual choices, but rooted in tradition
socialist revolution and central planning	temporary government protection and intervention	free market

	SCHUMPETERIAN	KEYNESIAN
The economy is made up of...	no particular view	classes
Individuals are...	no strong view, but emphasis on non-rational entrepreneurship	not very rational (driven by habits and animal spirits); ambiguous on selfishness
The world is...	no strong view but complex	uncertain
The most important domain of the economy is...	production	ambiguous, with a minority paying attention to production
Economies change through...	technological innovation	ambiguous, depends on the economist
Policy recommendations	ambiguous – capitalism is doomed to atrophy anyway	active fiscal policy, income redistribution towards the poor

INSTITUTIONALIST	BEHAVIOURALIST
individuals and institutions	individuals, organizations and institutions
layered (instinct – habit – belief – reason)	only bound-edly rational and layered
complex and uncertain	complex and uncertain
no strong view, but puts more emphasis on production than do the Neoclassicals	no strong view, but some bias towards production
interaction between individuals and institutions	no strong view
ambiguous, depends on the economist	no strong view, but can be quite accepting of government intervention

Further Reading

G. ARGYROUS AND F. STILLWELL
Readings in Political Economy (Annandale, NSW: Pluto Press, 2003).

P. DEANE
The State and the Economic System: An Introduction to the History of Political Economy (Oxford: Oxford University Press, 1989).

J. K. GALBRAITH
A History of Economics: The Past as the Present (London: Penguin, 1989).

R. HEILBRONER
The Worldly Philosophers: The Lives, Times, and Ideas of the Great Economic Thinkers (Harmondsworth: Penguin, 1983).

G. HODGSON
How Economics Forgot History: The Problem of Historical Specificity in Social Science (London: Routledge, 2001).

E. REINERT
How Rich Countries Became Rich, and Why Poor Countries Stay Poor (London: Constable, 2007).

A. RONCAGLIA
The Wealth of Ideas: A History of Economic Thought (Cambridge: Cambridge University Press, 2005).

CHAPTER 5

Dramatis Personae

WHO ARE THE ECONOMIC ACTORS?

'There is no such thing as society. There are individual men and women, and there are families.'
MARGARET THATCHER

'The corporations don't have to lobby the government any more. They are the government.'
JIM HIGHTOWER

Individuals as Heroes and Heroines

The individualist vision of the economy

The dominant Neoclassical view is that economics is the 'science of choice', as we saw in Chapter 1. According to this position, choices are made by individuals, who are assumed to be selfish, only interested in maximizing their own welfare – or at most that of their family members. In doing so, all individuals are seen to make rational choices, namely, they choose the most cost-efficient way to achieve a given goal.

As a consumer, each individual has a self-generated **preference system** that specifies what she likes. Using the preference system and looking at market prices of different things, she chooses a combination of goods and services that maximize her utility. When aggregated through the market mechanism, the choices made by individual consumers tell the producers what the demands are for their products at different prices (the **demand curve**). The quantity that the producers are willing to supply at each price (the **supply curve**) is determined by their own rational choices, made with a view to maximizing their profits. In making these choices, producers consider costs of production, given by technologies specifying different possible combinations of inputs, and the prices of those inputs. The market **equilibrium** is attained where the demand curve and the supply curve meet.

This is a story of the economy with individuals as the heroes and the heroines. Sometimes the consumers may be called 'households' and the producers 'firms', but they are essentially extensions of individuals. They are seen as making choices as single, coherent units. Some Neoclassical economists, following the pioneering work by Gary Becker, talk of 'intra-household bargaining', but this is conceptualized as a process between rational individuals ultimately seeking to maximize their personal utilities, rather than that between real-life family members, with their love, loathing, empathy, cruelty and commitments.

The appeal of the individualist vision of the economy and its limits

Even though this individualist vision is not the only way to theorize our economy (see Chapter 4), it has become the dominant one since the 1980s. One reason is that it has powerful political and moral appeals.

It is, above all, a parable of individual *freedom*. Individuals can get what they want, so long as they are willing to pay the right price for it, whether those are 'ethical' products (like organic food or fair trade coffee) or toys that children will forget by the following Christmas (I recall the Cabbage Patch Kids fever of 1983 and the Furby craze of 1998). Individuals can produce whatever will make money for them, using any method of production that maximizes profit, whether footballs made by child workers or microchips made with hi-tech machinery. There is no higher authority – king, pope or the planning minister – to tell individuals what they should want and produce. On this basis, many free-market economists have argued that there is an inseparable link between the freedom of individual consumers to choose and their broader political freedom. Friedrich von Hayek's seminal critique of socialism, *The Road to Serfdom*, and Milton Friedman's passionate advocacy of the free-market system, *Free to Choose*, are famous examples.

Moreover, the individualist view provides a paradoxical but very powerful *moral* justification of the market mechanism. We as individuals all make choices only for ourselves, the story goes, but the result is the maximization of social welfare. We don't need individuals to be 'good' to run an efficient economy that benefits all its participants. Or, rather, it is exactly because individuals are *not* 'good' and behave as ruthless maximizers of utility and of profit that our economy is efficient, benefiting everyone. Adam Smith's famous passage is the classic statement of this position: 'It is not from the benevolence of the butcher, the brewer, or the baker that we expect our dinner, but from their regard to their own interest.'

Appealing though they may appear, these justifications have serious problems. As for the political one, there is no clear relationship between a country's economic freedom and its political freedom. A lot of dictatorships have had very free-market policies, while a lot of democracies, such as the Scandinavian countries, have low economic freedom due to high taxes and plenty of regulations. In fact, many believers in the individualist view would rather sacrifice political freedom to defend economic freedom (this was why Hayek praised the Pinochet dictatorship in Chile). In the case of the moral justification, I have already discussed many theories, including the market failure approach based on the individualist Neoclassical vision, showing that unrestrained pursuit of self-interests through markets often fails to produce socially desirable economic outcomes.

Given that these limitations were well known even before its ascendancy, the current dominance of the individualist vision has to be at least partly explained by the politics of ideas. The individualist view gets so much more support and approval over alternative visions (especially the class-based ones like the Marxist or the Keynesian ones) from those who have power and money and therefore more influence. It gets such support because it takes the underlying social structure, such as property ownership or worker rights, as given, not questioning the status quo.*

Organizations as the Real Heroes: The Reality of Economic Decision-making

Some economists, most notably Herbert Simon and John Kenneth Galbraith, have looked at the reality, rather than the ideal, of economic decision-making. They found the individualistic vision to have been obsolete at least since the late nineteenth century. Since then, most important economic actions in our economies have been undertaken not by individuals but by large organizations with complex internal decision-making structures – corporations, governments, trade unions and increasingly even international organizations.

---

* In saying this, I am simplifying the relationship between people's economic position and the ideas they support; Warren Buffet, George Soros and plenty of other rich people have supported policies that would harm them personally. And I am certainly exaggerating the degree to which money and power can influence ideas. Nevertheless, it is important to recognize that the individualist vision of the economy has not become dominant purely on its intellectual merit.

Corporations, not individuals, are the most
important economic decision-makers

The most important producers today are large corporations, employing hundreds of thousands, or even millions, of workers in dozens of countries. The 200 largest corporations between themselves produce around 10 per cent of the world's output. It is estimated that 30–50 per cent of international trade in manufactured goods is actually **intra-firm trade**, or transfer of inputs and outputs within the same **multinational corporation** (MNC) or **transnational corporation** (TNC), with operations in multiple countries.[1] The Toyota engine factory in Chonburi, Thailand, 'selling' its outputs to Toyota assembly factories in Japan or Pakistan may be counted as Thailand's export to the latter countries, but these are *not* genuine market transactions. The prices of the products thus traded are dictated by the headquarters in Japan, not by competitive forces of the market.

Corporate decisions are not made like individual decisions

Legally speaking, we may be able to trace the decisions made by these large corporations to particular individuals, such as the CEO (chief executive officer) or the chairman of the board of directors. But those individuals, however powerful they may be, do not make decisions for their companies in the way in which individuals make decisions for themselves. How are corporate decisions made?

At the root of corporate decisions lie shareholders. Typically we say that shareholders 'own' corporations. Even though it would do as a shorthand description, it is, strictly speaking, not true. Shareholders own shares (or stocks), which give them certain rights concerning the management of the company. They do not own the company in the sense that I own my computer or my chopsticks. This point would become clearer if I explained that there are actually two types of shares – 'preferred' and 'ordinary' (or 'common').

Preferred shares give their holders priority in the payment of **dividends**, namely, profits distributed to shareholders, rather than 'retained' by the corporation. But that priority is bought at the cost of the right to vote for key decisions concerning the company – such as who to appoint as the top managers, how much to pay them and whether to merge with, take over or be taken over by another company. The shares that come with the right to vote on those things are called **ordinary shares**. The 'ordinary' shareholders (who are anything but ordinary in terms of decision-making power) make collective decisions through votes. These votes are usually according to the one-share-one-vote rule, but in some countries some shares have more votes than others; in Sweden, some shares could have up to 1,000 votes each.

Who are the shareholders?

These days, few very large companies are majority-owned by a single shareholder, like the capitalists of old. The Porsche-Piech family, which owns just over 50 per cent of the Porsche-Volkswagen group, is a notable exception.

There are still a considerable number of giant companies that have a **dominant shareholder**, who owns sufficient shares that he/she/it can usually determine the company's future. Such a shareholder is described as owning a **controlling stake**, usually defined as anything upwards of 20 per cent of the voting shares.

Mark Zuckerberg, who owns 28 per cent of Facebook, is a dominant shareholder. The Wallenberg family of Sweden is the dominant shareholder in Saab (40 per cent), Electrolux (30 per cent) and Ericsson (20 per cent).

Most large companies don't have one controlling shareholder. Their (share) ownership is so dispersed that no single shareholder has effective control. For example, as of March 2012, Japan Trustee Services Bank, the biggest shareholder of Toyota Motor Corporation, owned only just over 10 per cent of Toyota's shares. The next two biggest shareholders owned around 6 per cent each. Even acting in unison, these three together do not have one-quarter of the votes.

The separation of ownership and control

Dispersed ownership means that professional managers have effective control over most of the world's largest companies, despite not owning any significant stake in them – a situation known as the **separation of ownership and control**. This creates a **principal-agent problem**, in which the agents (professional managers) may pursue business practices that promote their own interests rather than those of their principals (shareholders). That is, professional managers may maximize sales rather than profit or may inflate the corporate bureaucracy, as their prestige is positively related to the size of the company they manage (usually measured by sales) and the size of their entourage. This was the kind of practice Gordon Gekko (you've met him in Chapter 3) was attacking in *Wall Street*, when he pointed out the company that he was trying to take over had no less than thirty-three vice presidents, doing God knows what.

Many pro-market economists, especially Michael Jensen and Eugene Fama, the 2013 Nobel Economics Prize winner, have suggested that this principal-agent problem can be reduced, if not eliminated, by aligning the interests of the managers more closely to those of the shareholders. They suggested two main approaches. One is making corporate takeover easier (so more Gordon Gekkos, please), so that managers who do not satisfy the shareholders can be easily replaced. The second is paying large parts of managerial salaries in the form of their own companies' stocks (stock option), so that they are made to look at things more from the shareholder's point of view. The idea was summarized in the term **shareholder value maximization**, coined in 1981 by Jack Welch, the then new CEO and chairman of General Electric, and has since ruled the corporate sector first in the Anglo-American world and increasingly in the rest of the world.

Workers and governments also influence corporate decisions

Though it is not common in the US and Britain, workers and the government also exercise significant influences on corporate decision-making.

In addition to trade union activities (which we'll explore below), workers in some European countries, such as Germany and Sweden, influence what their companies do through formal representation on company boards. In particular in Germany, large companies have a two-tier board structure. Under this system, known as the **co-determination system**, the 'managerial board' (like the board of directors in other countries) has to get the most important decisions, such as merger and plant closure, approved by the 'supervisor board', in which worker representatives have half the votes, even though the managerial side appoints the chairman, who has the casting vote.

Governments are also involved in managerial decisions in large corporations as shareholders. Government ownership of shares in private-sector companies is much more widespread than people think. Stora Enso, the world's largest paper and pulp manufacturer, is 25 per cent owned by the

Finnish government. Commerzbank, the second-biggest bank in Germany, is also 25 per cent owned by the German government. The list can go on.

Workers and governments have different goals from those of shareholders and professional managers. Workers want to minimize job losses, increase job security and improve working conditions. The government has to consider the interests of groups that go beyond the legal boundary of the company in question – for example, supplier firms, local communities or even environmental campaign groups. As a result, companies with strong worker and government involvement in management behave differently from companies dominated by shareholders and professional managers.

Volkswagen and the complexity of modern corporate decision-making

Volkswagen, the German car-maker, showcases the complexity of modern corporate decision-making. It has a majority owner, the Porsche-Piech family. Legally speaking, that family can bulldoze through any decision it takes. But that is not how things are done in Volkswagen. Like other large German companies, it has the two-tier board system, where workers have strong representation. Also, the company is 20 per cent owned by the government – or more precisely the state (Land) government of Lower-Saxony (Niedersachsen). As a result, decisions in Volkswagen are reached through very complicated processes of bargaining, involving shareholders, professional managers, workers and the population in general (through government ownership).

Volkswagen is an extreme example, but it powerfully illustrates how corporate decisions are made in a very different way from individual ones. We simply cannot understand the modern economy without having at least some understanding of the complexity involved in corporate decisions.

The cooperative as an alternative form of enterprise ownership and management

Some large companies are **cooperatives** owned by their users (consumers or savers), employees or independent smaller business units.

A **consumer cooperative**, the supermarket chain Coop, is the second-largest retailer in Switzerland. Its UK counterpart, Co-op, is the country's fifth-biggest supermarket chain. Consumer cooperatives allow consumers to get better prices by pooling their purchasing powers and negotiating for discounts from suppliers. Of course, getting discounts from suppliers by pooling consumers is exactly what many retailers, from Walmart to Groupon, do. But the difference is that, other things being equal, cooperatives can pass on more discounts to consumers, as they do not have shareholders to pay.

The **credit union** is a cooperative of savers. Nearly 200 million people around the world are members of credit unions. Some of the world's biggest banks, such as the Netherlands' Rabobank and France's Credit Agricole, are actually credit unions. Both of them started as savings cooperatives of farmers.

There are two types of **producer cooperatives**: worker cooperatives, owned by their own employees, and producer cooperatives, owned by independent producers that agree to do certain things together by pooling their resources.

Mondragon Co-operative Corporation (MCC) of Spain has nearly 70,000 employee-partners working in over 100 cooperatives and annual sales revenue of around $19 billion (as of 2010).[2] It is the seventh-biggest company in Spain, both by sales and employment. It is also the largest cooperative in the world. Another famous worker cooperative is John Lewis Partnership of Britain, the owner of John Lewis department stores and Waitrose supermarkets (the UK's sixth-biggest supermarket chain). It is of similar size to that of Mondragon – over 80,000 partners and a turnover of around $14 billion (as of 2011).

The most common examples of cooperatives of independent producers selectively working together are dairy farmers' cooperatives, in which farmers own their cows but together process and sell the milk and milk products (butter, cheese, etc.). Arla (the Swedish-Danish dairy cooperative that produces Lurpak butter and Lactofree milk), Land O'Lakes (the Minnesota-based American dairy farmer cooperative) and Amul (the cooperative of Indian dairy farmers) are the most famous examples.

One-person-one-vote: rules of cooperative decision-making

Being membership organizations, cooperatives make decisions based on the one-person-one-vote rule, rather than on the one-dollar(share)-one-vote rule of corporations. This results in decisions that are impossible to imagine in shareholder-owned corporations.

The Mondragon cooperative group is famous for having the wage rule in which the partner in charge of the top management position can be paid only three to nine times the minimum wage paid to a partner who does a front-line job, with the exact ratio being decided by votes among the partners of each cooperative. Compare this with the pay packages of top American managers, who get at least 300–400 times the *average* (not minimum) worker's wage.* Some cooperatives even rotate jobs, so that everyone has experiences in positions at different levels in the company.

Many workers do not make decisions as individuals any more

In modern economies, at least some workers do not make economic decisions as individuals any more. Many workers are organized into **trade unions**, or **labour unions**. Allowing workers to bargain as a group, rather than as individuals who may compete against each other, trade unions help workers extract higher wages and better working conditions from their employers.[3]

In some countries, trade unions are considered counter-productive, blocking the necessary changes in technologies and work organization. In others, they are seen as natural partners in any business. When Volvo, the Swedish vehicle manufacturer, bought the heavy construction equipment arm of Samsung in the aftermath of the 1997 Asian financial crisis, it is said to have asked the workers to set up a trade union (Samsung had – and still has – an infamous 'no-union' policy). The Swedish managers didn't know how to manage a company without a trade union to talk to!

Like cooperatives, trade unions are membership organizations, in which decisions are made according to the one-member-one-vote rule. These decisions by enterprise-level unions are usually aggregated by national-level unions, such as South Africa's COSATU (Congress of South African Trade Unions) and the UK's TUC (Trades Union Congress). In many countries, there is more than one national-level union, usually divided by political and/ or religious allegiances. For example, South Korea has two national-level unions, while France has as many as five.

In some countries, enterprise unions are also organized into industry-level unions. The most famous of these are IG Metall (Industriegewerkschaft

---

* Some estimates that include stock options – whose values are not easy to calculate – say that it could be over 1,000 times.

Metall), the German metal workers' union, and the UAW (United Auto Workers), the American auto-workers' union. In the case of IG Metall, its influence stretches over the metal-related industries (including the all-important automobile industry), because, as the most powerful union, what it does tends to set the trend for the other unions.

Some trade unions even play a part in national policy-making

In a number of European countries – Sweden, Finland, Norway, Iceland, Austria, Germany, Ireland and the Netherlands – trade unions are explicitly recognized as key partners in national-level decision-making. In those countries, they are involved in policy-making not just in 'obvious' areas like wages, working conditions and training, but also welfare policy, inflation control and industrial restructuring.

In some countries, such arrangements exist due to the fact that a very high proportion of workers are unionized. Around 70 per cent of workers in Iceland, Finland and Sweden belong to trade unions – the ratio is around 11 per cent in the US, to put it into perspective. However, the rate of unionization (known as 'union density') does not fully explain these arrangements. For example, more workers are unionized in Italy (around 35 per cent) or Britain (around 25 per cent) than in Germany and the Netherlands (both less than 20 per cent), but the Italian and the British unions have much weaker influence on national policy-making than do their German or Dutch equivalents. The political system (e.g., how strongly political parties are related to trade unions) and political culture (e.g., consensual or confrontational) matter too.

The government is the single most important economic actor

In all countries that are not in a virtual state of anarchy (the Democratic Republic of Congo and Somalia at the time of writing), the government is the single most important economic actor. We will discuss what it does in greater detail in Chapter 11, so let me just give you the big picture for now.

In most countries, the government is by far the single largest employer, employing anything up to 25 per cent of the national workforce in some cases.* Its expenditure is equivalent to anything between 10 and 55 per cent

---

* The fact that Walmart, the biggest private sector employer in the US, employs only about 1 per cent of the US labour force (1.4 million people) puts the number in perspective.

of national output, with the ratio generally higher in the richer countries than in the poorer ones. In many countries, the government owns and runs SOEs. These typically produce 10 per cent of national output, even though it could be over 15 per cent in countries like Singapore and Taiwan. The government also affects how other economic actors behave by creating, shutting down and regulating markets. Respective examples are the creation of the market for tradable permits for pollution, the abolition of slavery and various laws regarding working hours and conditions.

How the government makes its decisions:
compromises, compromises (and lobbying)

The process of government decision-making is far more complicated than that in even the largest corporations with the most complex ownership structures. It is because it does far more things than a corporation does, while having to accommodate far more actors with much more diverse goals.

When making decisions, even one-party states cannot override minority interests in the way the majority can in corporate decisions. Except in the most extreme cases, such as Pol Pot's Cambodia, political factions exist, and the competition between them can be quite intense, as it is in today's China.

In democracies, the decision-making process is even more complex. In theory, the majority party can impose its will on the rest of society. This is sometimes done, but in many countries the parliamentary majority is made up of independent parties in coalition, so compromises have to be made all the time. Anyone who has watched the Danish dramas *The Killing* or *Borgen* would appreciate this point.

Even after the politicians have made broad decisions, detailed policies have to be drawn up and implemented by civil servants, or bureaucrats. These people have their own decision rules, which are hierarchical, like those found in corporations, rather than deliberative, as found in parliaments.

Politicians and bureaucrats are lobbied by all sorts of groups to adopt particular policies. There are single-cause campaign groups, focusing on particular issues, such as the environment. Trade unions also have direct influences on politicians in some countries. But corporations exert the greatest influences. In some countries, such as the US, with weak restrictions on corporate lobbying, corporate influences are enormous. Jim Hightower, the

American political commentator, was certainly exaggerating, but not by much, when he said, 'The corporations don't have to lobby the government any more. They are the government.'

International organizations with money: the World Bank, the IMF and others

Some international organizations are important because – how shall I put it? – they have money. The World Bank and other 'regional' multilateral banks, predominantly owned by rich country governments, make loans to developing countries.* When they lend, they offer more favourable terms (lower interest rates, longer repayment periods) than do private-sector banks. The International Monetary Fund (IMF) makes large-scale loans on a short-term basis to countries in financial crises, which cannot borrow from the private market.

The World Bank, the IMF and other similar multilateral financial institutions demand the adoption of particular economic policies of their borrowing countries. Admittedly, all lenders attach conditions to their loans, but the World Bank and the IMF are particularly criticized for imposing conditions that the rich countries think are good, rather than those that would really help the borrowing countries. This happens because they are corporations with one-dollar-one-vote rule. The majority of their shares are owned by the rich countries, so they get to decide what to do. Most importantly, the US has de facto veto power in the Bank and the Fund, as the most important decisions in them require an 85 per cent majority, and the US happens to own 18 per cent of shares.

International organizations that set rules: the WTO and the BIS

Some international organizations have power because they set rules.[4] One example is the Bank for International Settlement (BIS), which sets international rules on financial regulations. But by far the most important of these rule-setting international organizations is the World Trade Organization (WTO).

The WTO sets rules on international economic interactions, including international trade, international investment and even the cross-border

---

* The most important regional multilateral banks are the Asian Development Bank (ADB), the African Development Bank (AfDB) and the Inter-American Development Bank (IDB).

protection of intellectual property rights, such as patents and copyrights. It is, importantly, the only international organization that is based on the one-country-one-vote rule. Thus, in theory, the developing countries, which have the numerical advantage, should dictate how things are done there. In practice, unfortunately, votes are almost never taken. Rich countries use all kinds of informal influences (e.g., issuing thinly disguised threats to reduce foreign aid to non-compliant poor countries) to avoid voting.

Those that promote ideas: UN agencies and the ILO

Some international organizations influence our economic life because they lend legitimacy to certain ideas. Various United Nations (UN) organizations belong to this category.

The UNIDO (United Nations Industrial Development Organization), for example, promotes industrial development. The UNDP (United Nations Development Programme) promotes poverty reduction on a global scale, and the ILO (International Labour Organization)[5] worker rights.

These organizations promote their causes mainly by offering a forum for public discussion on issues in their respective areas and by providing some technical assistance to countries that wish to implement their ideas. Sometimes they may issue declarations and conventions, but subscription to them is voluntary, so they have very little power. For example, virtually none of the immigrant-receiving nations have signed up to the ILO convention protecting migrant workers' rights (but then you cannot expect turkeys to vote for Christmas, as they say).

Not being backed by money and rule-setting power, the causes that these organizations promote are far less strongly promoted than the agenda of the IMF, the World Bank and the WTO.

Even Individuals Are Not What They Are Supposed to Be

Individualist economic theories misrepresent the reality of economic decision-making by downplaying, or even ignoring, the role of organizations. Worse, they are not even very good at understanding individuals.

The divided individual: individuals have 'multiple selves'

The individualist economists emphasize that the individual is the smallest irreducible social unit. It is obviously so in the physical sense. But philosophers, psychologists and even some economists have long debated whether the individual can be seen as an entity that cannot be divided up further.

Individuals don't need to suffer multi-polar disorder to possess conflicting preferences within themselves. This **multiple-self** problem is widespread. Even though the term may be unfamiliar, it is something that most of us have experienced.

We often see the same person behaving completely differently under different circumstances. A man may be a very selfish person when it comes to sharing domestic work with his wife but in a war may be willing to sacrifice his life for his comrades. This happens because people have multiple roles in their lives – a husband and a foot soldier in the above example. They are expected to, and do, act differently in different roles.

Sometimes it is due to weakness of will – we decide to do something in the future but fail to do it when the time comes. This bothered the old Greek philosophers sufficiently that they even invented a word for it – *akrasia*. For example, we decide to lead a healthier lifestyle but then see our willpower crumble in front of a tempting dessert. Anticipating this, we may devise tricks to prevent our 'other self' from asserting itself later, like Ulysses asking to be tied to his ship's mast in order not to be seduced by the Sirens. You declare at the beginning of dinner that you are on a diet and won't be having a dessert to be prevented from ordering one later, for fear of losing face (and you can always have a few compensatory chocolate cookies when you go back home).

The embedded individual: individuals are formed by their societies

The multiple-self problem shows that individuals are not atoms because they can be broken down further. They are not atoms also because they are not clearly separable from other individuals.

Economists working in the individualist tradition do not ask where individual preferences come from. They treat them as the ultimate data, generated from within 'sovereign' individuals. The idea is best summarized in the maxim 'De gustibus non est disputandum' ('Taste is not a matter of dispute').

Yet our preferences are strongly formed by our social environment – family, neighbourhood, schooling, social class and so on. Coming from different backgrounds, you don't just consume different things but you get to *want* different things. This process of **socialization** means that we cannot really treat individuals as atoms separable from each other. Individuals are – if we use a fancy term – 'embedded' in their societies. If individuals are products of society, Margaret Thatcher was seriously wrong when she famously (or infamously) said, 'There is no such thing as society. There are individual men and women, and there are families.' There *cannot* be such a thing as an individual without society.

In a scene from the 1980s cult BBC sci-fi comedy *Red Dwarf*, Dave Lister, the protagonist of the show, who is a Liverpudlian working-class slob, guiltily confesses that he's been to a wine bar once, as if he had committed some kind of crime (but then some of his friends would have called him a 'class traitor' for that). Some young people from poorer classes in Britain, even after decades of government policy encouraging university education for them, still believe that 'unis' are simply not for them. In most societies, women have been conditioned into believing that 'hard' professions such as science, engineering, law and economics are not for them.

It is an enduring theme in literature and cinema – *My Fair Lady* (the movie version of George Bernard Shaw's play *Pygmalion*), Willy Russell's *Educating Rita* (play and movie) and Marcel Pagnol's *La Gloire de mon père* (book and movie) – how education, and the resulting exposure to different lifestyles, will tear you away from your own people. You will want different things from what they want – and what you once wanted yourself.

Of course, people have free will and can – and do – make choices that go against what they are supposed to want and choose, given their backgrounds, as Rita did by choosing to do a university degree in *Educating Rita*. But our environment strongly influences who we are, what we want and what we choose to do. Individuals are products of their societies.

The impressionable individual: individuals are deliberately manipulated by others

Our preferences are not just shaped by our environment but often deliberately manipulated by others who want us to think and act in the ways they want. All aspects of human life – political propaganda, education, religious teachings, the mass media – involve such manipulation to one degree or another.

The most well-known instance is advertising. Some economists, following the works of George Stigler, a leading free-market economist of the 1960s and the 1970s, have argued that advertising is basically about providing information about the existence, prices and attributes of various products, rather than manipulation of preferences. However, most economists agree with John Kenneth Galbraith's seminal 1958 book *The Affluent Society* that much of advertising is about making potential consumers want the product more eagerly than they would otherwise do – or even want things that they never knew they needed.

Advertisements may associate a product with a celebrity, a sports team (which company logos does your favourite football or baseball team have on its uniform?) or with a fancy lifestyle. They may use memory triggers, which work on our subconscious. They may be aired at times when viewers are most susceptible (that's why you get TV advertisements for snacks around 9–10 p.m.). And not to forget product placements in movies, savagely satirized in the film *The Truman Show*: I still remember Mococoa, made with 'all natural cocoa beans from the upper slopes of Mount Nicaragua'.

Individual preferences are also manipulated at a more fundamental level through the propagation of free-market ideologies by those who want constraints on their profit-seeking minimized (so we're back to the politics of ideas again). Corporations and rich individuals generously finance think tanks that produce pro-market ideas, such as the Heritage Foundation in the US and the Institute of Economic Affairs in the UK. They donate campaign funds to pro-market political parties and politicians. Some big companies use their advertising spending to favour business-friendly media.

Once poor people are persuaded that their poverty is their own fault, that whoever has made a lot of money must deserve it and that they too could become rich if they tried hard enough, life becomes easier for the rich. The poor, often against their own interests, begin to demand fewer redistributive taxes, less welfare spending, less regulation on business and fewer worker rights.

Individual preferences – not just of consumers but also of tax-payers, workers and voters – can be, and often are, deliberately manipulated. Individuals are not the 'sovereign' entities that they are portrayed as in individualist economic theories.

The complicated individual: individuals are not just selfish

Individualist economic theories assume that individuals are selfish. When combined with the assumption of rationality, the conclusion is that we should let individuals do as they please; they know what is best for themselves and how to achieve their goals.

Economists, philosophers, psychologists and other social scientists have for centuries questioned the assumption of self-seeking individuals. The literature is huge, and many points are quite obscure, even if they are theoretically important. Let's stick to the main points.

Self-seeking itself is too simplistically defined, with the implicit assumption that individuals are incapable of recognizing long-term, systemic consequences of their actions. Some European capitalists in the nineteenth century argued for a ban on child labour, despite the fact that such regulation would reduce their profits. They understood that continued exploitation of children without education would lower the quality of the workforce, harming all capitalists, including themselves, in the long run. In other words, people can, and do, pursue **enlightened self-interest**.

Sometimes we are just generous. People care about other people and act against their self-interest to help others. Many people give to charities, volunteer for charitable activities and help strangers in trouble. A fireman enters a burning house to save an old lady trapped inside and a passer-by jumps into rough sea to save drowning children, even knowing that they themselves may be killed in the process. The evidence is endless. Only those who are blinded by a belief in the model of the self-seeking individual would try to ignore it.[6]

Human beings are complicated. Yes, most people are self-seeking much of the time, but they are also moved by patriotism, class solidarity, altruism, sense of fairness (or justice), honesty, commitment to an ideology, sense of duty, vicariousness, friendship, love, pursuit of beauty, idle curiosity and much else besides. The very fact that there are so many different words describing human motives is testimony to the fact that we are complicated creatures.

The bumbling individual: individuals are not very rational

Individualist economic theories assume individuals to be rational – that is, they know all possible states of the world in the future, make complicated calculations about the likelihood of each of these states and exactly know their preferences over them, thereby choosing the best possible course of action on each and every decision occasion. Once again, the implication is that we should let people be, because 'they know what they are doing'.

The individualist economic model assumes the kind of rationality that no one possesses – Herbert Simon called it 'Olympian rationality' or 'hyper-rationality'. The standard defence is that it does not matter whether a theory's underlying assumptions are realistic or not, so long as the model predicts events accurately. This kind of defence rings hollow these days, when an economic theory assuming hyper-rationality, known as the Efficient Market Hypothesis (EMH), played a key role in the making of the 2008 global financial crisis by making policy-makers believe that financial markets needed no regulation.

The problem is, simply put, that human beings are not very rational – or that they possess only bounded rationality.* The list of non-rational behaviour is endless. We are too easily swayed by instincts and emotion in our decisions – wishful thinking, panic, herd instinct and what not. Our decisions are heavily affected by the 'framing' of the question when they shouldn't be, in the sense that we may make different decisions about essentially the same problem, depending on the way it is presented. And we tend to over-react to new information and under-react to existing information; this is frequently observed in the financial market. We normally operate with an intuitive, heuristic (short-cut) system of thinking, which results in poor logical thinking. Above all, we are over-confident about our own rationality.

---

* There is a huge amount of evidence, well presented in accessible form in books like Peter Ubel's *Free Market Madness*, George Akerlof's and Robert Shiller's *Animal Spirits* and the psychologist and 2002 Nobel Economics laureate Daniel Kahnemann's *Thinking, Fast and Slow*.

Concluding Remarks: Only Imperfect Individuals Can Make Real Choices

A paradoxical result of conceptualizing individuals as highly imperfect beings – with limited rationality, complex and conflicting motives, gullibility, social conditioning and even internal contradictions – is that it actually makes individuals count more, rather than less.

It is exactly because we admit that individuals are products of society that we can appreciate more the free will of those who make choices that go against social conventions, prevailing ideologies or their class backgrounds. When we accept that human rationality is limited, we get to appreciate more the initiatives exercised by entrepreneurs when they embark on an 'irrational' venture that everyone else thinks is going to fail (which, when successful, is called an innovation). In other words, only when we admit the imperfect nature of human beings can we talk about 'real' choices – not the empty choices that people are destined to make in the world of perfect individuals, in which they always know which is the best course of action.

Emphasizing the importance of 'real' choices is not to suggest that we can make any choice we like. Self-help books may tell you that you can do or become anything if you choose to. But the options that people can choose from (or their **choice sets**) are usually severely limited. This could be because of the meagreness of the resources they command; as Karl Marx dramatically put it, the workers of early capitalism had only the choice between working eighty hours a week in harsh conditions and starving to death, because they had no independent means to support themselves. The limited choice set may also be, as I argued above, because we have been taught to limit the range of what we want and what we think may be possible through the socialization process and deliberate manipulation of our preferences.

Like all great novels and movies, the real economic world is populated by complex and flawed characters, both individuals and organizations. Theorizing about them (or about anything), of course, has to involve some degrees of generalization and simplification, but the dominant economic theories go too far in simplifying things.

Only when we take into account the multi-faceted and limited nature of individuals while recognizing the importance of large organizations with complex structure and internal decision mechanisms will we be able to build theories that allow us to understand the complexity of choices in real-world economies.

Further Reading

G. AKERLOF AND R. SHILLER
Animal Spirits: How Human Psychology Drives the Economy and Why It Matters for Global Capitalism (Princeton: Princeton University Press, 2009).

J. DAVIS
The Theory of the Individual in Economics: Identity and Value (London: Routledge, 2003).

B. FREY
Not Just For the Money: An Economic Theory of Personal Motivation (Cheltenham: Edward Elgar, 1997).

J. K. GALBRAITH
The New Industrial State (London: Deutsch, 1972).

F. VON HAYEK
Individualism and Economic Order (London: Routledge and Kegan Paul, 1976).

D. KAHNEMANN
Thinking, Fast and Slow (London: Penguin, 2012).

H. SIMON
Reason in Human Affairs (Oxford: Basil Blackwell, 1983).

P. UBEL
Free Market Madness: Why Human Nature Is at Odds with Economics – and Why It Matters (Boston, MA: Harvard Business School Press, 2009).

Moving On . . .

The first part of this book has been about 'getting used to' economics. In this part, we have discussed what economics is (a study of the economy), what the economy is, how our economy has become what it is today, how there are many different ways of studying it and who the main economic actors are.

Having become 'used to' economics, let us now discuss how we can 'use' it to understand the real world economy.

PART TWO

Using It

How Many Do You Want It to Be?

OUTPUT, INCOME AND HAPPINESS

WHEN: Sometime in the 1930s
WHERE: The office of the Gosplan, the central planning
        authority of the USSR
WHAT: Interview for the post of the chief statistician

The first candidate is asked by the interview board,
'What is two plus two, comrade?' He answers: 'Five.'
The chairman of the interview board
smiles indulgently and says: 'Comrade, we very much
appreciate your revolutionary enthusiasm, but this job
needs someone who can count.' The candidate is politely
shown the door.

The second candidate's answer is 'Three.' The
youngest member of the interview board springs up and
shouts: 'Arrest that man! We cannot tolerate this kind
of counter-revolutionary propaganda, under-reporting our
achievements!' The second candidate is summarily dragged
out of the room by the guards.

When asked the same question, the third candidate
answers: 'Of course it is four.' The professorial-
looking member of the board gives him a stern lecture
on the limitations of bourgeois science, fixated on
formal logic. The candidate hangs his head in shame and
walks out of the room.

The fourth candidate is hired.

What was his answer?

'How many do you want it to be?'

Output

Gross Domestic Product, or GDP

Output figures are rarely 'manufactured' blatantly, even in socialist countries, except in the most extreme political situations – such as the early days of Stalin's rule or the Great Leap Forward under Mao Zedong in China. Still, it would be wrong to think that we can measure economic output, or any other number in economics for that matter, in the way we measure things in natural sciences, such as physics or chemistry.

The economists' favoured measure for output is **Gross Domestic Product**, or GDP. It is, roughly speaking, the total monetary value of what has been produced within a country over a particular period of time – usually a year, but also a quarter (three months) or even a month.

I said 'roughly', because 'what has been produced' needs definition. In calculating GDP, we measure output – or product – by **value added**. Value added is the value of a producer's output minus the intermediate inputs it has used. A bakery may earn £150,000 a year by selling bread and pastries, but if it has paid £100,000 in order to buy various **intermediate inputs** – raw materials (e.g., flour, butter, eggs, sugar), fuel, electricity and so on – it has only added £50,000 of value to those inputs.

If we didn't take away the value of the intermediate inputs and simply added up the final outputs of all the producers, we would be double-, triple- and multiple-counting some components, inflating the actual output. The baker bought its flour from a milling company, so if we simply added up the output of the baker and the miller, the flour that the baker bought would be counted twice. The miller bought the wheat from a farmer, so if we added the output of the wheat farmer to those of the baker and the miller, the portion of the wheat output that the farmer had sold to the miller and then was sold on to the baker would be counted three times. Only by counting the 'added' value can we measure the true size of the output.*

What about the 'Gross' bit in GDP? It means that we still have *not* taken away something that could have been removed from the picture, as when a can of tuna specifies gross weight and net weight (that is, the weight of the

---

* A very rough but useful rule of thumb is that the value-added figure is usually around one-third of sales (turnover) figure of a company.

fish without the oil or brine). In this case, that something is the used-up parts of **capital goods** – basically machines, so we are talking the baker's ovens, dough mixers and bread slicers. Capital goods, or machines, are not 'consumed' and incorporated into the output in the same way in which flour is to bread, but they experience reduction in economic value with use – this is known as **depreciation**. If we take away the wear and tear of machines from GDP, we get **Net Domestic Product**, or NDP.

Net Domestic Product, or NDP

As NDP accounts for everything that has gone into producing the output – intermediate inputs and capital-goods inputs – it provides a more accurate picture of what the economy has produced than GDP does. But we tend to use GDP instead of NDP because there is no one agreed way of estimating depreciation (suffice it to say here there are several contending ways), which makes the definition of N in NDP quite tricky.

Then how about D in GDP? 'Domestic' here means being within the boundary of a country. Not all producers in a country are its own citizens or companies registered in it. Seen from the other side, not all producers produce in their home countries; companies run factories abroad, and people get jobs in foreign countries. The number that measures all the output produced by your nationals (including companies), rather than the output produced within your border, is called **Gross National Product**, or GNP.

Gross National Product, or GNP

In the US or Norway, GDP and GNP are more or less identical. In Canada, Brazil and India, with many foreign firms inside their borders and few domestic firms producing abroad, GDP could be more than 10 per cent bigger than GNP. For Sweden and Switzerland, which have more of their national firms operating abroad than foreign firms operating within their borders, GNP is bigger than GDP, around 2.5 and 5 per cent respectively as of 2010.

GDP is more frequently used than GNP, since, in the short run, it is the more accurate indicator of the level of productive activities within a country. But GNP is a better measure of an economy's long-term strength.

A country may have a higher GDP (GNP) than another, but that may be because it has a larger population than the other. So, we really need to look at GDP or GNP figures **per capita** (per head, or per person, if you like) if we want to know how productive the economy is – it is actually somewhat more complicated than that, but we can leave this aside; if you are interested, read the footnote.*

Limitations of GDP and GNP measures

A critical limitation of GDP and GNP measures is that they value outputs at market prices. Since a lot of economic activities occur outside the market, the values of their outputs need to be somehow calculated – 'imputed' is the technical word. For example, a lot of farmers in developing countries engage in subsistence farming in which they consume most of the food they produce. So we need to estimate that quantity and impute market values to what those farmers produced but did not sell in the market (and consumed themselves). Or, when people live in houses they own, we impute the value of the 'dwelling services' involved, as if the house-owners are paying the rents at market rates to themselves. Unlike outputs exchanged through markets, the imputation of market values to non-marketed outputs involves guesswork, imparting inaccuracy to the numbers.

Worse, there is a particular class of non-marketed output whose value isn't even imputed. Household work – including cooking, cleaning, care work for children and elderly relatives and so on – is simply not counted as part of GDP or GNP. The classic 'joke' among economists is that you reduce your national output if you marry your housekeeper. The standard excuse is that it is difficult to impute values to household work, but it is a very weak defence. After all, we impute values to all sorts of other non-marketed economic activities, including living in one's own house. As the vast bulk of household work is done by women, women's work is grossly under-valued as a result of this practice. Many estimates put the value of household work to be equivalent to around 30 per cent of GDP.

---

*   What really represents a nation's productivity is how much people have to work in order to produce a given amount of output, rather than what the output is for each person alive. Therefore, in order to judge an economy's productivity, ideally we have to look at GDP *per hour worked*, rather than per capita, but those numbers are not readily available, so we use GDP per capita figures as proxies for a country's productivity.

REAL-LIFE NUMBERS

Why do you need to know 'real-life numbers'?

Despite the common impression that it is a 'numbers' subject, economics as it is taught today is rather short on numbers. It is common that someone with an economics degree does not know some 'obvious' economic numbers, such as the GDP or the average working hours of her own country.

There is no way anyone can remember more than a handful of those numbers. Indeed, in this internet age, you don't have to remember any of them, because you can easily look them up. But I believe it is important that my readers familiarize themselves with some of these 'real-life numbers', even just to know what numbers to look up. More importantly, they need to develop a sense of what our economic world looks like in reality: when we talk about China's GDP, are we talking hundreds of billions or tens of trillions of US dollars? Are we talking 15 per cent or 30 per cent when we say that South Africa has one of the highest unemployment rates in the world? When we say that a high proportion of people in India live in poverty, do we mean 20 per cent or 40 per cent? Thus, in this and all subsequent chapters, I provide a selection of the most important real-life economic numbers.

Most of world output is produced by a small number of countries

The world GDP in 2010, according to the World Bank data, was around $63.4 trillion. The five largest economies by GDP were the US (22.7 per cent of the world economy), China (9.4 per cent), Japan (8.7 per cent), Germany (5.2 per cent) and France (4.0 per cent).* Thus these five economies accounted for half of world output.

In 2010, the 'high-income countries' in the World Bank classification (countries with above $12,276 per capita income) had collective GDP of $44.9 trillion.† They accounted for 70.8 per cent of the world economy. The rest of the world, or the developing world, collectively had a GDP of $18.5

---

* The GDP figures were $14.4 trillion for the US, $5.9 trillion for China, $5.5 trillion for Japan, $3.3 trillion for Germany and $2.5 trillion for France.

† This definition means that several countries that people wouldn't normally consider rich are included in the 'high-income' world – a few former socialist countries (Poland, Hungary, Croatia and Slovakia) and two of the poorer oil states (Saudi Arabia and Libya). But they are not large enough to alter the overall picture.

trillion, or 29.2 per cent of world GDP. But two-thirds (66.6 per cent) of this $18.5 trillion was accounted for by the five largest developing economies, China, Brazil, India, Russia and Mexico.* The rest of the developing world, with a collective GDP of $6.3 trillion, accounted for just under 10 per cent of the world economy.

Most developing economies produce tiny – I mean
tiny – fractions of what the richest countries produce

The typical GDP of very poor small developing countries (5–10 million people), such as the Central African Republic or Liberia, is in the region of one or two billion dollars, or $0.001 trillion to $0.002 trillion. These are not even 0.01 per cent of the US GDP, which was $14.4 trillion as of 2010.

The thirty-five low-income countries according to the World Bank classification (countries with less than $1,005 per capita GDP in 2010) collectively had a GDP of $0.42 trillion. This is 0.66 per cent of the world economy or 2.9 per cent of the US economy.

Even the larger middle-income developing countries (30–50 million people), such as Colombia or South Africa, may have GDP of $300–400 billion. These are only as large as the GDP of a mid-sized US state, such as Washington or Minnesota.

In terms of GDP per capita figures, we have a huge range. Since these figures are similar – actually identical in theory, although not necessarily so in practice – to income per capita figures that we discuss shortly, suffice it to say here that we are talking about differentials over 500 times.

Income

Gross Domestic Income, or GDI

GDP may be seen as a sum of incomes, rather than outputs, as everyone who is involved in the production activity is paid for his/her contribution (whether the amounts paid are 'fair' is another matter). Going back to the baker's example, having paid for flour, eggs and other intermediate inputs, the bakery will divide up its value-added between wages for its workers,

---

* GDPs were $5.9 trillion for China, $2.1 trillion for Brazil, $1.7 trillion for India, $1.5 trillion for Russia and $1.0 trillion for Mexico. These add up to $12.2 trillion.

profits for its shareholders, interest payments for the loan it may have contracted and the indirect taxes that are automatically included in the revenue that it generates (that is, value added tax (VAT) or sales tax).

The sum of these incomes is known as **Gross Domestic Income**, or GDI. In theory, GDI should be identical to GDP, as it is simply a different way of adding up the same thing. But in practice it is slightly different, as some of the data used in compiling the two of them may be collected through different channels.

Gross National Income, or GNI, and per capita GNI

Like GNP is to GDP, **Gross National Income**, or GNI, is to GDI. GNI is the result of adding up the incomes of a country's citizens, rather than the incomes of those who are producing within its border, which gives us GDI. The World Bank publishes GDP and GNI, rather than GNP and GDI. This is presumably on the reasoning that income, as a measure of earnings, is better measured according to the nationality of those who claim it, while product, as a measure of outputs, is better measured according to where the production activities are happening.

Per capita income, usually measured by GNI (or its product equivalent, GNP) per capita, is considered by many people to be the single best measure of a country's living standard. But saying that it is the best does not mean that it is good enough.

One obvious problem is that GNI per capita only measures the average income. But the average may conceal a much greater variation among different individuals and groups in one country than in another. To give a simple numerical example, Countries A and B may both have $5,000 per capita income and ten people (therefore GNI of $50,000 each), but A may consist of one person with $45,500 income and nine people with $500 each, while B may consist of one person with $9,500 income and nine people with $4,500 each. In this case, $5,000 per capita income will be a relatively accurate description of the standard of living in Country B but will be completely misleading for Country A. To use a more technical term, you would say that the average income is a more accurate indicator of the living standard for a country with a more equal distribution of income. (More on this in Chapter 9.)

Adjusting for different price levels: purchasing power parity

One important adjustment that is often made to the GNI (or GDP) figures is that for different price levels in different countries. The market exchange rate between the Danish krone and the Mexican peso may be around one krone to 2.2 pesos, but with 2.2 pesos you can buy more goods and services in Mexico than you can with one krone in Denmark (I will explain shortly why). So the official exchange rate between the Danish krone and the Mexican peso under-estimates the actual living standards in Mexico.

The problem is that market exchange rates are largely determined by the supply and demand for *internationally traded* goods and services, such as the Galaxy phones or international banking services, while what a sum of money can buy in a particular country is determined by the prices of *all* goods and services, including those that are not internationally traded, such as eating out or taking a taxi.[1]

To deal with this problem, economists have come up with the idea of an 'international dollar'. Based on the notion of **purchasing power parity** (PPP) – that is, measuring the value of a currency according to how much of a common set of goods and services (known as the 'consumption basket') it can buy in different countries – this fictitious currency allows us to convert incomes of different countries into a common measure of living standards.

The result of the conversion is that PPP incomes of countries with expensive service-sector workers (the rich countries, excluding a few with a lot of cheap immigrant labour, such as the US and Singapore) are significantly *lower* than their market-exchange-rate incomes, while those of countries with cheap service workers (the poor countries) tend to become much *higher* than their market-exchange-rate incomes.*

Sticking to the Denmark–Mexico comparison above, Danish PPP per capita income in 2010 is around 30 per cent lower than its market-exchange-rate income ($40,140 vs. $58,980), while the Mexican PPP per capita income is around 60 per cent higher than its market-exchange-rate income ($15,010 vs. $9,330). So the income gap of over six times ($58,980 vs. $9,330) is

---

* Note that we cannot, strictly speaking, directly compare these two different income figures.

reduced to the living standard gap of under three times ($40,140 vs. $15,010) after the PPP adjustments.

PPP adjustment is very sensitive to the methodology and the data used, not least because it relies on the rather heroic assumption that all countries consume the same basket of goods and services. And we are not talking about minor differences. By changing its method of estimating PPP incomes in 2007, the World Bank reduced China's PPP income per capita by 44 per cent (from $7,740 to $5,370) and increased Singapore's by 53 per cent (from $31,710 to $48,520) overnight.

Income figures do not fully represent living standards, even with PPP adjustments

Even with PPP adjustments, income figures, such as GNP per capita and GNI per capita, do not fully represent living standards. There are a number of reasons for this.

One obvious but important point is that we don't live by monetary income alone. We want political freedom, vibrant community life, self-fulfilment and many other things that money cannot buy. The increase in monetary income does not guarantee increases in these things and may even undermine them. For example, if higher income is gained at the cost of working longer and with greater intensity, we may have less time and energy for community life or self-fulfilment.

Another is that, as pointed out above, income figures do not reflect household work (including care work), which to a substantial part of the humanity – children, the elderly and the sick – are the most important things.

Even regarding things that can be bought with money, we often make poor decisions as consumers (recall Chapter 5). Influenced by advertising or in our desire to 'keep up with the Joneses' (or the Zhangs, the Patels, the Castros, or whoever, depending on where you live), most of us have bought things that we never knew we needed. Beyond providing the fleeting joy of purchase itself, these goods add little to our well-being.

Even if we are totally rational as consumers, the existence of **positional goods** makes income an unreliable gauge of true living standard (or happiness, satisfaction or what you will).[2] Positional goods are goods whose values derive from the fact that only a small proportion of potential consumers can have them.* Even if our personal income rises, we may still be unable to acquire things like houses in prime locations, Rembrandt's paintings or elite education that gives access to top jobs, if others have also become richer and are able to stump up even more money than we can. This problem is more severe in richer economies, as the finer things in life tend to be positional goods, while essential goods are usually not.

These limitations don't mean that income is unimportant in measuring living standards. Especially in the poorer countries, a higher income is largely a positive thing. In those countries, even a slightly higher income can make all the difference between eating properly and starvation, between working in a dangerous, back-breaking job and having just a hard job, and between having your child die at the age of one and seeing it grow up. In the richer societies, the positive impacts of a higher income on living standards are less certain. But even there, higher incomes will help people have higher standards of living, if they are used well. For example, a higher income will allow a country to reduce working hours and thus enable people to have more time with family and friends or get more adult education, while maintaining previous levels of material consumption.

REAL-LIFE NUMBERS

What are the income figures like in the real world? Here we will look at income per capita figures, given that we have already talked a lot about overall output figures, such as GDP and GNP, that are identical to overall income figures in theory and are very similar to them in practice.

Countries that we typically know as the richest countries have over $40,000 per capita income

According to the World Bank, in 2010, the country with the highest income (GNI) per capita in the world was Monaco ($197,460), followed

---

* Sheldon, the man-child physicist protagonist of *The Big Bang Theory*, the cult TV drama series, explained these goods beautifully, when he explained to his friend Raj why Howard, their friend, does what Raj calls 'lovey-dovey stuff' with his new girlfriend on the mobile phone in front of his friends: 'There's an economic concept known as a positional good in which an object is only valued by the possessor because it's not possessed by others. The term was coined in 1976 by economist Fred Hirsch to replace the more colloquial, but less precise, "neener-neener"' ('The Large Hadron Collision', season 3, episode 15). Hirsch's seminal work is the book *Social Limits to Growth*.

by Liechtenstein ($136,540). However, both of these are tax havens with tiny populations (33,000 and 36,000 respectively). So, if we exclude countries with a population of less than half a million, Norway, with a per capita income of $85,380, is the richest country (that is, it has the highest per capita GNI).

A selection of the richest countries is listed in Table 6.1. They are mostly in Western Europe and Western offshoots. A few Asian countries belong to this group, with Japan and Singapore firmly in the upper league. South Korea, together with a couple of Eastern European countries, is there too – only just.

The average person in the poorest four countries doesn't even earn $1 a day

At the other extreme, Burundi, with $160 per capita income, was the poorest country in the world in 2010. In several of the poorest countries, the average person did not even earn $1 of income per day ($365 per year).

Countries with less than $1,000 per capita income are officially classified as 'low-income' countries in the World Bank classification (the World Bank cut-off line is $1,005), or as **least-developed countries** (LDCs) by various international treaties and organizations.

Table 6.2 lists a selection of LDCs. It shows that most of them are in Africa, with a few in Asia (Nepal, Bangladesh, Cambodia, Tajikistan, Kyrgyz Republic) and only one in Latin America (Haiti).

Thus, the per capita income of the richest (Norway) is a staggering 534 times greater than that of the poorest (Burundi) as of 2010. Even if we take the less extreme cases of the US (no. 7 from the top with $47,140) versus Ethiopia (no. 8 from the bottom, with $380), the income differential is still 124 times.

There are poor countries and there are poor countries:
gaps between developing countries

In between these extremes lie the vast majority of countries that are called middle-income countries in the World Bank classification. People, including myself, often call them developing countries or simply poor countries, but there is poor and there is poor.

Table 6.3 provides per capita incomes of a selection of developing countries, to give the reader some idea of who belongs where and also the gaps that exist between developing countries themselves.

At the top of the developing country grouping are countries like Brazil and Mexico, with $8,001–$10,000 per capita incomes. These countries have per capita incomes that are fifty to sixty times higher than those of the poorest countries that we discussed in Table 6.2, when their own differentials with the richest countries are no more than ten times.

Countries that we typically think of when we hear the words 'developing countries' – such as Indonesia, Egypt, Sri Lanka, the Philippines, India and Ghana – are mostly found in the $1,001–$3,000 range of per capita income. Even these countries have per capita incomes that are five to ten times those of the poorest countries.

PPP adjustments show that gaps in living standards are not as severe as gaps in productivity

To more precisely learn about different countries' living standards instead of their productivity, we need to convert their incomes (outputs) into PPP terms. This adjustment results in significant changes in the rankings of countries.

In PPP terms, Luxembourg, at $63,850, becomes the richest country in the world, followed by Norway, Singapore, Kuwait, Switzerland and the US.* With PPP adjustments, per capita incomes of poor countries rise in relative terms, as non-traded services (and some goods) are cheaper in these countries. In PPP terms, the Democratic Republic of Congo (DRC) ($310), Liberia ($330) and Burundi ($390) are the three poorest countries in the world.†

With these PPP adjustments, the income differences between the rich and the poor countries are diminished, compared with the ones calculated in terms of market exchange rate incomes. The difference between the highest and the lowest GNI per capita is diminished from 534 times (Norway vs. Burundi) to 'only' 206 times (Luxembourg vs. the DRC).

---

* The PPP-adjusted per capita incomes are $57,130 in Norway, $54,700 in Singapore, $53,630 in Kuwait, $49,180 in Switzerland and ($47,020 in the US. They are followed by the Netherlands ($42,590), Denmark ($40,140) and Sweden ($39,600).

† They are followed by Eritrea ($540), Niger ($700), the Central African Republic ($760), Togo ($790) and Sierra Leone ($830).

INCOME RANGE	COUNTRIES (FROM THE RICHEST TO THE POOREST IN EACH GROUP)
$50,001 and above	Norway ($85,380), Switzerland ($70,350), Denmark ($58,980)
$45,001 – $50,000	Sweden ($49,930), the Netherlands ($49,720), Finland ($47,170), the USA ($47,140), Belgium ($45,420)
$40,001 – $45,000	Australia ($43,740), Germany ($43,330), France ($42,390), Japan ($42,150), Canada ($41,950), Singapore ($40,920)
$30,001 – $40,000	The UK ($38,540), Italy ($35,090), Spain ($31,650)
$20,001 – $30,000	New Zealand ($29,050), Israel ($27,340), Greece ($27,240)
$15,001 – $20,000	South Korea ($19,890), Czech Republic ($17,870), Slovakia ($16,220)

Table 6.1
Incomes of the richest countries (GNI per capita, 2010)
Source: World Bank, *World Development Report, 2012.*

INCOME RANGE	COUNTRIES (FROM THE POOREST TO THE RICHEST IN EACH GROUP)
$300 and below	Burundi ($160), Democratic Republic of Congo ($180), Liberia ($190)
£301 – $400	Malawi ($330), Eritrea ($340), Sierra Leone ($340), Niger ($360), Ethiopia ($380), Guinea ($380)
$401 – $500	Mozambique ($440), Togo ($440), Central African Republic ($460), Zimbabwe ($460), Uganda ($490), Nepal ($490)
$501 – $600	Tanzania ($530), Rwanda ($540), Burkina Faso ($550), Mali ($600)
$601 – $800	Bangladesh ($640), Haiti ($650), Benin ($750), Cambodia ($760), Tajikistan ($780)
$801 – $1,000	Kyrgyz Republic ($880)

Table 6.2

Incomes of the poorest countries (GNI per capita, 2010)

Source: World Bank, *World Development Report, 2012.*

INCOME RANGE	COUNTRIES (FROM THE RICHEST TO THE POOREST IN EACH GROUP)
$8,001 – $10,000	Chile ($9,940), Russia ($9,910), Turkey ($9,500), Brazil ($9,390), Mexico ($9,330), Argentina ($8,450)
$6,001 – $8,000	Malaysia ($7,900), Costa Rica ($6,580), Bulgaria ($6,240), South Africa ($6,100)
$4,001 – $6,000	Colombia ($5,510), Ecuador ($4,510), Algeria ($4,460), China ($4,260), Thailand ($4,210), Tunisia ($4,070)
$3,001 – $4,000*	Angola ($3,960), El Salvador ($3,360)
$2,001 – $3,000	Indonesia ($2,580), Egypt ($2,340), Sri Lanka ($2,290), the Philippines ($2,050)
$1,001 – $2,000	Bolivia ($1,790), India ($1,340), Ghana ($1,240), Vietnam ($1,100), Pakistan ($1,050)
$1,000 and below*	Least Developed Countries (LDCs)

Table 6.3
Incomes of selected developing countries (GNI per capita, 2010)
Source: World Bank, *World Development Report, 2012.*

* In the World Bank classification, a country is considered 'upper middle income' if it had GNI per capita higher than $3,975 and 'low' income if it had one lower than $1,005 in 2010.

Happiness

*Not everything that counts can be measured, not everything that can
be measured counts: can – and should – happiness be measured?*

Recognizing the limitations of using monetary income to measure living
standards, some economists have resorted to directly asking people how
happy they are. These 'happiness' studies allow us to get around a lot of
problems involved in measuring living standards: what needs to be included
in the measurement; how we assign values to difficult-to-measure elements
that affect our living standards (even though this has not stopped people
from coming up with things like 'political freedom index'); and what weight
to give to each element. The best-known of this type of study are the Gallup
Happiness Survey and the World Values Survey.

Many people question whether happiness can be, and indeed should be,
measured at all. The fact that happiness may be conceptually a better measure than income does not mean that we should try to measure it. Richard
Layard, the British economist who is a leading scholar trying to measure
happiness, defends such attempts by saying, 'If you think something matters you should *try to measure it* [italics added].'[3] But other people disa-
gree – including Albert Einstein, who once famously said, 'Not everything
that counts can be measured. Not everything that can be measured counts.'

We can try to quantify happiness, say, by asking people to rate their happiness on a scale of ten, and come up with numbers like 6.3 or 7.8 for the
average happiness of Countries A and B. But such numbers are not even half
as objective as $160 or $85,380 per capita incomes – and we've discussed
why even the income numbers are not totally objective.

*Adaptive preference and false consciousness: why we cannot
totally rely on people's judgements on their own happiness*

More importantly, it is debatable whether we can trust people's judgement on their own happiness. There are all kinds of **adaptive preferences**,
in which people reinterpret their situations to make them more bearable.
'Sour grapes', namely, deciding that what you could not get is actually not
as good as you had thought, is a classic example.

Many people who are oppressed, exploited or discriminated against
say – and they would not be lying – that they are happy. Many of them even

oppose changes that will improve their lot: many European women *opposed* the introduction of female suffrage in the early twentieth century. Some of them may even play an active part in perpetuating injustice and brutality – like those slaves who took a lead in the oppression of other slaves, such as Stephen, the character played by Samuel L. Jackson in the movie *Django Unchained*.

These people think they are happy because they have come to accept – 'internalize' is the fancy word here – the values of the oppressors/discriminators. Marxists call these cases of **false consciousness**.

The Matrix *and the limits of happiness studies*

The problem that false consciousness poses for happiness studies has been most brilliantly illustrated by the Wachowski siblings' mind-blowing 1999 movie *The Matrix*. In the movie, we have those, like Morpheus, who think that a happy life under false consciousness is unacceptable. Others, like Cypher, would rather live in false consciousness than lead a dangerous and hard life of resistance in reality. And who are we to say that Cypher's choice is necessarily the wrong one? What right does Morpheus have to 'rescue' people only to make them feel miserable?

The issue of false consciousness is a genuinely difficult problem that has no definite solution. We should not approve of an unequal and brutal society because surveys show that people are happy. But who has the right to tell those oppressed women or starving landless peasants that they shouldn't be happy, if they think they are? Does anyone have the right to make those people feel miserable by telling them the 'truth'? There are no easy answers to these questions, but they definitely tell us that we cannot rely on 'subjective' happiness surveys to decide how well people are doing.

Happiness studies with more objective measures

Given these limitations of subjective happiness measures, most happiness studies now combine more objective measures (e.g., income level, life expectancy) with some element of subjective assessment.

One good – and quite comprehensive – example in this category is the Better Life Index, launched in 2011 by the OECD. This index looks at people's subjective judgements on life satisfaction, together with ten other more (although not completely) objective indicators, ranging from income and jobs to community life and work–life balance (and each of these indicators has more than one constituent element).

Even while a happiness index that includes more elements is conceptually more defensible, its numerical outcome is more difficult to defend. As we try to incorporate more and more dimensions of our life into the happiness index, we are made to include more and more dimensions that are very difficult, if not impossible, to quantify. Civic engagement and the quality of community life in the OECD index are such examples. Moreover, as the number of elements grow in the index, it becomes more difficult to assign a weight to each element. It is interesting to note that, in open recognition of this difficulty, the OECD Better Life Index website lets you make up your own index by varying the weights between different elements according to your own judgements.

REAL-LIFE NUMBERS

Happiness index numbers, whether they are completely subjective or combined with more objective indicators, are not really meaningful in themselves. You simply cannot compare different types of happiness indexes with each other. The only thing that you can reasonably do with them is track changes in happiness levels for individual countries according to one index or, less reliably, rank countries according to one index.

Different happiness indexes include very different elements. As a result, the same country can rank very differently depending on the index. But some countries – the Scandinavian countries (especially Denmark), Australia and Costa Rica – tend to rank highly in more indexes than other countries do. Some countries – such as Mexico and the Philippines – tend to do better in indexes with greater weight given to subjective factors, suggesting higher degrees of 'false consciousness' among their people.

Concluding Remarks: Why Numbers in Economics Can Never Be Objective

Defining and measuring concepts in economics cannot be objective in the way such exercises in physics or chemistry can be. Even such an exercise regarding what are seemingly the most straightforward of economic concepts, such as output and income, is fraught with difficulties. A lot of value judgements are involved – for example, the decision not to include house-hold work in output statistics. There are many technical problems – especially in relation to the imputation of value to non-marketed activities and to the PPP adjustments. In the case of the poorer countries, there are also issues with data quality – collecting and processing the raw data require financial and human resources that these countries do not have.

Even if we do not dispute the numbers themselves, it is difficult to say that output/income figures correctly represent living standards, especially in richer countries, in which most people can meet their **basic needs** for food, water, clothing, shelter, basic health care and basic education. It is also necessary to make allowances for differences in purchasing power, working hours, non-monetary aspects of the standard of living, irrational consumer choices (whether due to manipulation or herd behaviour) and positional goods.

Happiness studies try to obviate these needs, but they have their own, even more serious, problems – the inherent immeasurability of happiness and the problem of adaptive preferences (especially of the false consciousness variety).

All of this does *not* mean that we should not use numbers in economics. Without having some knowledge of key numbers – like output levels, growth rates, unemployment rates and measures of inequality – an informed understanding of the real-world economy is impossible. But we need to use them in full awareness of what each number does and doesn't tell us.

Further Reading

J. ALDRED
The Skeptical Economist: Revealing the Ethics Inside Economics (London: Earthscan, 2009).

F. HIRSCH
Social Limits to Growth (London: Routledge and Kegan Paul, 1978).

M. JERVEN
Poor Numbers: How We Are Misled by African Development Statistics and What to Do about It (Ithaca: Cornell University Press, 2013).

R. LAYARD
Happiness: Lessons from a New Science (London: Allen Lane, 2005).

A. MADDISON
The World Economy: A Millennial Perspective (Paris: OECD, 2001).

D. NAYYAR
Catch Up: Developing Countries in the World Economy (Oxford: Oxford University Press, 2013).

J. STIGLITZ ET AL.
Mis-measuring Our Lives: Why GDP Doesn't Add Up (New York: The New Press, 2010).

CHAPTER 7

How Does Your Garden Grow?

THE WORLD OF PRODUCTION

You could say that Equatorial Guinea has been destined for obscurity. It is the smallest country in mainland Africa in terms of population, with just over 700,000 people. It is also a minnow in terms of landmass – the sixth smallest.[1] Who is going to notice such a small country? To add insult to injury, there are no less than five other countries with very similar names – not just Guinea and Guinea Bissau in its neighbourhood but also Papua New Guinea in the Pacific and Guyana and French Guiana in South America.

However, if Equatorial Guinea remains one of the most obscure countries in the world, it is not for lack of trying. It is the richest country in Africa, with a per capita GDP of $20,703, as of 2010. Over the last couple of decades, it has been one of the fastest-growing economies in the world. Between 1995 and 2010, its per capita GDP grew at the rate of 18.6 per cent per year – more than double the rate in China, the international growth superstar, which grew at 'only' 9.1 per cent per year.

Honestly, what more can a country do to get some attention? Invade the US? Make Scarlett Johansson the president? Paint the whole country pink? The world is really unfair.

Economic Growth and Economic Development

Economic development as the development of
productive capabilities

If Equatorial Guinea has grown so much faster than China, why have we not heard of the 'Equatorial Guinean economic miracle', when we hear about the 'Chinese economic miracle' all the time?

The difference in size is one reason – it is possible to ignore very small countries, even if they are doing very well. But most people do not take Equatorial Guinea's phenomenal income growth seriously mainly because it is due to a resource bonanza. Nothing about the country's economy changed other than finding a very large oil reserve in 1996. Without oil, the country would be reduced to one of the poorest in the world once again, which it used to be, as it cannot produce much else.[2]

I am not saying that all growth experiences based on natural resources, such as oil, minerals and agricultural products, are like that of Equatorial Guinea. The economic growth of the US in the nineteenth century benefited hugely from abundant natural resources, such as agricultural products and minerals. Finland, exploiting its position as a country with one of the world's most abundant forestry resources, relied heavily on logging for its exports well into the twentieth century. Australia's growth still depends critically on mineral exports.

What makes Equatorial Guinea different from those other cases is that its growth has not been achieved through an increase in its ability to produce. The US provides the best contrast.[3] In the late nineteenth century, the US was not only rapidly becoming the most powerful industrial nation in the world but was also the world's leading producer of almost all commercially relevant minerals. But this status had not been achieved simply because the US was in possession of a lot of mineral deposits. It was in large part because the country had developed impressive capabilities to locate, extract and process minerals efficiently; until the mid-nineteenth century, it had not been a world-leading producer of any mineral. In contrast, Equatorial Guinea not only cannot produce much else than oil, it does not even possess the ability to produce oil itself – its oil is all pumped out by American oil companies.

While it is an extreme example, Equatorial Guinea's experience powerfully illustrates how economic growth, that is, the expansion in the output (or income) of the economy, is not the same as **economic development**.

There is no universally agreed definition of economic development. But I define it as a process of economic growth that is based on the increase in an economy's productive capabilities: its capabilities to organize – and, more importantly, *transform* – its production activities.

An economy with low productive capabilities cannot
even be sure of the value of what it produces

When an economy has low productive capabilities and relies on natural resources or on products that are made with cheap labour (say, cheap T-shirts), it does not just earn low income. It cannot even be sure that in the long run what it produces will be as valuable as it is now.

Machines wiping out entire professions is such a recurring theme in economic development that it does not need further discussion. Just think of the professions that have disappeared except in name today, such as weavers, smiths, wheelwrights and so on.

More importantly, countries with superior productive capabilities can even develop substitutes for natural resources, vastly reducing the incomes of countries that rely on exporting them. After Germany and Britain developed technologies to synthesize natural chemicals in the mid-nineteenth century, some countries saw dramatic falls in their incomes. Guatemala used to earn quite a lot of money by being the main producer of cochineal (*cochinilla*), the crimson dye favoured by the Pope and the European royalties for their robes, until the invention of the artificial dye alizarin crimson. The Chilean economy was plunged into years of crisis when the Haber–Bosch process was developed in the early twentieth century to manufacture chemical substitutes for saltpetre (nitrate), the country's main export at the time.

Changes in technologies are at the root of economic development

Not so long ago, if someone could command a thousand horses at the same time, carry hundreds of books in his pocket, generate intense heat without any flame, turn thousands of litres of seawater into freshwater or make clothes out of stone, people would have said he was a magician. We are *not* talking about those witch-burning folks of medieval Europe. Even in the early twentieth century, when the world was not totally dissimilar to today's, all of those things would have been considered impossible. Today, they are done routinely in many countries. Most of you will have guessed how, except for the last one, which is, unbeknown to most people, done in North Korea, where they make a synthetic fibre called vinalon, or vinylon, out of limestone.*

---

* Just in case, the answers for the others are: the most powerful sports cars, which have engines with over 1,000 horse power; a USB memory stick or an e-reader, if his jacket pocket is large; the nuclear power station; and the desalination plant.

All these 'magical' developments have been possible only because we have constantly invented better technologies, namely, better machines and better chemical processes. Starting from Abraham Darby's coke-smelting technique in steel-making and John Kay's flying shuttle for textile weaving in the early eighteenth century, an endless stream of technologies has emerged to change the world. We discussed some of these in Chapter 3. The steam engine, the internal combustion engine, electricity, organic chemistry, steel ships, (wired and wireless) telegraphy, aeroplanes, computers, nuclear fission, semiconductors and fibre optics are only the most important examples. Today, genetic engineering, renewable energy, 'advanced' materials (e.g., graphene) and nano-technologies are emerging to transform the world yet again.

In the early days of the Industrial Revolution, new technologies were often developed by individual visionaries. As a result, until the late nineteenth and early twentieth centuries, many technologies were known by their inventors' names – Kay's flying shuttle, Watt's steam engine, the Haber–Bosch process and so on.

From the late nineteenth century, with technologies becoming increasingly complex, fewer and fewer of them have been invented by individuals. Companies started developing the capability to generate new technologies through R&D in their corporate labs. Around this time, governments also started investing actively in developing new technologies by either establishing public research labs (especially in agriculture) or subsidizing private-sector R&D activities.

Today, technological developments are the result of organized, collective efforts inside and outside productive enterprises, rather than of individual inspiration. The fact that few new technologies these days have their inventors' names attached to them is a testimony to the collectivization of the innovation process.

Technologies do not tell the whole story: the importance of work organization

Not all increases in our productive capabilities have come from technological development in the narrow sense: machines and chemicals. A lot of them are due to improvements in organizational skills – or, if you like, management techniques.

In the early nineteenth century, factory productivity was further raised by lining up the workers in accordance with the order of their tasks within the production process. The **assembly line** was born. In the late nineteenth century, the assembly line was put on a conveyor belt. The **moving assembly line** made it possible for capitalists to increase the pace of work simply by turning up the speed of the conveyor belt.

Outside industries like the automobile industry, in which one continuous assembly line basically decides who does what at which speed, improvements in the design of work flow have been an important source of productivity growth – how different machines are arranged, how different tasks are assigned to different workers, where parts and half-finished products are stored and so on. These things are taken for granted by economists, but they are still something that not every producer gets right, especially in developing countries.

The rise of Fordism, or the mass production system

In addition to organizing the flow of work more efficiently, attempts have been made to make workers themselves more efficient. The most important in this regard was **Taylorism**, named after Frederick Winslow Taylor (1856– 1915), the American engineer and later management guru. Taylor argued that the production process should be divided up into the simplest possible tasks and that workers should be taught the most effective ways to perform them, established through scientific analyses of the work process. It is also known as **scientific management** for this reason.

Combining the moving assembly line with the Taylorist principle, the **mass production system** was born in the early years of the twentieth century. It is often called *Fordism* because it was first perfected – but not 'invented', as the folklore goes – by Henry Ford in his Model-T car factory in 1908. The idea is that production costs can be cut by producing a large volume of standardized products, using standardized parts, dedicated machinery and a moving assembly line. This would also make workers more easily replaceable and thus easier to control, because, performing standardized tasks, they need to have relatively few skills.

Despite making them more easily replaceable, Ford paid his workers well because he realized that his production method would not work unless there was a 'mass' market with a lot of people with decent incomes who could buy the large 'mass' of output produced. When the mass production system was widely adopted in the US and Europe after the Second World War, rising wages expanded markets, which then enabled production at a higher volume, which then increased productivity further by spreading the **fixed costs** (of installing the production facilities) over a larger volume.

The mass production system was so effective that even the Soviet Union was attracted to it. In the beginning, there was a huge debate there about its adoption because of its obvious 'anti-worker' implications. It destroys the intrinsic value of work by making it simplistic and repetitive, while vastly reducing the worker's control over his/her **labour process**; standardized tasks make the monitoring of workers easier while the intensity of work can be easily increased by accelerating the assembly line. In the end, the efficiency of the system was so overwhelming that the Soviet planners decided to import it.

Modifications to the mass production system: the lean production system

The mass production system, a century after its invention, still forms the backbone of our production system. But since the 1980s it has been taken to another level by the so-called **lean production system**, first developed in Japan.

The system, most famously practised by Toyota, has its parts delivered 'just in time' for the production, eliminating inventory costs. By working with the suppliers to raise the quality of the parts they deliver (the so-called 'zero defect movement'), it vastly reduces the need for rework and fine-tuning at the end of the assembly line which had plagued Fordist factories. It also uses machines that allow quick change-overs between different models (e.g., by allowing a quick exchange of dies) and thus can offer a much greater variety of products than the Fordist system does.

Unlike the Fordist system, the Toyota system does not treat workers as interchangeable parts. It equips workers with multiple skills and allows them to exercise a lot of initiative in deciding work arrangements and suggesting minor technological improvements. Improvements thus generated are believed to have been crucial in establishing Japanese technological superiority in industries in which quality is important.

Productive capabilities beyond the firm level are also very important

Important as they are, improved technologies and better organizational skills at the firm level are not the only things that determine an economy's productive capabilities.

An economy's productive capabilities also include capabilities that non-enterprise actors – such as the government, universities, research institutes or training institutes – have in facilitating production and improving productivity. These they do by supplying productive inputs: infrastructure (e.g., roads, fibre optic network), new technological ideas and skilled workers.

Economy-wide productive capabilities are also determined by the effectiveness of economic institutions. The institutions of corporate ownership and financial transactions determine the incentives for long-term investments in productivity-enhancing machinery, worker training and R&D. Also important are institutions that affect economic actors' willingness to bear risk and accept change, such as bankruptcy law and the welfare state, as discussed in Chapter 3. Institutions that encourage socially productive cooperation matter too; industry associations to promote joint export marketing or government research institutes providing R&D for small farms or small firms are examples.

Also relevant are institutions that determine the effectiveness of dialogue between different economic actors – government, business, unions, CSOs (civil society organizations), such as poverty action groups or consumer watchdog groups, and universities and other educational institutions. Examples include formal and informal channels of government-business dialogue, government-CSO consultation, employer-union negotiation, and industry-university cooperation.

REAL-LIFE NUMBERS

Failing to check whether growth rates are overall or
per capita can distort your perspective

When you encounter growth rate figures, you need to check whether they are overall or per capita rates. This may sound like an obvious thing to do, but failure to do so can give you a rather distorted view of the world.

If you are monitoring a single economy's growth performance over a relatively short period of time, say several quarters or a few years, it may not be critical that you are using overall, rather than per capita, growth rate.

But, if you are comparing different economies over a relatively long period of time, it is important that you use per capita growth rates. Between 2000 and 2010, GDP grew at the rate of 1.6 per cent in the US and 1.0 per cent in Germany. With these figures, you may think that the US has done substantially better than Germany. However, during the same period population grew at the rate of 0.9 per cent in the US and -0.1 per cent in Germany. This means that Germany has actually done better in per capita terms – 1.1 per cent per year growth rate as opposed to 0.7 per cent in the US.[4]

Why a 6 per cent growth rate is a 'miracle'

In theory, there is no upper bound to the rate at which an economy can grow. In practice, it is not easy for it to grow at all.

In Chapter 3, we have seen that per capita yearly output growth rate used to be close to zero everywhere until the end of the eighteenth century. The Industrial Revolution saw it going up to around 1 per cent per year, the 'Golden Age of capitalism' saw it going up to 3–4 per cent per year. The East Asian economies have seen growth rates of 8–10 per cent per year during their growth peaks during their 'miracle' periods of three or four decades.

All in all, the rule of thumb is that per capita output growth rate above 3 per cent is good, while anything above 6 per cent is entering the 'miracle' territory. Anything substantially above 10 per cent for an extended period (say, more than a decade) is possible only through either resource bonanza, as in the case of Equatorial Guinea discussed above, or recovery from a war, as has been the case with Bosnia and Herzegovina in the last decade and a half.

The power of compound rates

The growth rates we use are **compound rates** (or exponential rates), meaning that the increased output of every year (or quarter or whatever period is the unit of measurement) is added to the existing output. If an economy of $100 billion is growing at the average rate of 10 per cent over ten years, it does *not* mean that its output increases by $10 billion every year and the size of the economy increases to $200 billion after ten years. 10 per cent growth rate in the first year increases the output to $110 billion, but the second year's 10 per cent growth is over $110 billion, not $100 billion, so the resulting output at the end of the second year is $121 billion, rather than $120 billion. Continuing like this, at the end of the ten-year period, the economy will be $259 billion, not $200 billion.

The use of compound rate means that what may seem to be a relatively small difference in growth rates can create a large gap, if sustained over a sufficiently long period of time. If a country grows at 3 per cent per year and another grows at 6 per cent for one year, it is no big deal. If, however, this difference persists for forty years, the faster-growing economy will have become 10.3 times richer, while the slower-growing one will have increased its income only by 3.3 times. Before they know it, the citizens of these two countries will be living in worlds of entirely different levels of comfort and opportunity.

It is useful to have a rule of thumb that enables you to project the future on the basis of today's growth rate. If you have a growth rate of a country and want to know how much time it will take for the size of its economy to double, divide seventy by the growth rate. So, if a country grows at 1 per cent per year, it will take it seventy years to double its output, while it will take somewhere between eleven and twelve years for the size of an economy growing at 6 per cent to double.

Unlike economic growth, economic development
cannot be measured by a single indicator

In Chapter 6, we saw how even the output figure may not be totally objective. But, given the output statistics, it is straightforward to calculate its growth rate. In contrast, there is no single number that allows us to measure economic development, defined as an increase in productive capabilities.

There are many different indexes of productive capabilities (under different names), published by international organizations, including the UNIDO (the United Nations Industrial Development Organization), the OECD, the World Bank and the World Economic Forum. These indexes are made up of dozens of different indicators that are thought to reveal various aspects of a country's productive capabilities. Most frequently included are indicators regarding the structure of production (e.g., share of hi-technology industries in total manufacturing output), infrastructure (e.g., broadband connections per capita), skills (e.g., the share of workers with a university degree) and innovation activities (e.g., R&D spending as a share of GDP or number of patents per capita).

However, being made up of such diverse elements, these indexes are difficult to interpret. Therefore, unless you are a professional economist, you are better off with simpler indicators that are easier to interpret. I talk about two of them below.

Share of investment in GDP is the key indicator of how a country is developing
In order to be used, most technologies have to be embodied in **fixed capital**, namely, machines and structures (e.g., buildings, railways). So, without high investment in fixed capital, technically known as gross fixed capital formation (GFCF),* an economy cannot develop its productive potential very much. Thus, the **investment ratio** (GFCF/GDP) is a good indicator of its development potential. Indeed, the positive relationship between a country's investment ratio and its rate of economic growth is one of the few undisputed relationships in economics.

For the world as a whole, the investment ratio is around 20–22 per cent. But there is a huge international variation. In China, this share has stood at a staggering 45 per cent in the last few years. At the other extreme, countries like the Central African Republic or the Democratic Republic of Congo can have an investment ratio as low as 2 per cent in some years, although typically they manage around 10 per cent.

No economy has achieved 'miracle' rates of growth (that is, over 6 per cent per year in per capita terms) over a period of time without investing at least 25 per cent of GDP. At the heights of such growth, countries invest at least 30 per cent of GDP. The investment ratio went above 35 per cent in Japan in the late 1960s and the early 1970s. During its 'miracle' growth period since the 1980s, China's investment rate has been 30 per cent and above, going above 40 per cent in the last decade.

This is not to say that a higher investment ratio is necessarily a good thing. Investment by definition sacrifices today's consumption and thus living standards, if only in the hope of achieving higher consumption in the future. So there can be such a thing as too much investment, even though how much is too much would depend on how much you value your

---

* The term 'gross' here means that we are not counting depreciation of capital, as explained in Chapter 6.

future income against today's income (this is known as *time preference*). Nevertheless, the investment ratio – and its evolution over time – is the best single indicator of how a country is developing its productive capabilities and thus its economy.

The R&D figure is a good indicator for the richer countries

Another simple but instructive indicator of a country's economic development, especially for countries at higher levels of income, is its R&D spending as a ratio of GDP – and its evolution over time.[5]

Rich countries spend a much higher proportion of their GDP on R&D than do poorer countries. The OECD average is 2.3 per cent, with several countries spending over 3 per cent of GDP on it.* Finland and South Korea top the list. These two countries are particularly impressive in that they have increased their R&D/GDP ratio very rapidly in the last few decades and achieved impressive progress in high-technology industries.

Most developing countries do practically no R&D. The ratio is 0.1 per cent in Indonesia, 0.2 per cent in Colombia and 0.5 per cent in Kenya. China's stood at 1.5 per cent in 2009 but has been on a fast rising trend, suggesting that the country is rapidly building up its capabilities to generate new technologies.[6]

Industrialization and Deindustrialization

In theory, we can achieve economic development by enhancing our productive capabilities in any economic activity, including agriculture and services. In practice, in the vast majority of cases, economic development has been achieved through industrialization, or, more precisely, the development of the manufacturing sector.† Albert Einstein was definitely right in saying: 'In theory, theory and practice are the same. In practice, they are not.'

---

* As of 2010, Finland spent 3.9 per cent of its GDP on R&D, with South Korea following closely at 3.7 per cent. Sweden (3.4 per cent), Japan (3.3 per cent), Denmark (3.1 per cent), Switzerland (3 per cent), the US (2.9 per cent) and Germany (2.8 per cent) are other economies with high R&D spending as a proportion of GDP.

† Industry includes things like mining, electricity generation and gas delivery, as well as manufacturing. Sometimes statistics are available only for 'industry' as a whole, rather than 'manufacturing' only.

Mechanization and chemical processes make it easier
to raise productivity in manufacturing

Raising productivity is much easier in manufacturing than in other eco-nomic activities, such as agriculture and services. Manufacturing activities are much less bound by nature and lend themselves much more easily to mechanization and chemical processing.

Agricultural productivity is very dependent on the physical environment, such as land mass, climate and soil. It is also very time-bound. Impressive ways to overcome all these natural constraints have been developed, such as irrigation, selective breeding and even genetic engineering, but there is a clear limit to them. No one has developed a way to grow wheat in six minutes instead of six months, which is roughly what should have happened, had the productivity in the wheat industry developed as fast as in pin-making over the last two and a half centuries.

By their very nature, many service activities are inherently impervious to increases in productivity. In some cases, the very increase in productivity will destroy the product itself; a string quartet cannot treble its productivity by trotting through a twenty-seven-minute piece in nine minutes. For some other services, the apparently higher productivity may be due to the debase-ment of the product. A lot of the increases in retail service productivity in countries like the US and the UK have been bought by lowering the quality of the retail service itself – fewer shop assistants, longer drives to the super-market, lengthier waits for deliveries and so on. The 2008 global financial crisis has revealed that much of the recent productivity growth in finance had been achieved through the debasement of the products – that is, the creation of overly complex, riskier and even fraudulent products.

The 'learning centre' of the economy

The manufacturing sector has been the 'learning centre' of capitalism. By supplying **capital goods** (e.g., machines, transport equipment), it has spread higher productive capabilities to other sectors of the economy, whether they are other manufacturing activities producing **consumer goods** (e.g., wash-ing machines, breakfast cereals), agriculture or services.

Many of the organizational innovations in the manufacturing sector have been transferred to the other sectors, especially to the service sector, and raised their productivities. Fast food restaurants, such as McDonald's, use 'factory' techniques, turning cooking into an assembly job. Some even deliver food on a conveyor belt, as in kaiten-zushi restaurants (for people living in Britain, that's Yo! Sushi). Large retail chains – be they supermarkets, clothes shop chains or online retailers – apply modern inventory management techniques developed in the manufacturing sector.

Even in the agricultural sector, productivity has been raised in some countries, such as the Netherlands (which is the third-largest exporter of agriculture in the world, after the US and France), through the application of manufacturing-style organizational knowledge, such as computer-controlled feeding.

The rise of the post-industrial society?

It has recently become fashionable to argue that the manufacturing sector does not matter very much any more, as we have entered the era of **post-industrial society**.

In the early days of industrialization, many assumed that the manufacturing sector would keep growing. And for a long time, it looked to be the case. The share of manufacturing both in output and in employment was almost constantly rising in most countries. However, from the 1960s, some countries started experiencing **deindustrialization** – a fall in the share of manufacturing, and a corresponding rise in the share of services, in both output and employment. This prompted the talk of a post-industrial society. Many economists have argued that, with rising income, we begin to demand services, such as eating out and foreign holidays, relatively more than we demand manufactured goods. The resulting fall in the relative demand for manufacturing leads to a shrinking role for manufacturing, reflected in lower output and employment shares.

This view got a boost in the 1990s, with the invention of the worldwide web and the alleged rise of the 'knowledge economy'. Many argued that the ability to produce knowledge, rather than things, was now critical, and high-value knowledge-based services, such as finance and management consulting, would become the leading sectors in the rich countries that were experiencing deindustrialization. The manufacturing industry – or the 'bricks and mortar' industry – was viewed as second-rate activity that could be shifted to cheap-labour developing countries, such as China.

More recently, even some developing countries have bought into the discourse of the post-industrial economy. They have started believing that, with the rise of the post-industrial economy, they can more or less skip industrialization and become rich through services. They look to India, which is supposed to have become – through its success in the export of services like software, accountancy and the reading of medical scanning images – 'the office of the world' to China's 'workshop of the world' (a title which had originally been conferred on Britain after its Industrial Revolution).

Deindustrialization doesn't mean that we are producing fewer manufactured products

While many people, including key policy-makers, have been seduced by it, the discourse of post-industrial society is highly misleading. Most rich countries have indeed become 'post-industrial' or 'deindustrialized' in terms of employment; a decreasing proportion of the labour force in these countries is working in factories, as opposed to shops and offices. In most, although not all, countries this has been accompanied by a fall in the share of manufacturing in output.

But this does not necessarily mean that those countries are producing fewer manufactured goods in absolute terms. Much of this apparent fall is due to the decline in the prices of manufactured goods, compared to the prices of services. This is thanks to the faster productivity growth in their production. Just think how computers and mobile phones have become cheaper (holding the quality constant), compared with the costs of haircuts or eating out. When this relative price effect is taken into account and the shares of different sectors are recalculated in **constant prices** (that is, applying the prices of the starting year to the quantities produced in subsequent years), as opposed to **current prices** (today's prices), the share of manufacturing has not fallen very much in most rich countries. It has even risen in several countries, as I will show later.

Some deindustrialization is due to 'optical illusions'

The extent of deindustrialization has also been exaggerated due to the 'optical illusions' created by the way in which statistics are compiled. A lot of services that used to be provided in-house in manufacturing firms (e.g., catering, security guards, some design and engineering activities) are now **outsourced**, that is, supplied by independent companies (at home or abroad; in the latter case this is called **off-shoring**). This gives the illusion that services have become more important than they actually have. These outsourced services are still the same activities. But they are now counted as part of service output, rather than of manufacturing output.

In addition, seeing the share of manufacturing in their output falling, some manufacturing firms have applied to be reclassified as service firms, even though they still conduct some manufacturing. A UK government report estimates that up to 10 per cent of the fall in manufacturing employment between 1998 and 2006 in the UK may be due to this 'reclassification effect'.[7]

Making things still matters

The view that the world has now entered a new era of the 'knowledge economy', in which making things does not confer much value, is based upon a fundamental misreading of history. We have *always* lived in a knowledge economy. It has always been the quality of knowledge involved, rather than the physical nature of the things produced (that is, whether they are physical goods or intangible services), that has made the more industrialized countries richer. This point can be seen more clearly if you recall that woollen manufacturing, which used to be one of the most hi-tech sectors until the eighteenth century, is now one of the lower-tech sectors. In this regard, it is useful to remember that 'There are no condemned sectors; there are only outmoded technologies,' as a French minister of industry once eloquently put it.[8]

Recently, some service activities, such as finance and transport, have experienced high productivity growths, which have caused many people to say that countries can generate economic development on the basis of such service activities. Like Britain, they can export high-value services and use the earnings from them to buy necessary manufactured products from abroad. This strategy may be viable for a period. In the decade or so up to the 2008 financial crisis, Britain indeed managed to generate a decent rate of growth despite a rapid process of deindustrialization, thanks to a booming financial industry. But the 2008 crisis was a rude reminder that a lot of this faith in services as the new engine of growth has been illusory.

Moreover, many of these high-productivity services are 'producer services', such as engineering, design and management consulting, for which the main customers are manufacturing firms. So, a weakening manufacturing base will eventually lead to a decline in the quality of those services, which will make their export more difficult.

Agriculture is still surprisingly important

Until the late nineteenth century, agriculture was the mainstay of the economy in almost all countries.[9] Even in many of today's rich countries, nearly three-quarters of people worked in agriculture until a few generations ago. In 1870, 72 per cent of the workforce was employed in agriculture in Sweden. The corresponding figure was 73 per cent in Japan in 1885.

Being a lower productivity sector than manufacturing or services, agriculture has rarely accounted for more than half of output, even when most of the people were working there. In 1870, agriculture accounted for 50 per cent of output in Denmark and 47 per cent in Sweden. South Korea's agriculture accounted for 47 per cent of output until as late as 1953.

Today, agriculture plays a very small role, in terms of both output and employment, in the rich countries. Only 1–2 per cent of their GDP is produced in agriculture, while only 2–3 per cent of people work there. This has been possible because agricultural productivity in those countries has risen enormously in the last century or so. The fact that the US, France and the Netherlands – and not some large developing economies, such as India or Indonesia – are the three largest exporters of agriculture in the world is a testimony to the height of agricultural productivity in the rich countries.

In many poorer developing countries, agriculture is still very important. In a handful of poorest countries, more than half the output is still produced in agriculture.* Even in the richer developing countries, agriculture still accounts for 20–40 per cent of output.

Agriculture plays an even more important role when it comes to employment. It employs 80–90 per cent of people in some of the poorest countries, such as Burundi (92 per cent), Burkina Faso (85 per cent) and Ethiopia (79

---

* According to the World Bank, they are, as of 2009, Sierra Leone (59 per cent), Liberia (58 per cent), the Central African Republic (57 per cent) and Ethiopia (51 per cent).

per cent). Despite the country's impressive industrialization in the last three decades, 37 per cent of people in China still work in agriculture.

Manufacturing in the rich countries is less important than before . . .

At their peaks (between the 1950s and the 1970s, depending on the country), nearly 40 per cent of the workforce in the then industrialized countries of Western Europe and the US worked in the manufacturing sector. The number reached nearly 50 per cent if you looked at industry as a whole.

Today, in most rich countries, less than 15 per cent of people work in manufacturing. Exceptions are countries such as Taiwan, Slovenia and Germany, where upwards of 20 per cent are still employed in manufacturing.* In some of them, such as the UK, the Netherlands, the US and Canada, the corresponding number is only around 9–10 per cent.

The fall in employment share of manufacturing has been accompanied by a fall in output share. In some countries, such as Austria, Finland and Japan, the share of manufacturing in GDP used to be around 25 per cent until the 1970s. Today, in none of the richest countries does it account for more than 20 per cent.[10]

. . .But it is still far more important than people think it is

I have explained above that much of the apparent decline in the share of manufacturing in GDP is due to the faster productivity growth in manufacturing, which makes manufacturing products relatively cheaper compared to other things (services and agricultural products). This means that the share of manufacturing can be very different, depending on whether it is calculated in constant prices (to remind you, the prices at the beginning of the period we are looking at) or current prices.

During the last two decades, in some rich countries, such as Germany, Italy and France, the fall in the share of manufacturing in GDP has been quite large in current prices (by 20 per cent in Germany, 30 per cent in Italy and 40 per cent in France), but not been so large in constant prices (by less than 10 per cent in all three).[11] In several rich countries, the share of manufacturing has actually risen, if calculated in constant prices: in the US

---

* The shares in 2011 were 28 per cent in Taiwan, 23 per cent in Slovenia and 20 per cent in Germany.

and Switzerland, its share has risen by around 5 per cent in the last couple of decades;[12] in Finland and Sweden, the share has actually risen by as much as 50 per cent over the last few decades.[13]

An important exception is the UK, in which the share of manufacturing has fallen dramatically in the last couple of decades, even in constant prices.[14] This suggests that the UK's deindustrialization has largely been the result of the absolute decline of its manufacturing industry due to loss of competitiveness, rather than the relative price effect due to differential productivity growth rates.

'Premature' deindustrialization in developing countries

In the last three decades, many developing countries have experienced 'premature' deindustrialization. That is, the share of manufacturing (and industry in general) in their outputs and employments started falling at a much earlier stage of economic development than had been the case for the rich countries.

Latin America's share of manufacturing in GDP rose from 25 per cent in the mid-1960s to 27 per cent in the late 1980s but has fallen dramatically since then. It stands at only 17 per cent today. In Brazil, the industrial powerhouse of the continent, deindustrialization has been even more dramatic. The share of manufacturing in GDP has fallen from 34 per cent in the mid-1980s to 15 per cent today. In Sub-Saharan Africa, the share has fallen from 17–18 per cent during the 1970s and much of the 1980s to 12 per cent today.[15]

This premature deindustrialization is largely the result of neo-liberal economic policies implemented in these countries since the 1980s (see Chapter 3).[16] Sudden trade liberalization has destroyed swathes of manufacturing industries in those countries. Financial liberalization has allowed banks to redirect their loans to (more lucrative) consumers, away from producers. Policies geared towards inflation control, such as high interest rates and over-valued currencies, have added to the agony of manufacturing firms by making loans expensive and exports more difficult.

Service-based success stories?: Switzerland, Singapore and India

When talking about the post-industrial economy, people frequently cite Switzerland and Singapore as the examples of service-based success stories.

Haven't these two countries shown, they say, that you can become rich – very rich – through services such as finance, tourism and trading?

Actually these two countries show the exact opposite. According to the UNIDO data, in 2002, Switzerland had the highest per capita manufacturing value added (MVA) in the world – 24 per cent more than that of Japan. In 2005, it ranked the second, after Japan. Singapore ranked the third in that year. In 2010, Singapore ranked the first, producing 48 per cent more MVA per capita than the US. Switzerland ranked the third, after Japan. Switzerland produced 30 per cent more MVA than the US in that year.

As for the claim that India has shown how countries can skip industrialization and achieve prosperity through services, it is very much exaggerated. Before 2004, India had a **trade deficit** in services (namely, it imported more services than it exported). Between 2004 and 2011, it did run a **trade surplus** (opposite of trade deficit) in services, but that was equivalent only to 0.9 per cent of GDP, covering only 17 per cent of its trade deficit in goods (5.1 per cent of GDP). It is hardly a service-based success story.

Running Out of the Planet?: Taking Environmental Sustainability Seriously

We need to take environmental constraints
extremely seriously

Before we leave the world of production, we must address the looming question of the environmental limits to economic growth. There is no doubt that climate change, mainly caused by our material production and consumption activities, threatens human existence. Moreover, many non-renewable resources (such as oil and minerals) are rapidly being depleted. Even the earth's capacity to produce renewable resources, such as agricultural products or forestry products, may be outpaced by the increase in demand for those resources. Given all of this, we are going to run out of the planet, so to speak, if we do not find ways to control the impacts of our economic activities on the environment.

But doesn't this mean that we should stop economic development, which I have defined as the increase in our capabilities to produce? If so, doesn't that negate a lot of things I have said so far in the chapter?

*Technological developments can be solutions, as well as
causes, of environmental problems . . .*

It must have been 1975 or 1976, as I think I was twelve or thirteen. I came across this book, *The Limits to Growth*, by a curiously named author, the Club of Rome. Flicking through the book, even though I couldn't fully understand it, I became very depressed. It said that the world will run out of oil in 1992 or thereabouts. So, even before I turn thirty, I thought, I am supposed to start riding around in bullock carts and burn wood for heating? That seemed mightily unfair, especially when my family had moved to a house with oil-burning central heating system only five or six years earlier.

The prediction by the Club turned out to be right. We *have* run out of oil – that is, the oil that was accessible with the technologies of the 1970s. But we are still burning oil in huge quantities because we have become much more efficient in locating and extracting oil from places that were just not accessible forty years ago, especially the deep sea.

Technology does not only give us access to formerly inaccessible resources but it expands the definition of what is a resource. Sea wave, formerly only a destructive force to be overcome, has become a major energy resource, thanks to technological development. Coltan used to be a rare mineral of relatively little value until the 1980s. Today, it is one of the most valuable minerals in the world – to the extent that many rebel groups in the Democratic Republic of Congo are said to finance their wars with slave labour in coltan mines. Tantalum, one of the component elements of coltan, is a key ingredient in the making of parts used for mobile phones and other electronic goods.

At a less dramatic level, technological development allows us to produce renewable resources with greater efficiency. As I pointed out earlier in the chapter, over the last century, humanity's ability to produce food – and other natural raw materials (e.g., cotton) – has been enormously increased by mechanization, use of chemicals, selective breeding and genetic engineering. We have also become more efficient in the use of given resources. Car and aircraft engines and power stations use less oil and coal to get the same amount of energy. We recycle an increasingly higher proportion of our materials.

. . . but there are limits to technological solutions

However fast our technologies develop, there are still definite limits to the availability of non-renewable resources, even including those natural substances that are yet to become resources.

We won't completely run out of any of the major resources in the near future. But their declining availability can make them unaffordable to poorer people, threatening their welfare or even existence. The rising price of water is already hurting poor people by increasing waterborne diseases and reducing their agricultural yields. Higher food prices would increase hunger and malnutrition. More expensive fuel would cause extra deaths of poor elderly people in winter even in the rich countries. As in the world of Neal Stephenson's science-fiction novel *The Diamond Age*, poor people may be forced to cope with flimsy synthetic substitutes made with nano-technology, rather than real natural materials.

Far more urgent, of course, is the challenge of climate change, whose consequences are already being felt and certain to become extremely serious, if not necessarily catastrophic, within the next generation or two. And given this, it is extremely unlikely, if not logically impossible, that humanity will be able to come up with a purely technological solution to climate change in time that does not require any significant change in the way in which we live.

Developing countries still need more economic development in order to
raise their living standards and to better adapt to climate change

All of this does not mean that we need to stop economic development, especially for developing countries. To begin with, developing countries still need more output – that is, economic growth – provided that it is not totally appropriated by a tiny minority. Higher income for these countries doesn't just mean another TV but working in less back-breaking and dangerous conditions, not having to see your children die as babies, living longer, falling ill less often and so on. Such changes would be more sustainable if they came from economic development (that is, increase in their productive capabilities) rather than simple growth, but even growth coming from a resource bonanza would be valuable for these countries.

Developing countries also need to increase their productive capabilities to be able to deal with the consequences of climate change (**climate**

adaptation is the technical term). Due to their climate, locations and geography, many developing countries are going to bear the brunt of the impacts of global warming, despite having very little, if not necessarily minimal, responsibility for causing it. Despite this, these are exactly the countries with the least capability to deal with those impacts.* In order to better deal with the consequences of climate change, poor countries need to equip themselves with better technologies and organizational capabilities, which can only be acquired through economic development.

The case for having more economic growth and development in the least-developed countries is overwhelming, as growing their income to a certain level (say, where China is today) would make at most a marginal difference to climate change, as, for example, discussed in the Greenhouse Development Rights (GDR) framework, developed by two think tanks, Eco-Equity and the Stockholm Environmental Institute.[17]

Rich countries should continue to develop their economies but radically change their production and consumption priorities

Given that they are already consuming the vast bulk of the world's resources and they have far fewer needs to increase consumption, the rich countries need to reduce their consumption, if we are to dampen the extent of climate change. But even with lower aggregate consumption, human welfare need not go down. In highly unequal countries like the US, Britain and Portugal, reduction in inequality will allow more consumption for more people. Even in relatively equal societies, welfare can be increased without increase in consumption by consuming differently, rather than consuming more.[18] Increase in the consumption of collective services, especially public transport and leisure facilities, can improve welfare by reducing the resources wasted in fragmented individualistic consumption: time wasted in sitting in a car in a traffic jam or duplication of services between small private libraries that are popular in countries like Korea.

In addition to reducing the amount of consumption, its energy intensity can be reduced. Stricter energy efficiency requirements on buildings, cars

---

* The physical intensity of a natural disaster is much less important than the adaptability of the human community that it affects in determining its impacts. For example, the 2010 earthquake in Haiti, which killed over 200,000 people and has scarred the country for a generation, was only 7 on the Richter scale, which would have killed no more than a handful of exceptionally unlucky people in Japan.

and electrical equipment may be imposed. Out-of-town shopping centres and suburban developments could be discouraged, while investments in better public transport are made, so that people drive less. Cultural shifts may also be needed if people are to find more joy in having quality time with family and friends than buying things. Continued, or even increased, use of nuclear power should be contemplated outside major earthquake areas (such as Japan, parts of the US and Chile) as a transitional measure before we completely shift to renewable energy sources.[19]

But all of this does *not* mean that the rich countries should stop economic development, at least in the sense in which I have defined it in this chapter. They can still increase their productive capabilities but use them not to increase material consumption but to reduce working hours while producing the same amount as, or even more than, before. They can develop – and transfer to developing countries at affordable prices – their productive capabilities in activities that combat climate change and other environmental problems, such as better renewable energy technologies, more efficient but environmentally friendly agriculture and more affordable desalination technology.

Concluding Remarks: Why We Need to Pay More Attention to Production

Production has been seriously neglected in the mainstream of economics, which is dominated by the Neoclassical school. For most economists, economics ends at the factory gate (or increasingly the entrance of an office block), so to speak. The production process is treated as a predictable process, pre-determined by a 'production function', clearly specifying the amounts of capital and labour that need to be combined in order to produce a particular product.

Insofar as there is interest in production, it is at the most aggregate level – that of the growth in the size of the economy. The most famous refrain along this line, coming from the debate on US competitiveness in the 1980s, is that it does *not* matter whether a country produces potato chips or micro-chips. There is little recognition that different types of economic activity may bring different outcomes – not just in terms of how much they produce but more importantly in terms of how they affect the development of the country's ability to produce, or productive capabilities. And in terms of the latter effect, the importance of the manufacturing sector cannot be over-emphasized, as it has been the main source of new technological and organizational capabilities over the last two centuries.

Unfortunately, with the rise of the discourse of post-industrial society in the realm of ideas and the increasing dominance of the financial sector in the real world, indifference to manufacturing has positively turned into contempt. Manufacturing, it is often argued, is, in the new 'knowledge economy', a low-grade activity that only low-wage developing countries do.

But factories are where the modern world has been made, so to speak, and will keep being remade. Moreover, even in our supposed post-industrial world, services, the supposed new economic engine, cannot thrive without a vibrant manufacturing sector. The fact that Switzerland and Singapore, which many people consider to be the ultimate examples of successful service-led prosperity, are actually two of the three most industrialized countries in the world (together with Japan) is a testimony to this.

Contrary to conventional wisdom, development of productive capabilities, especially in the manufacturing sector, is crucial if we are to deal with the greatest challenge of our time – climate change. In addition to changing their consumption patterns, the rich countries need to further develop their productive capabilities in the area of green technologies. Even just to cope with the adverse consequences of climate change, developing countries need to further develop technological and organizational capabilities, many of which can only be acquired through industrialization.

Further Reading

M. ABRAMOVITZ
Thinking about Growth (Cambridge: Cambridge University Press, 1989).

F. ACKERMAN
Can We Afford the Future?: The Economics of a Warming World (London: Zed Books, 2009).

H.-J. CHANG
23 Things They Don't Tell You about Capitalism (London: Allen Lane, 2010).

T. JACKSON
Prosperity without Growth: Economics for a Finite Planet (London: Earthscan, 2009).

S. KUZNETS
Modern Economic Growth: Rate, Structure and Speed (New Haven and London: Yale University Press, 1966).

N. ROSENBERG
Inside the Black Box: Technology and Economics (Cambridge: Cambridge University Press, 1982).

R. ROWTHORN AND J. WELLS
De-industrialization and Foreign Trade (Cambridge: Cambridge University Press, 1987).

J. SCHUMPETER
Capitalism, Socialism and Democracy (London: Routledge, 2010).

CHAPTER 8

Trouble at the Fidelity Fiduciary Bank

FINANCE

Michael does not understand. Even though he has given back to his father the very thing that has caused all the trouble, it has not made things right again. Why are grown-ups so strange? Michael wanted to use his tuppence coin to buy bird feed from that old lady sitting on the steps of St Paul's Cathedral, but his father tricked him out of it. His father said he would show what more interesting things could be done with Michael's money when he and the children (Michael was with his sister, Jane) get to his work.

When Michael and Jane got there, this very old man called Mr Dawes, the 'directors' (as he called them) and even their father started singing about depositing his tuppence in Dawes, Tomes, Mousely, Grubbs Fidelity Fiduciary Bank (what a name). They said that this money will make him part of all these things he has never heard of in strange places – 'railways through Africa; dams across the Nile; fleets of ocean greyhounds; majestic, self-amortizing canals; and plantations of ripening tea'. Mesmerized by the song, Michael momentarily lost concentration and opened his fist, at which point Mr Dawes, surprisingly quickly for such an old man, snatched the coin.

Naturally, Michael shouted 'give me back my money!', but this somehow made all the bank's customers rush to withdraw their money. The bank refused to pay them, and chaos ensued. He and Jane in the end managed to grab the coin back from the old man and ran away, but upon returning home they found out that his father had been fired from work for what had happened. Michael has given the tuppence coin back to his father, but his father has not got his job back.

Why did what he said cause such a problem? Why did all those people want their money back too? More confusingly, how could the bank refuse to pay the customers their own money?

Banks and the 'Traditional' Financial System

Banks make promises that they cannot quite keep

The above is a retelling of the famous bank scene and its aftermath in the Disney movie *Mary Poppins* from the point of view of Michael Banks, the boy to whom Mary Poppins is the magical nanny. And the scene is by far the best summary of what banking is about: confidence.

What caused trouble at the Fidelity Fiduciary Bank is, to put it bluntly, that it had made promises that it could not quite keep. Like all other banks, it had promised the holders of deposit accounts that they would be paid in cash upon demand, when it had only enough cash to pay a proportion of them.*

A bank making such a 'false' promise is usually *not* a problem. At any given point of time, only a small proportion of the depositors would want to withdraw their money, so it is safe for the bank to have cash (or 'near cash', such as government bonds that can be quickly sold) that is only a fraction of the amount in its deposit accounts.

But if a deposit account holder develops any doubt about the bank's ability to pay her back, she has the incentive to withdraw her money as soon as possible. She knows that her bank actually does *not* have the cash to pay all her fellow depositors, should a sufficient number of them want to withdraw their deposits in cash at the same time. Even though the belief may be totally unfounded – as was the case with the Fidelity Fiduciary Bank – it will become a 'self-fulfilling prophecy' if enough account holders think and act in this way.

This situation is known as a **bank run**. We have seen examples of it in the wake of the 2008 global financial crisis. Customers queued up in front of Northern Rock bank branches in the UK, while online depositors in the UK and the Netherlands clogged up the website of Icesave, the internet arm of the collapsing Icelandic bank Landsbanki.

---

* It is important to note that depositors of a bank include its borrowers. When you borrow money from a bank, it opens a deposit account for you, credited with the agreed sum, rather than paying you that amount in cash. So, by borrowing money from a bank, you also become one of its depositors.

Banking is a confidence trick (of a sort), but a
socially useful one (if managed well)

So, is banking a confidence trick? It is – sort of. Strictly speaking, a confidence trick involves making the victim believe in something that is false. In the case of banking, it involves making people believe in something that *could be true or false, depending on how many others believe in it.* If enough savers in a bank believe that their bank will be able to pay them back any time they want, it will indeed be able to do so. If they don't, it won't.*

The fact that banking involves a confidence trick (of a sort) has prompted some people to argue for 'narrow banking', which requires banks to hold enough cash to pay all its depositors at the same time. But, when you think about it, the confidence trick is actually the whole point of banking – creating more money than they have in cash by taking advantage of the fact that, while we all want the flexibility, or the liquidity, provided by cash, we don't all need it at the same time.

The banks' ability to create new money (that is, credit) is bought exactly at the cost of instability – that is, the risk of having runs. But the added difficulty is that, once there is a run on some banks, there could be a **contagion** across all the banks.

This is not just about people becoming hyper-sensitive and suspecting all banks because they are, well, banks. It is also because banks borrow from and lend to each other in the inter-bank loan market and, increasingly, buy and sell financial products from each other (more on this below). This means that confidence in banks has to be managed at the level of the whole banking system, rather than at the level of individual banks.

---

* This special kind of confidence trick is actually used quite often in economic management. Another prominent example is the use of government deficit spending in a recession. The government initially spends 'money it does not have' and runs a budget deficit. But the spending increases demand in the economy, which stimulates business and makes consumers more optimistic. If enough businessmen and consumers begin to form positive expectations for the future as a result, they will invest and spend more. Increased investment and consumption then generate higher incomes and thus higher tax revenues. If tax revenues increase sufficiently, government deficit may be eliminated, which means that the government had the money that it spent after all.

*The central bank is the most important tool of
managing confidence in the banking system*

The classic solution to this confidence problem is to have a central bank
that can 'print money' at will, using the monopoly it has in issuing notes (and
coins), and let it lend without limit to a bank that is experiencing a confidence
problem. However, this 'trick' works only insofar as the confidence problem
is one of cash flows – or what is called a **liquidity crisis**. In this situation, the
bank in trouble owns assets (loans that it has made, bonds and other financial
assets it has bought, etc.) whose values are greater than its liabilities (deposits,
bonds it has issued, loans from another bank, etc.) but it cannot immediately
sell those assets and meet all liabilities that are due.

If the bank has a **solvency crisis**, which means that the total value of its
liabilities exceeds that of its assets, no amount of central bank lending will
fix the problem. Either the bank will go bankrupt or require a government
bail-out, which happens when the government injects new capital into the
troubled bank (as happened with Northern Rock and Icesave). Government
bail-out of banks has become highly visible after the 2008 crisis, but it is a
practice that has been going on throughout the history of capitalism.

Shoring up confidence further: deposit insurance and prudential regulation

A country can also shore up confidence in its banks through **deposit
insurance**, as well as through central banking. Under this insurance scheme,
the government commits itself to compensate all depositors up to a certain
amount (for example, €100,000 in the Eurozone countries at the moment),
if their banks are unable to pay their money back. With this guarantee, savers
do not have to panic and withdraw their deposits at the slightest fall in confidence in their banks. This significantly reduces the chance of a bank run.

Another way to manage confidence in the banking system is to restrict
the ability of the banks to take risk. This is known as **prudential regulation**.
One important measure of prudential regulation is the 'capital adequacy
ratio'. This limits the amount that a bank can lend (and thus the liabilities it
can create in the form of deposits) to a certain multiple of its equity capital
(that is, the money provided by the bank's owners, or shareholders). Such
regulation is also known as 'leverage regulation', as it is a regulation on how
much you can 'leverage' your original capital. Another typical measure of
prudential regulation is 'liquidity regulation', that is, to demand that each

bank holds more than a certain proportion of its assets in cash or other highly 'liquid' assets (assets that can be quickly sold for cash, such as government bonds).

The 'traditional' financial system (as of the mid-twentieth century)

By the middle of the twentieth century, the advanced capitalist countries had acquired a fairly well-functioning financial system, which facilitated the Golden Age of capitalism. At the heart of the system was the banking sector, which we have just discussed. The other key elements were the stock market and the bond market, which can be divided into the government bond market and the corporate bond market.

Stock markets enabled companies to raise money on a large scale by allowing them to sell their shares to investors that they don't know – or, if you like, anonymous investors (this is why the limited liability company in some countries is called the 'anonymous society', as in Sociedad Anónima in Spain).

When a company sells its shares for the first time to outsiders and turns itself from a **private company** (a company whose shares are *not* sold to the general public) into a **public company** (a company whose shares are), we call it the **initial public offering** (or the IPO). You may have heard of the term in the contexts of the 'tech' giants Google and Facebook 'going public' in 2004 and 2012 respectively. Sometimes companies that are already public issue new shares, to raise additional money.

Allowing companies to raise money by selling new shares is only one of the functions of the stock market. Another important function of it – actually the more important function in some countries, such as the US and the UK – is to allow companies to be bought and sold; the **market for corporate control** is the fancy term. If a new shareholder (or a group of shareholders working together) gains the majority of shares of a company, she (or the group) will become its new owner(s) and dictate its future. This is known as an **acquisition** or takeover (as in 'hostile takeover', which we discussed in Chapter 3). General Motors (GM) was created out of a series of acquisitions in the early twentieth century.* The purchase of Nokia mobile phone division by

---

* The original GM, established in 1908, produced Buick. Between 1908 and 1909, it acquired a series of companies producing Oldsmobile, Cadillac and other brands, as well as what subsequently became its truck division. It acquired Chevrolet in 1918.

Microsoft is the most high-profile corporate acquisition in the recent period. Sometimes two or more companies may fuse themselves into a single new entity by pooling their shares. This is known as a **merger**. The most famous, or rather infamous, merger was the one between Time Warner, the giant of traditional media, and AOL, the internet service pioneer, in 2001.*

The New York Stock Exchange (NYSE) (founded in 1817), the London Stock Exchange (LSX) (founded in 1801) and the Tokyo Stock Exchange (TSE) (founded in 1878) have been the largest stock markets during much of the post-Second World War period. The NASDAQ (National Association of Securities Dealers Automated Quotation), another US stock exchange founded as a 'virtual' market in 1971 (it did not have a physical marketplace, like the NYSE, in the beginning), has grown rapidly since the 1980s, thanks to the fact that many fast-growing information technology firms were 'listed' there. It is at the moment the second-biggest stock exchange in the world, after the NYSE (the TSE is the third-largest). The price movements in a stock market are usually represented by a **stock market index**, recording average price movements of the shares of a selection of important companies, weighted by their relative sizes. The NYSE price movements are captured by the S&P 500 (compiled by Standard and Poor, the credit rating agency), the LSX ones by FTSE 100 (compiled by the *Financial Times*) and the TSE ones by Nikkei 225 (compiled by the *Nihon Keizai Shimbun*, or *Japan Economic Times*).†

There were also bond markets, which allowed companies or governments to borrow directly from investors by issuing IOUs (bonds) that are transferable to anyone and pay fixed amounts of interest. However, the government bond market was not very developed except in the US (the market for Treasury bills, or 'T-bills' for short), while the corporate bond market was not very significant even in the US. The list of corporate bond issuers in the US apparently fitted into three pages in the 1968 classic by Sidney Homer, *The Bond Buyer's Primer*.[1]

Within this broad framework, there were important international variations. In the US and the UK, these (stock and bond) 'markets' were bigger

---

* This merger did not work – to the extent that it was described as 'the biggest mistake in corporate history' by the current Time-Warner CEO, Jeff Bewkes – and was undone (this is known as 'de-merger') in 2009. AOL's business failed to grow as predicted at the time of the merger (it was at the height of the dot.com bubble) and there were irreconcilable differences between the corporate cultures of the two companies.

† The numbers in their names denote the number of companies whose share prices make up the index.

(in relative terms) and more influential than in countries like Germany, Japan or France, where banks played a much more important role. For this reason, the former countries were known to have 'market-based' financial systems and the latter 'bank-based' ones. The former system is said to generate greater pressure for short-term profits on the part of enterprises than the latter, as shareholders (and bondholders) have less commitment to the companies they 'own' than banks do to the companies they lend to.

Investment Banks and the Rise of the New Financial System

Banks that we do not see: investment banks

So far I have talked about the banks we see: the ones with branches on every high street. These are banks like HSBC or NatWest that actively advertise themselves on TV, on billboards and on websites. They remind us how nice they are to their depositors (a free railcard for students! Only UK call centres!). They tell us how willing they are to give us a loan, should we wish to, say, take an impulsive foreign holiday or fulfil our life-long dream of opening a muffin shop. These banks are known as **commercial banks** or **deposit banks**.*

But then there are banks we do *not* see. These are known as **investment banks**. Some of them share brands with their commercial bank siblings. Barclays has a commercial bank, but also has an investment bank named Barclays Capital. Or it could be one company engaged in both, using different brands: JP Morgan Chase has an investment banking arm, using the brand of JP Morgan, and a commercial banking arm, using the brand of Chase Manhattan. Other investment banks – Goldman Sachs, Morgan Stanley, the now-defunct Lehman Brothers, etc. – do not have commercial siblings. Most of us have heard of them – especially Goldman Sachs, who have been infamously likened to a 'vampire squid' by the journalist Matt Taibbi – but don't fully understand what they do.

Investment banks have existed since the nineteenth century – sometimes as independent entities but often as parts of **universal banks** that perform both

---

* When commercial banks deal with individuals, taking deposits from them or lending them money to buy houses or cars, they are said to engage in 'retail banking'. When they deal with businesses – lending them money, taking deposits from them – they are said to engage in 'corporate banking'.

types of banking. German banks, such as Deutsche Bank or Commerzbank, are the quintessential examples. In the US, due to the Glass-Steagall Act, the combination of investment banking and commercial banking in a single entity was not allowed between 1933 and 1999. Since the 1980s, these banks have played the leading role in reshaping the financial system on a global scale.

Investment banks' key role is (or used to be) to facilitate the creation and the trading of shares and bonds

Investment banks are so called because they help companies raise money from investors – at least that was their original purpose. They arrange the issuance of shares and corporate bonds by their client companies and sell them on their behalf.

When they sell shares and bonds for their client companies, investment banks do not deal with 'retail' investors, namely, small individual investors who only buy small quantities. They only deal with large investors, such as extremely rich individuals ('high net worth individuals' is the jargon) or **institutional investors**, that is, large *funds* created by individual investors pooling their money.

The most important types of funds include: **pension funds**, investing money that individuals save for their pensions; **sovereign wealth funds**, which manage state-owned assets of a country (Government Pension Fund of Norway and Abu Dhabi Investment Council are two of the biggest examples); **mutual funds** or **unit trusts**, which manage money pooled by small individual investors that buy into them in the open market; **hedge funds**, which invest actively in high-risk, high-return assets, using a pool of large sums given to them by very rich individuals or other, more 'conservative', funds (e.g., pension funds); **private equity funds**, which are like hedge funds, but make money solely out of buying up companies, restructuring them and selling at a profit.

In addition to selling shares and bonds for their client companies, investment banks buy and sell shares and bonds with their own money, hoping to make a profit in the process. This is known as **proprietary trading**. Investment banks also earn money from helping companies to engage in **mergers and acquisitions** (or **M&A**). But the service that investment banks provide in this process is more of a consulting service than a 'banking' service.

Since the 1980s, and especially since the 1990s, investment banks have increasingly focused on the creation and the trading of new financial products, such as **securitized debt products** and derivative financial products, or simply **derivatives**.* These new financial products became popular among investment banks because, to put it bluntly, they let them make more money than did 'traditional' businesses, such as selling shares and bonds or advising on M&A. Exactly how they do so is rather complicated, as I shall explain below.

Securitized debt products are created by pooling individual loans into a composite bond

In the old days, when someone borrowed money from a bank and bought something, the lending bank owned the resulting debt and that was that. But 'financial innovations' in the last few decades have led to the creation of a new financial instrument called **asset-backed securities** (ABSs) out of these debts. An ABS pools thousands of loans – for homes, cars, credit cards, university fees, business loans and what not – and turns them into a bigger, 'composite', bond.

If you are dealing with an individual loan, its repayment would dry up if the particular borrower defaulted. Given this risk, these loans cannot be easily sold to someone else. However, if you create an ABS by pooling, for example, thousands of home mortgage loans – which is known as a **Residential Mortgage Backed Security** (RMBS) – you can be sure that on average the borrowers will make repayments, even if individually they have relatively high risks of default (known in the US as 'subprime' mortgage borrowers). In technical terms, these products pool risk among a large number of borrowers, like insurance products do among the insured.

In this way, illiquid assets that cannot easily be sold (such as a mortgage for one particular house, a loan for a particular car) are turned into something (a composite bond) that can be easily traded. Until the rise of ABSs, bonds could be issued only by governments and by very large companies. Now, anything – down to a humble student loan – could be behind a bond. Having sold off the original loans by packaging them into an ABS, the lender can use the money that it has got from the sale to extend even more loans.

Until the 1980s, ABSs were mainly confined to the US and mostly created out of residential mortgages. But, from the early 1990s, ABSs made of

---

* Even though people, including myself elsewhere, have called both these products 'financial derivatives', it is more accurate to separate the two types of products for reasons I explain below.

other loans came on stream in the US and then gradually took off in other rich countries, as they abolished regulations that restricted the ability of lending banks to sell off their loans to a third party.

You can make ABSs more complicated – and
supposedly safer – through 'structuring'

More recently, these financial products have become even more complex since ABSs have become 'structured' and been turned into **Collateralized Debt Obligations** (or CDOs). Structuring in this context involves combining a number of ABSs, such as RMBSs, into yet another composite bond, such as CDO, and dividing the new bond into a few **tranches** (slices) with differential risks. The most 'senior' tranche would be made safer by, say, the guarantee that its owners will be asked to bear losses the last (that is, only after the owners of all other, more 'junior', tranches have absorbed their losses), should any loss occur. In this way, a very safe financial product could be created out of a pool of relatively unsafe assets – that was at least the theory.* A derivative product called a credit default swap (CDS) was created to supposedly protect you from default on the CDOs by acting as an insurance policy against the risk of default of particular CDOs (I will discuss what the 'swap' is a bit later).

Pooling and structuring simply shift and obscure risk, not eliminate it

All of this was deemed to have reduced risk for the financial products concerned – first through safety in numbers (pooling), and then through the deliberate creation of safety zones within that pool (structuring).

The 'senior' tranches of CDOs thus created were frequently given AAA credit ratings, traditionally reserved for the safest of the financial assets, such as the government bonds of a handful of rich countries and a tiny minority of super-safe companies.

Having been given AAA ratings, these assets could now be sold to pension funds, insurance companies and charitable foundations, which are mandated to be conservative in their asset choices. Commercial banks also

---

* Things got more complicated over time. CDOs-squared were created by pooling tranches from CDOs and structuring them in the way described above. And then CDOs-cubed were created by creating a structured debt product out of tranches of CDOs-squared. Even more high-powered CDOs were created.

bought these assets in large quantities. CDOs, having AAA ratings and thus easily sellable, helped banks meet the aforementioned liquidity regulation while being paid higher interest rates than traditional AAA-rated financial assets (which usually brought lower returns, in return for the safety they offered). The markets for structured debt products exploded.

But the fact still remained that these bonds were ultimately based on shaky assets – mortgage loans given to workers with unstable employment or credit card debts of consumers with a chequered financial history. When the US housing bubble burst, even the supposedly super-safe senior tranches of CDOs proved exactly the opposite.

Derivatives are essentially bets on how 'other things' are going to unfold over time [2]

In addition to the 'pooled' and 'structured' financial products, investment banks have played a key role in generating and trading derivative financial products, or simply derivatives, in the last three decades.

Derivatives are so called because they do *not* have any intrinsic value of their own and 'derive' their values from things or events external to themselves, in much the same way in which someone in Manchester can derive value from a boxing match in Las Vegas by entering into a bet on it with a bookmaker or even a friend.[3] You could say that derivatives are bets on how other things are going to unfold over time.

In the beginning, derivatives were confined to commodity markets

These days, derivative contracts can involve anything – commodities (e.g., rice, oil), financial assets (e.g., shares, foreign exchange), prices (e.g., stock market indexes, property prices), or even weather. But, in the beginning, they were basically confined to commodity markets.

A classic example is a rice farmer and a rice merchant going into a contract specifying that the farmer will sell his rice to the merchant at a pre-agreed price when he harvests his rice. This type of contract is known as a forward contract, or simply a **forward**. A forward is not the only type of derivative, but let's stick to it for the moment, as it is the 'prototype' derivative.

Once the contract is established, a derivative becomes like a bet on the real-world thing upon which it is based. In this example, holding a forward contract for rice becomes like holding a bet on the future price of rice.

*Over-the-counter vs. exchange-traded: custom-
made vs. standardized derivatives*

Many derivatives are 'custom-made' – that is, they are between two particular contracting parties, such as the rice farmer and the rice merchant in the example above. A more modern example might be a company protecting itself from fluctuations in exchange rates by going into a forward contract with an investment bank to convert a particular currency at a pre-agreed exchange rate in, say, twenty-three days' time. These custom-made derivatives are called **over-the-counter** (OTC) derivatives.

Derivatives contracts may be 'standardized' and sold in exchanges, or become **exchange-traded** – the Chicago Board of Trade (CBOT), set up in the mid-nineteenth century, being the most important example. In the case of a forward, it is re-christened when standardized – these are called **futures**. An oil futures contract might specify that I will buy from whoever happens to hold that contract, say, in a year's time 1,000 barrels of a particular type of oil (Brent Crude, West Texas Intermediate, etc.) at $100 a barrel.

Derivatives allow hedging against risk but also enable speculation

The standard justification for derivatives is that they allow economic actors to 'hedge' against risk. If I am an oil refinery, I can protect myself against the possibility that the oil price may go above $100 a barrel in a year's time by buying an oil futures contract that I have just described above. This means that I will lose out if the oil price falls below $100 a barrel (as I *have to* buy the oil at $100 a barrel, even if it is only $90 a barrel, unless I have already sold the contract on to someone else). Naturally, I would buy such a contract only if I believed that the chance of the price falling below $100 a barrel is small.

This hedging, or protective, function is, however, not the only – or these days not even the main – function of derivatives. They also allow people to speculate (that is, bet) on the movements of oil prices. In other words, someone who has no inherent interest in the price of oil itself, whether as a consumer or as an oil refinery, can make a bet on the movements of oil prices. Thus, in a provocative but insightful analogy, Brett Scott, a financial activist, points out that '[saying] that derivatives exist to allow people to hedge themselves . . . [is] a bit like arguing that the horse betting industry exists to help horse owners protect themselves from risk [of their horses losing a race].'[4]

Other types of derivatives have evolved – options and swaps

Over time, derivative families other than forward/futures have evolved. There are two main types – options and swaps.

An **option** contract would give a contracting party the right (but not the obligation) to buy (or sell) something at a price fixed now at some particular date. The option to buy is called a 'call' option, and the option to sell is called a 'put' option. Options have become more widely known through 'stock options' – that is, the right to buy a certain number of stocks (shares) at a pre-agreed price at some future date – given to top managers (and sometimes other employees), to encourage them to manage companies in a way that raises share prices.

Where a forward is like a bet on a single future event, a **swap** is like a bet on a series of future events; it is like a number of forward contracts linked together. For example, it allows you to replace a series of variable future payments or earnings with a series of fixed payments or earnings, like contracts for your mobile phone or fixed-price electricity deals over a period, according to Scott's instructive analogy.[5] The variation in payments or earnings could be due to variations in all sorts of things, so there are many different types of swaps; interest rates (interest rate swaps), exchange rates (currency swaps), commodity prices (commodity swaps), share prices (equity swaps), or even default risk of particular financial products (CDSs).

At this point, your head may be spinning at the complexity of things, but that is in a way the point. The complexity of these new financial products is exactly what made them so dangerous, as I shall explain later.

Derivative trade took off in the 1980s

Derivative markets were not very significant until the early 1980s, although exchanges for currency futures and stock options had been established by the Chicago Board of Trade in the 1970s.[6]

Then a historic change came in 1982. In that year, two key US financial regulatory bodies, the Securities and Exchange Commission (SEC) and the Commodity Futures Trading Commission (CFTC) agreed that the settlement of a derivative contract does not have to involve the delivery of the underlying goods (e.g., rice or oil) but can be settled in cash.

This new regulatory rule enabled the proliferation of derivative contracts that are derived from 'notional' things, such as the stock market index, which can never be physically delivered, and not just commodities or particular financial assets.[7] From then on, your imagination was the limit to what kind of derivative contract you could create.

REAL-LIFE NUMBERS
The explosive growth of finance

Until the 1990s, there were very few securitized debt products (ABS, CDO, etc.) around in Europe. But, according to the OECD, by 2010, the market for those products in Europe was estimated to have grown to around $2.7 trillion. This was still much smaller than the market in the US, estimated to be around $10.7 trillion, where such products had a longer history, especially when considering that the EU had a GDP that was over 10 per cent bigger than that of the US.[8]

Derivative markets have grown even faster. They were marginal markets until the 1980s. By 2011, the IMF estimated the global OTC derivative market to be $648 trillion in terms of 'outstanding value' (that is, the total value of the 'bets', which usually exceed the value of underlying assets by many multiples). The 'market value' of the contracts themselves was estimated to be $27 trillion, as against $110 trillion of global banking assets and $70 trillion of world GDP (these numbers are not really comparable with each other; they are given to provide a sense of magnitude).[9]

Rapid growth was not confined to the new financial products. The rest of the financial sector has also grown fast. Between 1980 and 2007, the ratio of the stock of financial assets to world output rose from 1.2 to 4.4, according to the calculation by Gabriel Palma.[10]

The relative size of the financial sector was even greater in many rich countries, especially – but not exclusively – the US and the UK. According to Palma, the ratio of financial assets to GDP in the UK reached 700 per cent in 2007.* Using different data sources, Lapavitsas estimates that the UK

---

* France, which often styles itself as a counterpoint to Anglo-American finance capitalism, has not lagged far behind the UK in this respect – the ratio of its financial assets to GDP is only marginally lower than that of the UK.

number rose from around 700 per cent in the late 1980s to over 1,200 per cent by 2009 – or 1,800 per cent, if we included assets owned abroad by UK citizens and companies.[11] James Crotty, using American government data, calculated that the ratio of financial assets to GDP in the US fluctuated between 400 and 500 per cent between the 1950s and 1970s, but that it started to shoot up from the early 1980s, following financial deregulation. It broke through the 900 per cent mark by the early 2000s.[12]

The New Financial System and Its Consequences

The new financial system was to be more efficient and safer

All this meant that a new financial system has emerged in the last three decades. We have seen the proliferation of new and complex financial instruments through financial innovation, or financial engineering, as some people prefer to call it. This process was enormously facilitated by **financial deregulation** – the abolition or the dilution of existing regulations on financial activities, as I shall discuss later.

This new financial system was supposed to be more efficient *and* safer than the old one, which was dominated by slow-witted commercial banks dealing in a limited range of financial instruments, unable to meet increasingly diverse demands for financial risk. The belief was that greater freedom of contract would maximize the chance that financial market actors could come up with innovative ways to assess risk and price assets more efficiently, thereby enhancing the stability of the system.

The possibility that these new financial instruments might be too complicated to be handled safely was brushed away. Pro-market economists argued that, in a free market, a contract will be signed only when the contracting parties know that they would benefit from it, especially when they are 'largely sophisticated financial institutions that would appear to be eminently capable of protecting themselves from fraud and counterparty insolvencies', according to Larry Summers, the then deputy secretary of the Treasury, in his testimony to the US Congress in 1998.*

---

* Summers, a professor of economics on leave from Harvard and a former chief economist of the World Bank (1991–3), subsequently became the Treasury secretary (July 1999–January 2001) during Bill Clinton's second presidency and then was the director of the National Economic Council (January 2009–December 2010) during Barack Obama's first term.

One of those 'sophisticates' – a certain Joe Cassano, who was then the chief financial officer of AIG, the American insurance company bailed out by the US government in the fall of 2008 – said only six months before the collapse of his company, 'It is hard for us, without being flippant, to even see a scenario within any kind of realm of reason that would see us losing one dollar in any of the [CDS] transactions.'

This belief in the infallibility of the market was shared by the regulators. At the height of the housing bubble in the US, key policy-makers kept denying that there was a bubble. In June 2005, while admitting that there are 'signs of froth in some local markets', Alan Greenspan, the then Fed chairman, assured the members of the US Congress that 'a "bubble" in home prices for the nation as a whole does not appear likely'. A few months later, in October 2005, Ben Bernanke – the then chairman of the Council of Economic Advisers to the President (George W. Bush) and the Fed chairman between February 2006 and January 2014 – stated in his Congressional testimony that the 25 per cent increase in home prices that the US had seen in the previous two years 'largely reflect strong economic fundamentals'.

Increasing complexity has made the financial
system more inefficient and unstable

Despite these assurances, the US housing bubble burst in 2007 and 2008 – the prices were simply too high, given the performance of the underlying economy, and could not be sustained any more. With it came the collapse of the markets for CDOs and CDSs that fed on it, resulting in the biggest financial crisis since the Great Depression. Following the 2008 global financial crisis, so much information has come out that shows how those running Summers's 'sophisticated' financial institutions and the confident regulators really did not understand what was going on.

This was because of the vast increase in complexity of the financial system. And we are not talking about things getting a little more complicated. Andy Haldane, the executive director of financial stability at the Bank of England, once pointed out that in order to fully understand a CDO[2] – one of the more, but not the most, complicated new financial products – a prospective investor needs to absorb more than one billion pages of information.[13] I have also come across bankers who confessed that they had frequently got derivative contracts running a few hundred pages, which they naturally didn't have the time to read. Complicated mathematical models were developed to deal with this information overload, but in the end events have proved them to be, at best, woefully inadequate and, at worst, sources of a false sense of control. According to these models, the chances of what happened in 2008 actually happening were equivalent to winning the lottery twenty-one or twenty-two times in a row.[14]

Increasing interconnectedness has also heightened the instability of the financial system

The more liberal definition of what is a legitimate financial contract (e.g., allowance of index-based derivatives) and the pooling, structuring and vastly increased trading of those products have occurred in the context of a general deregulation of the financial sector.

Starting from the US and the UK in the early 1980s, country after country has relaxed, or even abolished, a wide range of financial regulations: prudential regulation for commercial banks, especially liquidity regulation and leverage regulation; ceilings on interest rates that lenders can charge; restrictions on asset types that different financial firms can hold, such as pre-1980s restrictions on US Savings & Loan institutions against making consumer loans and commercial real estate mortgage loans; rules on how aggressive the lending can be (e.g., rules on loan-to-house-value ratio for mortgage loans); and the relaxation, and frequently abolition, of restrictions on cross-border movement of capital (for further discussion on the last, see Chapter 12).

The result has been the proliferation of connections between different parts of the financial system like never before. This was not only across different sectors – for example, commercial banks and insurance companies getting deeply involved in derivatives trading – but also across different countries – the first sign of problems with American CDOs in 2008 were noticed by German and Swiss banks who had bought them. With this increase in interconnectedness, a problem in one part of the system rapidly spread to other parts, vastly increasing the instability of the system.

The point is that, however deftly you may pool, structure and derive your financial products, it is in the end the same subprime mortgage borrower in Florida, the same small company in Nagoya and the same guy who borrowed money to buy his car in Nantes who have to pay back the loans that underlie all those new financial products. And by creating all sorts of financial products that link different bits of the system, you actually increase the intensity with which the failure by these people to repay their loans affects the system.

How the new financial system has made non-financial corporations more short-term-oriented

The rise of new finance has not just affected the financial sector. It has also significantly changed the way in which non-financial corporations are run. The change was particularly pronounced in the US and the UK, in which new finance has advanced the furthest and in which, unlike in Germany or Japan, stakeholders other than shareholders have had little influence on how companies are managed.

The first important change has been a further shrinking time horizon in management. With the rise of hostile takeovers in the 1980s (recall Gordon Gekko from Chapter 3), companies had already been put under increasing pressure to deliver short-term profits, if necessary at the cost of long-term competitiveness. But with the proliferation of so many financial instruments that provide quick and high returns, shareholders have become even more impatient in the last couple of decades. For example, in the UK, the average period of shareholding, which had already fallen from five years in the mid-1960s to two years in the 1980s, plummeted to about 7.5 months at the end of 2007.[15]

This has resulted in the formation of an 'unholy alliance' between the professional managers of corporations and the growing band of short-term shareholders, under the rallying call of 'shareholder value maximization' (see Chapter 5). In this alliance, astronomical salaries were paid to managers in return for maximizing short-term profits – even at the cost of product quality and worker morale – and distributing the biggest possible proportions of those profits to the shareholders, in the form of dividends and **share buy-backs** (companies buying up their own shares in order to prop up the share price).

Such practices left very few resources with which the company could invest in things like machines, R&D and training, reducing its long-term productivity and thus competitiveness. When the company gets into trouble, most of the professional managers and short-term shareholders who orchestrated the demise are not even with the company any more.

The financialization of non-financial corporations

The new financial system has not just made non-financial corporations operate with a shorter time horizon. It has also made them more 'financial-ized' – that is, more dependent on financial activities of their own. Given the higher returns that financial assets bring compared with traditional busi-nesses, many companies have increasingly diverted their resources to the management of financial assets. Such a shift in focus has made those com-panies become even less interested in building up technology-based long-term productive capabilities than what was made necessary by the increasing pressure from short-term-oriented shareholders.

In the last couple of decades, some of them have aggressively expanded their financial arms – for example, GE Capital by General Electric, GMAC by GM and Ford Finance by Ford. Some of them have become so significant that, in the summer of 2013, the Financial Stability Oversight Council of the US government designated the biggest of them, GE Capital, as one of the 'system-atically important financial institutions' (SIFIs) – a status usually reserved for only the biggest banks.

The over-development of the financial sector and its consequences

Under the new regime, the financial sector has become much more prof-itable than the non-financial sector, which had not always been the case.[16] This has enabled it to offer salaries and bonuses that are much higher than those offered by other sectors, attracting the brightest people, regardless of the subjects they studied in universities. Unfortunately, this leads to a misal-location of talents, as people who would be a lot more productive in other professions – engineering, chemistry and what not – are busy trading deriva-tives or building mathematical models for their pricing. It also means that a lot of higher-educational spending has been wasted, as many people are not using the skills they were originally trained for.*

The disproportionate amount of wealth concentrated in the financial sector also enables it to most effectively lobby against regulations, even when they are socially beneficial. The growing two-way flow of staff between

---

* A few years ago, Professor David King, the eminent Cambridge chemist and the chief scientific advisor to the British government between 2000 and 2007, told me that probably 60 per cent of his former PhD students are working in the financial industry.

the financial industry and the regulatory agencies means that lobbying is often not even necessary. A lot of regulators, who are former employees of the financial sector, are instinctively sympathetic to the industry that they are trying to regulate – this is known as the problem of the 'revolving door'.

More problematically, the revolving door has also encouraged an insidious form of corruption. Regulators may bend the rules – sometimes to the breaking point – to help their potential future employers. Some top regulators are even cleverer. When they leave their jobs, they don't bother to look for a new one. They just set up their own private equity funds or hedge funds, into which the beneficiaries of their past rule-bending will deposit money, even though the former regulators may have little experience in managing an investment fund.

Even more difficult to deal with is the dominance of pro-finance ideology, which results from the sector being so powerful and rewarding to people who work in – or for – it. It is not simply because of the sector's lobbying power that most politicians and regulators have been reluctant to radically reform the financial regulatory system after the 2008 crisis, despite the incompetence, recklessness and cynicism in the industry which it has revealed. It is also because of their ideological conviction that maximum freedom for the financial industry is in the national interest.

REAL-LIFE NUMBERS

There has been a vast increase in the frequency of financial crises

For most people, the 2008 global financial crisis is probably proof enough that the new financial system has failed to deliver on its promises for greater efficiency and stability. But it is important to note that the 2008 crisis was presaged by many earlier, smaller crises in the last three decades. The list, even counting only the major ones, is impressive.

In 1982, Chile got into a major banking crisis, following the radical financial market liberalization in the mid-1970s under the Pinochet dictatorship. In the late 1980s, the Savings and Loan (S&L) companies in the US – also known as 'thrifts' – got into massive trouble, having been allowed by the government to move into more risky, but potentially higher-yielding, activities, such as commercial real estate and consumer loans. The US government had to close down nearly one-quarter of S&Ls and inject public money equivalent to 3 per cent of GDP to clean up the mess.

The 1990s started with banking crises in Sweden, Finland and Norway, following their financial deregulations in the late 1980s. Then there was the 'tequila' crisis in Mexico in 1994 and 1995. This was followed by crises in the 'miracle' economies of Asia – Thailand, Indonesia, Malaysia and South Korea – in 1997, which had resulted from their financial opening-up and deregulation in the late 1980s and the early 1990s. On the heels of the Asian crisis came the Russian crisis of 1998. The Brazilian crisis followed in 1999 and the Argentinian one in 2002, both in large part the results of financial deregulation.

These are only the prominent ones, but the world has seen so many more financial crises since the mid-1970s. According to a widely cited study,[17] virtually no country was in banking crisis between the end of the Second World War and the mid-1970s, when the financial sector was heavily regulated. Between the mid-1970s and the late 1980s, the proportion of countries with banking crisis rose to 5–10 per cent, weighted by their share of world income. The proportion then shot up to around 20 per cent in the mid-1990s. The ratio then briefly fell to zero for a few years in the mid-2000s, but went up again to 35 per cent following the 2008 global financial crisis.

The 'unholy alliance' between short-term-oriented shareholders and professional managers has reduced the ability of corporations to invest

The rise of the 'shareholder value maximization' model in the era of new finance has dramatically reduced the resources available for long-term investments in non-financial corporations.

The era has seen a dramatic rise in **distributed profits**, that is, profits given to shareholders in the forms of dividends and share buy-backs. For example, distributed profits as a share of total US corporate profits stood at 35–45 per cent between the 1950s and 70s.[18] Between 2001 and 2010, the largest US companies distributed 94 per cent of their profits and the top UK companies 89 per cent of their profits.[19]

This has significantly reduced the ability of corporations in these countries to invest. Contrary to the popular perception, it is not the issuing of new shares or bank loans but **retained profits** (that is, profits not distributed to shareholders) that is the main source of investment financing. Given this, the dramatic fall in retained profits – from 55–65 per cent to just 6 per cent in the case of US corporations – has meant a huge reduction in the capacity of corporations to make long-term-oriented investments.

Non-financial companies, at least in the US, have become increasingly dependent on their financial activities for their profits

Especially in the US, non-financial companies have enormously increased their financial assets. The ratio of financial assets to non-financial assets owned by non-financial corporations gradually rose from 30 per cent in 1950 to 40 per cent in 1982. Then it started to shoot up, reaching 100 per cent in 2001. Since then it fell – down to 81 per cent in 2008. It sharply rose again in 2009, reaching a new height at 104 per cent, essentially staying at the same level.[20]

For some companies, their financial arms have been the main source of profits in the recent period, dwarfing their original manufacturing arms. In 2003, 45 per cent of GE's profit came from GE Capital. In 2004, 80 per cent of the profits of GM were from its financial arm, GMAC, while Ford made all its profits from Ford Finance between 2001 and 2003.[21]

Concluding Remarks: Finance Needs to Be Strictly Regulated Exactly Because It Is So Powerful

Capitalism would not have developed in the way it has without the development of the financial system. The spread of commercial banking, the rise of the stock market, the advance in investment banking and the growth of the corporate and the government bond markets have enabled us to mobilize resources and to pool risk on an unprecedented scale. Without such developments, we would still be living in a world full of small factories run and financed by Ricardo's 'master manufacturers', supported by poorly financed and inadequate governments.

Unfortunately, following the rise of 'new finance' in the last three decades, our financial system has become a negative force. Our financial firms have become very good at generating high profits for themselves at the cost of creating asset bubbles whose unsustainability they obscure through pooling, structuring and other techniques. When the bubble bursts, these firms deftly use their economic weight and political influence to secure rescue money and subsidies from the public purse, which then has to be refilled by the general public through tax hikes and spending cuts. This scenario has been playing out on a gargantuan scale since the 2008 global financial crisis, but it had already been repeated dozens of times on smaller scales all over the world – Chile, the US, Sweden, Malaysia, Russia, Brazil, you name it – in the last three decades.

Unless we regulate our financial system much more strictly, we will see the repeat of these crises. Many of the regulations that I have described as having been weakened or abolished since the 1980s need to be brought back or even strengthened. These regulatory changes involve technical discussions that need not detain the reader here, but there is one clear principle that needs to be borne in mind in thinking about the reform. It is that our financial system needs to be made simpler.

As discussed above, our financial system has become too complex to control – not just for supposedly clueless regulators but also for those supposed 'sophisticates' of the financial industry. We need to reduce this complexity by limiting the proliferation of overly complicated financial products, especially when their creators cannot prove beyond reasonable doubt that their benefits outweigh their costs.

This principle may sound very radical, but it is not. We do this kind of thing all the time in relation to medicine; given the complexity of the human body and the seriousness of potential damage new drugs might do, we demand that the manufacturers prove to the rest of society that their products have more benefits than costs.[22] Indeed, the boundaries of legitimate financial contracts have been constantly redrawn through political decisions, as I have shown above (recall the case of derivatives).

Arguing for a stricter regulation of the financial system does not imply that it is not an important part of the economy. On the contrary, it needs to be regulated exactly because of its power and importance. We didn't have traffic lights, ABS brakes, seat belts and air bags in the days when most people walked, used bullock carts and at most sprinted on horses. Today we have – and started demanding through regulation – those things exactly because we have cars that are powerful and fast but that can do a lot of damage if something – even a small thing – goes wrong. Unless the same reasoning is applied to finance, we will keep having the economic equivalents of car crashes, hit-and-runs or even motorway pile-ups.

Further Reading

Y. AKYUZ
The Financial Crisis and the Global South: A Development Perspective (London: Pluto Press, 2013).

G. EPSTEIN (ED.)
Financialization and the World Economy (Cheltenham: Edward Elgar, 2005).

G. INGHAM
The Nature of Money (Cambridge: Polity, 2004).

C. KINDLEBERGER
Manias, Panics, and Crashes: A History of Financial Crises (London: Macmillan, 1978).

J. LANCHESTER
Whoops!: Why Everyone Owes Everyone And No One Can Pay (London: Penguin, 2010).

C. LAPAVITSAS
Profiting without Producing: How Finance Exploits Us All (London: Verso, 2013).

F. MARTIN
Money: The Unauthorised Biography (London: Bodley Head, 2013).

B. SCOTT
The Heretic's Guide to Global Finance: Hacking the Future of Money (London: Pluto Press, 2013).

CHAPTER 9

Boris's Goat Should Drop Dead

INEQUALITY AND POVERTY

'The peasant Ivan is jealous of his neighbour Boris, because Boris has a goat. A fairy comes along and offers Ivan a single wish. What does he wish for? That Boris's goat should drop dead.'

D. LANDES, *THE WEALTH AND POVERTY OF NATIONS*

Inequality

Ivan is not alone – pursuit of equality as a driver of human history

Ivan is not alone. In Korea, there is a saying that you get a bellyache when your cousin buys a plot of land. And I am sure many readers know similar jokes or proverbs about people becoming irrationally jealous with other people doing better.

The pursuit of equality is a very natural human emotion and has been a powerful driver of human history. Equality was one of the ideals behind the French Revolution, one of whose most famous mottos was 'Liberté, égalité, fraternité ou la mort' (liberty, equality, brotherhood or death). In the Russian Revolution, and other socialist revolutions that followed it, equality was *the* driving motive. Many industrial strikes, demonstrations, revolutions and countless other human conflicts would not have happened without the pursuit of equality.

'You know, I think it's just about envy'

The advocates of free-market policies, however, warn us against letting such a base instinct take over. They tell us that politicians who try to make richer people pay more taxes or restrain bonuses in the banking industry are engaged in the 'politics of envy'. They tell us not to pull down people higher up just so that we can all be equal. Inequality is an inevitable outcome of different productivities of different people. Rich people are rich because they are better at creating wealth. Trying to go against this natural outcome, we will only create equality in poverty, they warn us. What Mitt

Romney, the 2012 Republican presidential candidate, said about the concern about inequality sums up this position very well: 'You know, I think it's just about envy.'

In the last few decades, the advocates of the free market have success-fully persuaded many others that giving a bigger slice of national income to the top earners will benefit everyone. The aphorism 'a rising tide lifts all boats', originally attributed to John F. Kennedy but made popular recently by Robert Rubin, the US treasury secretary under Bill Clinton, has been their favoured slogan.

When the rich have more money at their disposal, they will invest more and generate more income for others; they will hire more work-ers for their businesses, and their businesses will buy more from their suppliers. With higher personal incomes, the rich will spend more, gen-erating more income for those companies that sell, say, sports cars or designer clothes to the rich. The companies supplying those things will increase demand for, say, car parts and textiles, while their workers will earn higher wages and spend more on their own food and (non-designer) clothes. And so on. Thus, if there is more income at the top, more of it will eventually 'trickle down' to the rest of the economy, making every-one richer than before. Even though the shares that poorer people get in the national income may be smaller, they will be better off in absolute terms. This is what Milton Friedman, the guru of free-market econom-ics, meant when he said: 'Most economic fallacies derive from . . . the tendency to assume that there is a fixed pie, that one party can gain only at the expense of another.'[1]

The belief in the trickle-down effect has prompted many governments to employ – or at least has provided them with the political cover for – pro-rich policies in the last three decades. Regulations on product, labour and finan-cial markets were relaxed, making it easier for the rich to make money. Taxes on corporations and high-income earners were cut, making it easier for them to keep the money they thus make.

Too much inequality is bad for the economy: instability and reduced mobility

Few, if any, people would advocate the extreme egalitarianism of China under Mao or Cambodia under Pol Pot. Nevertheless, many people argue that too much inequality is a bad thing, not just ethically but also in economic terms.*

Some economists have emphasized that high inequality reduces social cohesion, increasing political instability. This, in turn, discourages investments. Political instability makes the future – and thus the returns on investments, which are by definition in the future – uncertain. Reduced investments reduce growth.

Greater inequality also increases economic instability, which is bad for growth.[2] A larger share of national income going to the top earners may increase investment ratio. But an increased share of investment also means that the economy is more subject to uncertainty and thus becomes less stable, as Keynes pointed out (see Chapter 4). Many economists have also pointed out that rising inequality played an important role in the making of the 2008 global financial crisis. Especially in the case of the US, top incomes have soared while real wages have been stagnant for most people since the 1970s. Stagnant wages made people incur high levels of debts to keep up with the ever-rising consumption standard at the top. The increase in household debts (as a proportion of GDP) made the economy more vulnerable to shocks.

Others have argued that high inequality reduces economic growth by creating barriers to social mobility. Expensive education that only a tiny minority can afford but that you need in order to get a well-paid job, personal connections within a small privileged group (the French sociologist Pierre Bourdieu famously called it **social capital**)† or even the 'subculture' among the elite (e.g., accents and attitudes you acquire in expensive schools) can act as barriers to social mobility.

Reduced social mobility means that able people from poorer backgrounds are excluded from high-end jobs and thus have their talents wasted from both

---

* Ethical arguments against inequality include the following: a high degree of inequality is morally unacceptable because a large part of what you earn is down to luck (e.g., to which parents you were born) rather than a 'just desert' (e.g., efforts you have made); a group with too many discrepancies between its members cannot function as a true community; too much inequality undermines democracy by allowing the rich to exercise disproportionate political influence.

† Another definition of the term, popularized by the American political scientist Robert Putnam, refers to the collection of social bonds among the members of a society.

an individual and a social point of view. It also means that some of the people filling the top jobs are not the best that the society could have got, had it had higher social mobility. If sustained over generations, such barriers make able youngsters from less privileged backgrounds give up even *trying* for higher-end jobs (recall Chapter 5). This leads to cultural and intellectual 'inbreeding' among the elite. If you believe that big changes require fresh ideas and unconventional attitudes, a society with an 'inbred' elite is likely to become bad at generating innovation. The result is reduced economic dynamism.

Inequality leads to inferior social outcomes

Recently, studies have come out to show that inequality leads to poor outcomes in health and other social indicators of human well-being. And this is independently of the sheer effect of higher inequality producing a higher number of poor people, who are bound to perform worse in these regards.

This argument has been made popular recently by the book *The Spirit Level*, by Richard Wilkinson and Kate Pickett. The book examined the data from two dozen or so rich countries (roughly countries with per capita incomes above the level of Portugal, which is around $20,000). It argues that more unequal countries definitely do worse in terms of infant mortality, teenage births, educational performance, homicide and imprisonment, and also possibly in terms of life expectancy, mental illness and obesity.[3]

More egalitarian societies have grown faster in many cases

Not only is there a lot of evidence showing that higher inequality produces more negative economic and social outcomes, there are quite a few examples of more egalitarian societies growing much faster than comparable but more unequal societies.[4]

During their 'miracle' years between the 1950s and the 1980s, Japan, South Korea and Taiwan grew much faster than comparable countries despite having lower inequalities. Japan grew much faster than the US, while Korea and Taiwan did so too in relation to the much more unequal countries in Africa and Latin America.

Despite being one of the most equal societies in the world, more equal than even the former Soviet bloc countries in the days of socialism, Finland has grown much faster than the US, one of the most unequal societies in the rich world. Between 1960 and 2010, Finland's average annual per capita income growth rate was 2.7 per cent, against 2.0 per cent in the US. This means that, during this period, the US's income rose 2.7 times while Finland's rose by 3.8 times.

These examples do *not* prove that higher inequality leads to lower growth. There are other examples where more egalitarian societies have grown more slowly than comparable but more unequal countries. But they are enough to let us reject a simplistic 'greater inequality is good for growth' story. Moreover, the majority of statistical studies looking at a large number of countries show a negative correlation (which does *not* necessarily mean a causality) between a country's degree of inequality and its growth rate.

Analysis of the same society over time also lends support to the view that inequality has negative effects on growth. During the last three decades, despite the income shares of those at the top rising in most countries, investment and economic growth have slowed down in most of them.

Some animals are more equal than others: too much equality is bad too

Of course, all of this evidence does not mean that the lower the inequality the better it is. If there is *too little* income inequality, it can discourage people from working hard or creating new things to earn money, as used to be the case in the socialist countries – most notoriously in the agricultural communes in Mao's China.

What made things worse was that the low degrees of income inequality were often seen as charades. Low income inequality in these countries co-existed with high inequality in other dimensions (e.g., access to higher-quality foreign goods, opportunities to travel abroad), based upon ideological conformity or even personal networks.

George Orwell had seen through this in the very early days of socialism, when he coined the slogan 'some animals are more equal than others' in *Animal Farm*, his satire of the Russian Revolution. By the 1970s, this recognition led to widespread cynicism in those countries, summarized in the joke 'They pretend to pay us and we pretend to work.' When things started to unravel in the late 1980s, few wanted to defend a system that could now only be described as hypocritical.

The most reasonable conclusion to draw from the review of various theories and empirical evidence is that neither too little nor too much inequality is good. If it is excessively high or excessively low, inequality may hamper economic growth and create social problems (of different kinds).

The Kuznets hypothesis: inequality over time

Simon Kuznets, the Russian-born American economist, who won one of the first Nobel Prizes in Economics (in 1971 – the first one was in 1969), proposed a famous theory about inequality over time. The so-called **Kuznets hypothesis** is that, as a country develops economically, inequality first increases and then decreases. This hypothesis has very strongly influenced the way in which the study of inequality has been conducted over the last half century, so it is important to know what it is about.

According to Kuznets, in the earliest stage of economic development income distribution remains quite equal. It is because most people are poor farmers at that stage. As the country industrializes and grows, more and more people move out of agriculture and into industry, where wages are higher. This increases inequality. As the economy develops even further, Kuznets argued, inequality begins to decrease. Most people now work in the industrial sector or in the urban service sector that serves the industrial sector, while few remain in the agricultural sector with low wages. The result is the famous inverted-U-shaped curve, known as the **Kuznets curve**, as shown below.

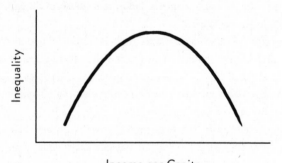

Income per Capita

The Kuznets hypothesis does not hold up . . .

Despite its popularity, the evidence for the Kuznets hypothesis is rather weak. Until the 1970s, it seemed to have been borne out by the experiences of today's rich countries. They saw rising inequality in the early days of their industrialization, peaking, for example, in the mid-nineteenth century in England and in the early twentieth century in the US, and then a fall later. However, since the 1980s, most of these countries have experienced an increase in inequality – dramatically in some cases, such as the US and the UK – starting a new upswing in the curve at the tail end, so to speak.

The hypothesis has not really held up well in today's developing countries either. Inequality has increased with the start of economic development in most of them (exceptions include Korea and Taiwan), but it has hardly decreased with further economic development in the majority of them.

. . .because economic policy matters

The main explanation for the lack of evidence for the Kuznets hypothesis is that economic policy matters hugely in determining the level of inequality.

I have already mentioned that the recent dramatic upswings in inequality in the US and the UK can mainly be explained by deregulation and tax cuts for the rich.

The absence of inequality upswing in Korea or Taiwan in their early stages of economic development between the 1950s and the 1960s can also be explained by policies. During this period, these countries implemented programmes of **land reform**, in which landlords were forced to sell most of their land to their tenants at below-market prices. Their governments then protected this new class of small farmers through import restrictions and the provision of subsidized fertilizer and irrigation services. They also heavily protected small shops from competition by large stores.

Indeed, Kuznets himself did *not* believe that the decrease in inequality in the later stage of economic development would be automatic. While believing that the nature of modern economic development made the inverted-U curve likely, he emphasized that the actual degree of the decrease in inequality would be strongly affected by the strengths of trade unions and, in particular, of the welfare state.

The importance of the welfare state in determining the level of inequality is proven by the fact that, *before* taxes and transfers through the welfare state, some European countries have income inequality that is as high as that of the US (France, Austria and Belgium) or even higher than that of the US (Germany and Italy). As we shall see below, they are far more equal than the US, after taxes and transfers.

Different types of inequality

Though it is the most commonly discussed one, income inequality is only one type of economic inequality. We can also talk of economic inequality in terms of distribution of **wealth** (e.g., ownership of assets, such as real estates or shares) or of **human capital** (that's the fancy – and controversial – word for skills that individuals acquire through education and training).

There are also inequalities in terms of non-economic factors. In many societies, people with a 'wrong' caste, ethnicity, religion, gender, sexuality or ideology have been denied access to things like political office, university places or high-status jobs.

Measuring inequality: the Gini coefficient and the Palma ratio

Of all these inequalities, only income and wealth inequalities are readily measurable. Of these two, the data on wealth are much poorer, so most of the information on inequality we see is in terms of income. Income inequality data are sometimes derived from surveys on consumption, rather than actual incomes, which are harder to capture.

There are number of different ways of measuring the extent to which income is unequally distributed.[5] The most commonly used measure is known as the **Gini coefficient**, named after the early twentieth-century Italian statistician Corrado Gini. As can be seen in the following graph, it compares real-life income distribution (denoted in the graph by the **Lorenz curve**)[6] with the situation of total equality (denoted by the forty-five-degree line in the graph). The Lorenz curve plots the proportion of the overall income in the economy that is cumulatively earned by the bottom x per cent of the population. The coefficient is calculated as a proportion of the area between the Lorenz curve and the forty-five-degree line over the lower triangle in the graph (A/A+B).

More recently, my Cambridge colleague Gabriel Palma has proposed the use of the ratio between the income share of the top 10 per cent and that of the bottom 40 per cent as a more accurate – and easier to calculate – measure of a country's income inequality.[7] Noting that the share taken by the middle 50 per cent of income distribution is remarkably similar across countries regardless of the policies they use, Palma argues that looking at the

Gini coefficient = A / (A+B)

$$= \frac{\text{(area between 45-degree line and Lorenz curve)}}{\text{(area under 45-degree line)}}$$

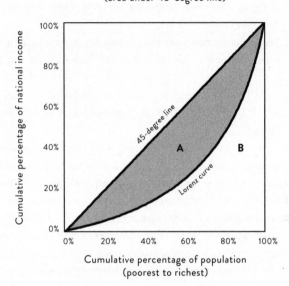

shares at the extremes that differ more across countries gives us a quicker and better idea of inequalities in different countries. Known as the **Palma ratio,** this number overcomes the Gini coefficient's over-sensitivity to the changes in the middle of the income distribution, where it is more difficult to make a difference through policy intervention anyway.[8]

Inequality among whom?

Most inequality figures, like the Gini coefficient, are calculated for individual countries. However, with increasing integration of national economies through globalization, people have become more interested in the changes in the income distribution for the world as a whole. This is known as the global Gini coefficient and calculated by treating each individual in the world as if they are the citizens of the same country.

Some people, myself included, think that the global Gini coefficient is really not terribly relevant, as the world is *not* (at least yet) a true community. Income inequality matters only because we have feelings – positive, negative, solidaristic, murderous – in relation to those others who are included in the statistics; this is known as the **reference group**. We actually don't really care that much how well people who do not belong to our own reference groups are doing.*

Indeed, Ivan in our opening story did not wish the czar to become a poor man because the czar wasn't in his reference group; he wanted the tiny edge that his neighbour Boris had over him to be wiped out. Likewise, his Korean counterpart – let's call him Youngsoo – did not get jealous of some big landlord acquiring a huge tract of land; he was jealous of his own cousin getting one small additional plot.

It is true that global inequality is becoming more relevant, as people are increasingly aware of what is happening in other parts of the world, thanks to the development of mass media and the internet, and thus are beginning to develop a sense of global community. However, it will be a long time before we can tell a poor Chinese peasant not to get too upset about the runaway inequality in his country because the world as a whole has become a slightly more equal place – especially given that it is in large part thanks to the top earners in China pulling away from the rest of the country.

REAL-LIFE NUMBERS

In theory, the Gini coefficient can be anything between 0 and 1. In practice, these extreme values are impossible. No society, however egalitarian it may be in spirit and policies, can make everyone exactly equal, which is what is needed for a Gini coefficient of 0. In a society with a Gini of 1, everyone except one person who has everything will soon be dead.† In real life, no country has a Gini coefficient below 0.2 and none has one above 0.75.

---

* To see this point more clearly, do a little thought experiment. Suppose that you are told that scientists have identified fifty-five planets with sentient beings within our galaxy that are all vastly richer than the earth and also have huge income gaps between themselves, giving a very high galactic Gini coefficient. Would you be terribly upset about it? Probably not – because you don't really know those beings and cannot even imagine how they live.

† Thereby reducing its Gini coefficient to 0, as it will be a perfectly equal society – of one person.

Lowest and highest inequalities: Europe vs. Southern Africa and Latin America

Gini coefficients can differ quite a lot even for the same country, depending on the estimate you look at. For the late 2000s, the OECD gives an income Gini of around 0.25 for Denmark, while the ILO gives a slightly higher figure at around 0.28. In the case of the US, the gap is significant – the OECD estimate is around 0.38 but the ILO puts it around 0.45.[9] In the text below, I cite the ILO data, given that the OECD membership is much smaller than the ILO one.[10]

The most equal societies, mainly found in Europe, have Gini coefficients between 0.2 and 0.3. Many of these are advanced capitalist countries with a strong welfare state. They are, in alphabetical order, Austria, Belgium, Denmark, Finland, France, Germany, the Netherlands, Norway (the most equal country in the world) and Sweden. As mentioned above, before taxes and social spending, some of them are more unequal than the US but they tax and redistribute such a large part of their GDPs that they end up being much more equal than the US. Some of the most equal countries are former socialist bloc economies, whose egalitarian legacies have held. Croatia, Czech Republic, Hungary, Slovakia and Slovenia belong to this group.

At the other extreme, we have countries whose Gini coefficients go up above 0.6. They are, in alphabetical order, Botswana, Madagascar, Namibia and South Africa. They are all in Southern Africa.

Any country with a Gini coefficient above 0.5 can be considered very unequal. Many of these are Latin American countries: Bolivia, Brazil, Chile, Colombia, Costa Rica, Honduras, Panama and Paraguay. But some of them are in Africa (Côte d'Ivoire, Mauritania and Rwanda) and in Asia (Cambodia, the Philippines and Thailand). There is even one country in the former socialist bloc that belongs to this group. It is Georgia, which is, very ironically, Stalin's native country.

Gini coefficients in most other countries are distributed between 0.3 and 0.5. The US and China are found at the more unequal end of that distribution (0.45–0.5). Countries like Uganda, Poland, New Zealand and Italy are at the other end of that range (around 0.3). Roughly speaking, Gini of 0.35 is the dividing line between relatively equal countries and ones that are not.[11]

Wealth inequality is much higher than income inequality

The data on wealth inequality are much less readily available and less reliable than those on income inequality. But it is clear that wealth inequality is much higher than income inequality in all countries for the main reason that accumulating wealth is much more difficult than earning income.

According to the UNCTAD (United Nations Conference on Trade and Development), the wealth Gini coefficient for the fifteen countries studied, including poor countries like India and Indonesia as well as rich countries like the US and Norway, ranged between 0.5 and 0.8.[12] The gap between a country's income inequality and wealth inequality was particularly large for European countries with low income inequality, such as Norway and Germany.[13]

Income inequality has risen in the majority of countries since the 1980s

Since the 1980s, income inequality has risen in the majority of countries.[14] The most marked increase was seen in the UK and especially the US, which led the world in pro-rich policies. In the US, the share of income for the top 1 per cent used to be around 10 per cent between the 1940s and the 1970s, but rose to 23 per cent by 2007.[15] The top 0.1 per cent increased its share from 3–4 per cent to over 12 per cent during the same period.[16]

The trend of rising inequality has slowed down somewhat since around 2000. Inequality has fallen slightly in many countries in the traditionally high-inequality regions of Latin America and Sub-Saharan Africa, although they still remain very unequal by international standards. At least in Latin America cases, this was mainly due to policy interventions, such as increased taxes for the rich, increase in minimum wages, and increased social welfare spending – once again supporting the conclusion we drew from our discussion of the Kuznets hypothesis.

Global inequality has risen for the last two centuries

According to the widely used estimate by Bourguignon and Morrisson, the global Gini coefficient was around 0.5 in 1820 and rose to 0.61 in 1910, 0.64 in 1950 and 0.66 in 1992.[17] According to the above-cited study by the UNCTAD, it has fallen slightly from around 0.7 in the late 1980s and the early 1990s to around 0.66 in the second half of the 2000s.[18] But these numbers are less reliable than national Gini coefficients.

This means that, if the world were a country, two centuries ago it started off as a very unequal one, like Panama or Rwanda, and has become an extremely unequal one, like South Africa, although it may have become slightly – only slightly – less unequal since 1990, largely thanks to China becoming rapidly more prosperous.

Poverty

Poverty has been the dominant human condition for most of history

Poverty has been a consistent oppressive presence throughout human history. Except when we talk of kings and queens and heroes, much of our folklore and literature before the nineteenth century is about poverty and its consequences. And we are not just talking about being a bit hard up. We are talking about the kind of poverty that makes people steal bread (as in *Les Misérables*), eat boiled earth (as in *The Good Earth*) and even abandon children to get rid of mouths to feed (as in *Hänsel and Gretel*). In today's terms, it is the kind of poverty that you see in movies like *Slumdog Millionaire*, set in the slums of Mumbai, India, in which even going to the toilet is a major struggle.

Economists call this kind of poverty **absolute poverty**. It is the failure to be in command over income to fulfil the most basic human needs for survival – such as nutrition, clothing and shelter. This human condition started to change only in the nineteenth century, with the Industrial Revolution. But, as I discussed in Chapter 3, in the beginning, things got worse for some.

Different definitions of poverty: absolute vs. relative poverty

Today, few people in the rich countries, such as the US or Germany, suffer from absolute poverty. But we still talk about poverty in those countries, because every society has certain standards of consumption which are considered necessary to maintain 'decency'.

This view dates back to Adam Smith, who argued that things become necessities when it becomes 'indecent for creditable people, even of the lowest order, to be without'. So, in a famous example, he argued that a linen shirt is 'not a necessary of life' but 'in the present times, through the greater part of Europe, a creditable day-labourer would be ashamed to appear in public without a linen shirt, the want of which would be supposed to denote that disgraceful degree of poverty'.

This notion of poverty is known as that of **relative poverty**. Using this notion of poverty, today most countries have their own national **poverty line**, which is usually set around some proportion (usually 50–60 per cent) of median (rather than average) income. For example, in 2012, the US government set the poverty line at $23,050 for a family of four.

Defined in this way, relative poverty is inherently related to inequality. It is possible for a country to have no absolute poverty, even if it is very unequal, if it is sufficiently rich. In such a country, however, relative poverty will be high.

Different dimensions of poverty: income poverty vs. multidimensional poverty

So far, we have defined poverty – absolute or relative – only in terms of income, but we can also talk of what is known as **multidimensional poverty**. This is to reflect the fact that some people may have – just – enough income to eat sufficiently and clothe themselves but may have no or little access to things like education and health care. There is no agreement on what should be included in this measure, but this measure naturally increases the number of people living in poverty.

Measuring the extent of poverty: head count or poverty gap

Having established the poverty line – whether absolute or relative, whether income-based or multidimensional – we can tell how many people fall below that line. This is known as the **head count measure of poverty**.

The obvious shortcoming of the head count measure is that it does not distinguish between people who are just below the poverty line and those that fall well below it. Thus some economists measure the **poverty gap**, by weighing each poor person by the distance he/she falls short of the poverty line. This measure obviously requires more information than simple head count, so it is less easily available.

Whichever measure we use, snapshot pictures of poverty, at a given point of time, may not give us the full picture, as many people fall in and out of poverty. So, in the long run, many more people experience poverty than poverty figures measured at any given point of time suggest. Those who are in poverty all or most of their lives are said to be in 'chronic poverty'.

What is wrong with poor people?: causes of poverty

Starting from Disney animations that we watch as young children telling us that if we believe in ourselves, we can achieve anything, we are bombarded with the message that individuals, and they alone, are responsible for what they get in their lives. We are persuaded to accept what I call the L'Oréal principle – if some people are paid tens of millions of pounds per year, it must be because they are 'worth it'. The implication is that, if people are poor, it must be because they are either not good enough or not trying hard enough.

Individuals are in the end responsible for what they make out of their lives. Even if they are from broadly the same backgrounds, different people end up in different positions because they have different talents in different things and make different levels and types of efforts. It will be silly to blame everything on the 'environment' or luck. Attempts to suppress the effects of individual talents and efforts too much, as in the former socialist countries, can create societies that are ostensibly equal but fundamentally unfair, as I discussed above. There are, however, causes of poverty that are 'structural' in the sense that they are beyond the control of the individual concerned.

Inadequate childhood nutrition, lack of learning stimulus and sub-par schools (frequently found in poor neighbourhoods) restrict the development of poor children, diminishing their future prospects. Parents may have some control over how much nutrition and learning stimulus their children get – and some poor parents, to their credit, make great efforts and provide more of those things than do other parents in similar situations – but there is a limit to what they can do. They are by definition under great financial stress. Many of them are totally exhausted from juggling two or three insecure jobs. And most of them had a poor childhood and poor education themselves.

All of this means that poor children start the race of life already weighed down by sandbags on their legs. Unless there are social measures to at least partially compensate for these disadvantages (e.g., income support for poor parents, subsidized childcare, greater investments in schools in poor areas), those children won't be able to fully realize their innate potentials.

Even when they overcome childhood deprivation and aspire to climb the social ladder, people from poorer backgrounds are likely to meet more obstacles. Lack of personal connections and cultural gap with the elite often mean that people from underprivileged backgrounds are unfairly discriminated in hiring and in promotion. If those people also happen to have other 'wrong' characteristics – in terms of gender, race, caste, religion, sexual orientation and what not – they will have an even harder time to get a fair chance to demonstrate their abilities.

Rigged markets

With these disadvantages, the poor find it difficult to win the race even in the fairest of markets. But markets are routinely rigged in favour of the rich, as we have seen from a series of recent scandals surrounding deliberate misselling of financial products and the lies told to the regulators.

Money gives the super-rich the power even to rewrite the basic rules of the game by – let's not mince our words – legally and illegally buying up politicians and political offices (more on this in Chapter 11). Many deregulations of the financial and the labour markets, as well as tax cuts for the rich, have been the results of such money politics.

REAL-LIFE NUMBERS

1.4 billion people live in absolute poverty – most of them citizens of middle-income countries

At the moment, the international (absolute) poverty line is set at PPP $1.25 per day. People below this line are seen as having such little income that they are unable to reach the critical minimum even in terms of nutrition. This is the definition of poverty that is used when Oxfam campaigns to 'make poverty history' or when the world leaders pledge to 'eradicate extreme poverty and hunger', as the United Nations' first Millennium Development Goals declare.

Translated into yearly income, this is PPP $456, which means that the average PPP incomes in the world's three poorest countries in PPP terms (the DRC, Liberia and Burundi) are below this line.

Currently, around 1.4 billion people – or about one in five people in the world – live with less than $1.25 per day. The number goes up to around 1.7 billion people, or one in four people in the world, if we adopt the multidimensional definition of poverty.

One counterintuitive fact is that most poor people do *not* live in the poorest countries. Over 70 per cent of people in absolute poverty actually live in middle-income countries. As of the mid-2000s, over 170 million people in China (around 13 per cent of its population) and 450 million people in India (around 42 per cent of its population) lived with incomes below the international poverty line.

Poverty according to national poverty lines can
be anything between 5 and 80 per cent

In terms of relative poverty, we can talk about poverty rates in countries according to each country's official poverty line.

In the rich countries, the proportion of people living under the national poverty line – known as the **poverty rate** – ranges between 5–6 per cent (Ireland, France and Austria) and 20 per cent (Portugal and Spain).

In many poor countries, the majority of the population is below the national poverty line, which is invariably higher than the PPP $1.25 threshold. In some countries, the poverty rate according to the national poverty line could reach up to 80 per cent. The poverty rate in Haiti is 77 per cent according to the World Bank and 80 per cent according to the CIA (a surprisingly good source of economic statistics!).

The poverty rate figures based on national poverty line, however, cannot be directly compared across countries, because some countries set their poverty lines more generously than others.

According to its national poverty line, the latest available poverty rate in Canada was 9.4 per cent, while that in Denmark was 13.4 per cent. However, if you look at the OECD statistics, which adopt a 'universal' (relative) poverty line, defined as the proportion of population living with less than 50 per cent of median household income in each country (after taxes and transfers), Denmark has a much less serious poverty problem than Canada does (a poverty rate of 6.0 per cent against Canada's 11.9 per cent).

Actually, of the OECD member countries with more than $20,000 per capita income in 2011, Denmark had the lowest poverty rates, followed by Iceland, Luxembourg and Finland. The ones with the highest poverty rates were Israel (20.9 per cent), followed by the US, Japan and Spain.*

---

* Poverty rates were 6.4 per cent in Iceland, 7.2 per cent in Luxembourg and 7.3 per cent in Finland. They were 17.4 per cent in the US, 16.0 per cent in Japan and 15.4 per cent in Spain.

Concluding Remarks: Why Poverty and Inequality Are Not Beyond Human Control

Poverty and inequality are disturbingly widespread. One in five people in the world still live in absolute poverty. Even in a number of rich countries, such as the US and Japan, one in six people live in (relative) poverty. Outside a handful of countries in Europe, income inequality ranges between serious and shocking.

Far too many people accept poverty and inequality as inevitable results of natural differences in abilities among individuals. We are told to live with these realities in the way we live with earthquakes and volcanoes. But, as we have seen in this chapter, these things are subject to human intervention.

Given the high inequality in many poor countries, absolute poverty (and relative poverty) can be reduced without an increase in output, if there is appropriate redistribution of income. In the longer run, however, a significant reduction of absolute poverty requires economic development, as has been shown by China in the recent period.

The rich countries may have virtually got rid of absolute poverty, but some of them suffer from high incidences of relative poverty and high inequality. The fact that (relative) poverty rates (5–20 per cent) and Gini coefficients (0.2–0.5) vary wildly among these countries suggests that the more unequal and poverty-ridden rich countries, such as the US, can significantly reduce inequality and poverty through public intervention.

Who ends up being poor also depends a lot on public intervention. Even to allow poor individuals to get out of poverty through their own efforts, we need to provide more equal childhood conditions (through better welfare provision and education), improve access to jobs by poor people (by reducing discrimination and 'clubbiness' at the top) and prevent the rich and the powerful from rigging markets.

In pre-industrial Korea, they used to say that 'even the almighty king cannot do anything about poverty'. This is not true any more, if it ever was. The world now produces enough to eliminate absolute poverty. Even without worldwide income redistribution, all countries except the poorest produce enough to do so. Inequality will always be present, but with appropriate policies, we can live in very equal societies, as many Norwegians, Finns, Swedes and Danes can tell you.

Further Reading

A. BANERJEE AND E. DUFLO
Poor Economics (London: Penguin Books, 2012).

D. HULME
Global Poverty: How Global Governance Is Failing the Poor (London: Routledge, 2010).

B. MILANOVIC
The Haves and the Have-Nots (New York: Basic Books, 2011).

A. SEN
Development as Freedom (Oxford: Oxford University Press, 2001).

J. STIGLITZ
The Price of Inequality (London: Allen Lane, 2012).

D. STUCKLER AND S. BASU
The Body Economic: Why Austerity Kills (London: Basic Books, 2013).

R. WILKINSON AND K. PICKETT
The Spirit Level: Why Equal Societies Almost Always Do Better (London: Allen Lane, 2009).

CHAPTER 10

I've Known a Few People Who've Worked

WORK AND UNEMPLOYMENT

'*Lady Glossop*: Do you work, Mr Wooster?

Bertie: What, work, as in honest toil, you mean?

Lady Glossop: Yes.

Bertie: Hewing the wood and drawing the old wet stuff and so forth?

Lady Glossop: Quite.

Bertie: Well, I've known a few people who've worked. Absolutely swear by it, some of them.'

JEEVES AND WOOSTER, BBC SERIES, SEASON 1, EPISODE 1, 'JEEVES' ARRIVAL'

Work

Work as the defining condition of humanity

For Bertie Wooster – the kind-hearted but clueless aristocratic dandy (played by a young Hugh Laurie of *House* fame) in the 1980s BBC TV adaptation of P. G. Wodehouse's classic *Jeeves and Wooster* novels – work is what other people do. However, except for a tiny minority of idle rich, or the **leisure class,*** like him, work has been the defining condition of humanity throughout most of its history.

Until the nineteenth century, most people in today's rich Western countries typically worked seventy to eighty hours a week, with some people working over 100 hours. Since they often (not always) had the Sunday morning off for church attendance, this meant that they were working at least eleven hours, and possibly up to sixteen hours, per day, except on Sundays.

Today, few work that long even in poor countries. The average working week ranges between thirty-five and fifty-five hours. Even so, the majority of the adult population spends around half of their waking hours at work (more, if we add the time for commuting), outside weekends and paid holidays.

---

* The term has become famous in economics thanks to *The Theory of the Leisure Class* by Thorstein Veblen (whom we met in Chapter 4), a savage critique of what he called *conspicuous consumption* (consumption to show off one's wealth, rather than for the pleasure of it).

The dog that didn't bark: the curious absence of work in economics

Despite its overwhelming presence in our lives, work is a relatively minor subject in economics. The only major mention of work is, somewhat curiously, in terms of its absence – unemployment.

Insofar as work is discussed, it is basically treated as a means to get income. We are seen to value income or leisure, but not work in and of itself. In the dominant Neoclassical view, we put up with the disutility from work only because we can derive utility from things we can buy with the resulting income. In this framework, we work only up to the point where the disutility from an additional unit of work is equalized with the utility that we can derive from the additional income from it.

But for most people, work is a lot more than simply a means to earn income. When we spend so much time on it, what happens in the workplace affects our physiological and psychological well-being. It may even shape our very selves.

Many have worked – and are still working – with
their basic human rights violated

For many people, work is about basic human rights – or, rather, the lack of them. For much of human history, huge numbers of people were deprived of the most basic human right of 'self-ownership' and were bought and sold as commodities – that is, as slaves.

After the abolition of slavery in the nineteenth century, around 1.5 million Indians, Chinese (the 'coolies') and even Japanese went overseas as **indentured labourers** to replace the slaves. People like V. S. Naipaul, the Indian-Trinidadian novelist who was the 2001 winner of the Nobel Prize in Literature, Yat-sen Chang, the Chinese-Cuban ballerino at the English National Ballet, and Vijay Singh, the Indian-Fijian golfer, are reminders of this history.

Indentured labour was not slavery, in the sense that the worker was not owned by the employer. But an indentured labourer had no freedom to change jobs and had only minimal rights during the contract period (three to ten years). In many cases, their working conditions were scarcely better than those of the slaves whom they came to replace; many were put in the exact same barracks that the slaves used to live in.

But we shouldn't make the mistake of thinking this is all in the past.

There are still a lot of people whose work is founded upon the violation of their fundamental human rights. There may be few legal slaves, but still a lot of people are engaged in other forms of **forced labour**. Some of them would have been coerced into those jobs (that is, trafficked). Others may have voluntarily signed up for them initially, but they may be prevented from leaving their jobs, due to either violence (most common among domestic workers) or debts to the employer, artificially inflated by over-charging on their recruitment, travel, food or accommodation. Some international migrant workers toil under conditions similar to the indentured labourers of the late nineteenth and the early twentieth centuries.

How work shapes us

Even when it does not involve violation of basic human rights, work can so fundamentally affect us that it really 'forms' us.

Nowhere is this more evident than in relation to **child labour**.* When children work in adult jobs, their mental and physical developments are arrested. Thus, by working from a young age, individuals may not fulfil their potential to the full.

Work forms adults too. Adam Smith, while praising the positive productivity effects of the finer division of labour (see Chapter 2), was concerned that excessive division of labour might cripple the worker's mental capacity. This point was later hilariously but poignantly depicted in Charlie Chaplin's classic movie *Modern Times*, in which he plays a worker who, having been reduced to performing simple repetitive tasks at high speed, has a mental breakdown and runs amok.

Work can also form us positively. People who like their jobs often have a greater sense of self-fulfilment. It is well understood that factory work, compared to work in shops or even agricultural work, makes workers more politically aware and disciplined because of its very nature – a large number of people working in a closely connected and synchronized way in a confined and organized space.

---

* The ILO defines child labour as children under the age of fifteen (or twelve, for some jobs) doing jobs that hamper their physical development and education, thereby excluding cases such as children helping with domestic chores or doing paper rounds.

Work affects our physical, intellectual and
psychological well-being

Even when it does not affect us so deeply that it actually 'forms' us, work greatly affects our well-being in physical, intellectual and psychological terms.

Some jobs are more physically demanding, dangerous and harmful for health than others. Working longer makes people more tired and harms their health in the long run.

There are jobs – crafts, arts, design, teaching, research, etc. – that are often considered more intellectually interesting, thanks to their higher creative contents.

The psychological dimension relates to the employer–employee relationship, rather than to the physical or intellectual nature of the work per se. Even if the job is identical, those who are provided with fewer breaks during work, put under excessive pressure to perform or made to feel insecure are less happy than their counterparts working for more decent employers.

'Working as long as one wishes': labour
standards vs. free choice

If people's welfare can be so dramatically affected by what happens at their work, then it is going to be affected hugely by the **labour standards** we set in relation to things like the length of working hours, safety at work or job security.

Many economists are against such standards – especially if they are imposed through government regulation, rather than through employers' 'codes of conduct' or through voluntary agreements with trade unions. However 'excessively long' or 'overly dangerous' some jobs may appear, they argue, we have to accept them as they are, insofar as they have been taken by free workers with full mental faculties. If a worker has taken a 'bad' job, these economists argue, it is because he has concluded that the 'bad' conditions he has to put up with are more than compensated by the wage he gets. Indeed, it was exactly on these grounds that in 1905 the US Supreme Court declared (in the Lochner vs. New York case) that a ten-hour restriction on the working hours for bakery workers introduced by the New York state was unconstitutional, as it 'deprived the bakers of the liberty of working as long as they wished'.[1]

This is, in itself, not an unreasonable argument. If someone freely chooses to do something, it must, by definition, mean that that person prefers that to other options. But the question we need to ask is whether that choice was made under conditions that ought to be – and can be – changed. Most workers who willingly take 'bad' jobs do so because the alternative is starvation. Perhaps there is very high unemployment, and they cannot find any other job. Perhaps they are not attractive to any other employer because they are physically stunted or illiterate due to childhood deprivation. Perhaps they are migrants from rural areas who have lost everything in a flood and thus are desperate for work – any work. But can we really call choices made under such circumstances 'free'? Aren't these people acting under compulsion – of having to eat?

In this context, we should bear in mind what the Brazilian archbishop of Olinda and Recife, Dom Hélder Câmara, a leading figure of the left-wing Catholic 'liberation theology' especially popular in Latin America between the 1950s and the 1970s, said: 'When I give food to the poor, they call me a saint. When I ask why the poor have no food, they call me a Communist.' Perhaps we should all be a bit of a 'Communist' and question whether the underlying conditions that make the poor so desperate to voluntarily sign up for 'bad' jobs are acceptable.*

REAL-LIFE NUMBERS
Forced labour

The ILO estimates that, as of 2012, around 21 million people in the world are engaged in forced labour. This is only 0.6 per cent of the estimated global workforce of 3.3 billion (or 0.3 per cent of the world population), but it is still too high by 0.6 per cent points.

According to the ILO, the frequency of forced labour is the highest in the former socialist countries in Europe and in the former Soviet Union (0.42 per cent of the population) and Africa (0.40 per cent). Even in the rich countries, 0.15 per cent of the population is estimated to be engaged in forced labour.[2]

---

* This point is discussed in the 'Unrealistic individuals, over-acceptance of the status quo and neglect of production: limitations of the Neoclassical school' section in Chapter 4.

Child labour

The ILO also estimates that there are 123 million child labourers, aged between five and fourteen, around the world – equivalent to 3.7 per cent of the global workforce. However, this is only the global picture, and in a number of the poorest countries around half the children are believed to be child labourers. Guinea Bissau (57 per cent) tops the list, followed by Ethiopia (53 per cent) and then by the Central African Republic, Chad, Sierra Leone and Togo (all at 47 per cent or 48 per cent). Most other countries with very high incidences of child labour (say, over 30 per cent) are in Africa. But some of them are in Asia (Cambodia 39 per cent, Nepal 34 per cent) and Latin America (Peru 34 per cent).

The ratio of child labour is obviously related to the country's poverty but is *not* determined by it. The child labour ratio in Burundi is 19 per cent, despite the country having the lowest per capita income in the world in 2010. This is only around half the level found in Peru, whose per capita income in the same year, at $4,710, was nearly thirty times higher. For another example, in the 1960s, South Korea, despite being one of the poorest countries in the world at the time, virtually eliminated child labour for children under twelve by making primary education compulsory and enforcing it with determination. These examples show that poverty is not an excuse for the prevalence of child labour, although it may limit the extent to, and the speed at, which you can reduce it.

People in poor countries work much longer than those in rich countries

In most rich countries, people work around thirty-five hours per week, although the working week is considerably longer in the East Asian countries (Japan, forty-two hours; Korea, forty-four hours; Singapore, forty-six hours).[3] People in those countries are working half, or even less than half, the length of the time that their great-grandparents or great-great-grandparents worked (seventy to eighty hours per week).

In today's poorer countries, people do not work as long as people at comparable levels of income did in today's rich countries in the eighteenth and nineteenth centuries, but they work much longer than their modern-day counterparts in rich countries. Some of them can work up to fifty-five hours per week on average, as in Egypt (fifty-five to fifty-six hours) and

Peru (fifty-three to fifty-four hours). Average weekly working hours are also long – forty-five to fifty hours – in countries such as, in alphabetical order, Bangladesh, Colombia, Costa Rica, India, Malaysia, Mexico, Paraguay, Sri Lanka, Thailand and Turkey.

These numbers underestimate the time we are occupied with work (as opposed to actually 'at' work). In countries with poor public transport and sprawled-out living spaces, the long hours spent by people commuting to and back from work can severely reduce their welfare. In South Africa, you can spend up to six hours a day simply commuting, if you are a poor black worker living in one of the far-flung black townships and working in one of the still mostly white cities. On another front, the increasing use of the internet in business has forced many white-collar workers to work outside the traditional working hours.

Drought or flood?: uneven distribution of working hours

When looking at the data regarding working hours, we have to bear in mind that all these numbers are averages. In many countries, some people are working excessively long hours (the ILO defines this as above forty-eight hours per week), which exposes them to potential health risks. Others are in **time-related underemployment**; that is, they are working part-time even when they want to work full-time, as many people have done since the outbreak of the 2008 global financial crisis. In developing countries, many people are in **disguised unemployment** in the sense that they have a job that adds very little, if anything at all, to output and mainly acts as a way to get some income. Examples include rural people working on an over-crowded family farm and those poor people in the **informal sector** (the collection of unregistered small – often one-person – businesses) 'inventing' jobs so that they can beg without appearing to beg (more on these later). These people 'cannot afford to be unemployed', as the saying goes.

The proportion of the workforce working excessively long hours is the highest in Indonesia (51 per cent) and Korea (50 per cent), with countries such as Thailand, Pakistan and Ethiopia all having proportions over 40 per cent. The proportions are the lowest in Russia (3 per cent), Moldova (5 per cent), Norway (5 per cent) and the Netherlands (7 per cent).

How long people really work: paid vacations and annual hours of work

These weekly working hours, however, do not provide us with the full picture. In some countries, people work every week of the year, while in others they can have several weeks of paid vacation; in France and Germany, paid vacations can be as many as five working weeks (twenty-five working days) per year. Thus we need to look at annual working hours to get the full picture of how much people work in different countries.

Such data exist only for the OECD member countries. Of these, the ones with the shortest annual working hours are, as of 2011, the Netherlands, Germany, Norway and France.[4] At the other extreme, the longest working hours are found in South Korea, Greece, the US and Italy.[5] The OECD data set also includes a number of countries that cannot be considered rich. In one of these countries – Mexico (2,250 hours) – the yearly working hours are longer than those in South Korea (2,090 hours).[6] Chile, another developing country member of the OECD, at 2,047 hours per year, is between Korea and Greece (2,039 hours).

Who are the 'lazy' ones?: the myths and the realities of working hours

These numbers reveal that the cultural stereotypes of which people work hard and which don't are often completely wrong.

Mexicans, seen as the archetypal 'lazy Latinos' in the US, actually work longer than the 'worker ant' Koreans. Recall that the Latin American countries are very strongly represented in the above-mentioned list of countries with longest working weeks (five out of twelve). It is simply not true that the Latin Americans are laid-back people who do not work hard, as the stereotype goes.

In the ongoing Eurozone crisis, the Greeks have been vilified as lazy 'spongers' living off hard-working Northerners. But they have longer working hours than every country in the rich world apart from South Korea. The Greeks actually work 1.4 and 1.5 times longer than the supposedly workaholic Germans and Dutch. Italians also defy the myth of 'lazy Mediterranean types' by working as long as the Americans and 1.25 times longer than their German neighbours.

Why are harder-working people poorer?

One explanation for these misperceptions is that they are sometimes based on hopelessly out-dated information. Take the case of the Dutch, whose stereotypical image is that of hard-working, penny-pinching Puritans. However, this stereotype is based on information that is out-dated at least by fifty and possibly eighty years. Between the 1870s and the 1920s, the Netherlands indeed did have among the longest working hours of today's rich countries, but this started changing in the 1930s and radically changed after the 1960s, since when it has become the 'laziest' country in the world – that is, the country with the shortest annual working hours in the world.

Another explanation for the faulty stereotypes is that people often mistakenly believe that poverty is the result of laziness and thus automatically assume that people in poorer countries are lazier.[7] But what makes those people poor is their low productivity, which is rarely their own fault. What is most important in determining national productivity is the capital equipment, technologies, infrastructure and institutions that a country has, which are really things that the poor themselves cannot provide. So, if anyone is to blame, it is the rich and the powerful in countries such as Greece and Mexico, who have control over those determinants of productivity but have done a poor job in delivering them in sufficient quantity and quality.

The hazard of work: industrial accidents and job insecurity

As for the quality of work, there are no good indicators of the intellectual dimension, but we can at least get some indicators for the physical and the psychological dimensions.

In terms of the physical dimension of quality of work, the most readily available indicator is the rate of fatal injuries at work (usually measured per 100,000 workers). Countries such as, in alphabetical order, Australia, Finland, Norway, Sweden, Switzerland and the UK offer the safest work environment – only one or two of their workers out of 100,000 die every year from workplace injuries. The corresponding ratio is in the region of thirty to forty in El Salvador and India and around twenty in Ethiopia and Turkey. The rates in most other developing countries for which data are available (they often are not) range between ten and fifteen.

The most readily available indicators of the psychological aspects of work are, as I mentioned, those related to job security.[8] There is no single agreed way to measure job security, but the most reliable measure is probably the share of employees with less than six months' tenure, published by the OECD for its member countries. According to this, as of 2013, Turkish workers have the least job security (at 26 per cent), followed by those in Korea (24 per cent) and Mexico (21 per cent). According to this measure, workers in Greece, Slovakia and Luxembourg have the securest jobs (all around 5 per cent).

Unemployment

Giacomo should remain unemployed for the greater good:
how we have become used to high unemployment

In 2009, I met Giovanni Dosi, the eminent Italian industrial economist, at a conference. He related a story that a friend of his had experienced in the city of Bolzano in Alto Adige, the German-speaking part of Italy. Knowing that it is a very prosperous town, Giovanni's friend (not an Italian) casually asked his taxi driver how many unemployed people he knows. The driver shocked him by saying that there was only one unemployed person in the whole town – a certain Giacomo. Giovanni's friend protested – even though the town had only about 100,000 people, it seemed impossible that there was only one unemployed person. Disagreeing, the cab driver pulled up at a taxi rank and asked other drivers to back him up. After a short impromptu conference, the other cabbies not only confirmed their colleague's assertion but also added that they thought Giacomo should remain unemployed for the greater good – if he got a job, they explained, the government job centre would have to be shut down and its four employees made redundant.

Perhaps the cabbies of Bolzano were taking the mickey out of a foreigner. Perhaps they were telling the truth. But the point of this story is that we have become so used to high unemployment in the last three decades that we find it shocking to hear that a society can exist with virtually no unemployment, even though it is only a small city.

However, there was a time – during the Golden Age – when many developed capitalist countries had very low unemployment. They strived to have none and sometimes very nearly succeeded; in the early 1970s, there were less than ten unemployed people in the Swiss city of Geneva (population of around 200,000 at the time). Exceptional the Golden Age may have been, but it still shows that full employment can be achieved. There is nothing 'inevitable' about unemployment.

Individual costs of unemployment: economic
hardship, loss of dignity and depression

Even if you are unemployed, you may be just about OK financially if you live in one of those European countries where **unemployment benefits** (that is, pay-outs from unemployment insurance) are 60–75 per cent of previous wages for up to two years. But they are exceptions on a global scale. In the US, they give only 30–40 per cent of your previous salary (depending on the state you live in). In most developing countries, it is non-existent.

Unemployment is about dignity too. Kurt Vonnegut, the American writer, in his 1952 classic novel *Player Piano*, depicts a world in which no one has to do any manual work. Machines now do all of that; in his story, those machines run on instruction sheets like the ones you feed into the player piano, which gives the book the title. Despite not wanting in their basic material needs and having all the leisure time in the world, people of that world, except a tiny minority of engineers and managers, are actually desperately unhappy – they have been deprived of the dignity they derived from being useful members of the society.

Unemployment also has significant negative health, especially mental health, effects. The combination of economic hardship and loss of dignity makes unemployed people more depressed and more likely to commit suicide.[9]

Social costs of unemployment: waste of resources,
social decay and skills erosion

Unemployment is a huge waste of resources from a social point of view. It creates a situation in which some people are unable to find a job while there are machines lying around idle.

Long-term unemployment concentrated in certain regions can lead to social decay and urban degeneration. Some areas of the American 'rust belt' and the Northern (formerly) industrial areas of the UK still have not fully recovered from the consequences of high unemployment in the late 1970s and 1980s.

If people remain unemployed for long, their skills become out-dated and their confidence is eroded, making them less productive in the future. As long-term unemployment (say, over a year) dramatically reduces a worker's chance of re-employment, those workers get into a vicious circle of ever-falling employability and ever-lengthening periods of unemployment.

People in between jobs: frictional unemployment

There are quite a few different types of unemployment – at least five of them, as I shall discuss below.

First of all, there is unemployment that happens 'naturally'. Jobs appear and disappear as companies are born, grow, shrink and die. Workers decide to change their jobs for various reasons; they may have grown dissatisfied with their current job or they decide to move to another town, say, to take care of elderly parents who cannot take care of themselves any more or to live with a new partner. So it is natural that people move in and out of jobs.

The trouble is that this process is not instantaneous. It takes time for people to search for new jobs and for companies to find the right people. The result is that some people end up spending some time unemployed in the process. This is known as **frictional unemployment**.

Some skills are not wanted any more: technological unemployment

Then there is unemployment due to the mismatch between the types of workers demanded and the available workers. This is usually known as **technological unemployment** or **structural unemployment**. This is unemployment that we have seen in movies like *Roger and Me*, the first movie made by Michael Moore, in which he documents the consequence of the closure of a GM car factory in his town, Flint, Michigan, or in *The Full Monty*, in which six unemployed steel workers in Sheffield, UK, after a draining period of unemployment, launch themselves as a male stripper group.

According to standard economic theory, these workers could have acquired skills in 'sunrise' industries and moved to other areas – the electronics industry in California and investment banking in London would have been, respectively, the obvious alternatives. In reality, smooth transitions almost never happen, if you leave things to the market alone. Even with systematic government subsidies and institutional supports for retraining and relocation (e.g., a bridging loan to buy a house where the new job is before the current one is sold), as used in the Scandinavian countries, it is a struggle to eliminate technological unemployment.

Governments and unions create unemployment: political unemployment

Believing in the modern version of Say's Law, many Neoclassical economists have argued that, except in the short run, the law of supply and demand ensures that everyone who wants to work will find a job at the going wage rates. If some people are unemployed, these economists argue, it is because something – the government or trade unions – is preventing them from accepting the wage rates that will clear the market.

Some workers in the rich countries refuse to accept the going wage rate and remain unemployed because they can live on government welfare payments. Trade unions make it impossible for the wage rate to go down. At the same time, government labour market regulations (e.g., minimum wages, brakes on firing, requirements for severance payments) and employment taxes, such as employers' social security contribution, all make workers more expensive than they really should be. This reduces the incentive on the part of employers to hire them. The result is higher unemployment.

In that it is due to the interferences of 'political' entities like the government or trade unions, this type of unemployment may be called **political unemployment**. The solution offered is to make the labour market more 'flexible' through measures like the reduction in trade union power, the abolition of minimum wages and the minimization of worker protection against dismissal.

There may not be enough demand: cyclical unemployment

As we talked about when discussing Keynes in Chapter 4, there are instances of involuntary unemployment that arise from deficiencies in the aggregate demand, as during the Great Depression or in today's Great Recession, as the aftermath of the 2008 global financial crisis is often called. For such unemployment, known as **cyclical unemployment**, the above-mentioned supply-side solutions, such as lowering wages or retraining workers with redundant skills, are powerless.

The main solution to cyclical unemployment is to boost demand through government deficit spending and loose monetary policy (such as the lowering of interest rates) until the private sector recovers and starts creating enough new jobs.*

Capitalism needs unemployment: systemic unemployment

While the Keynesians see unemployment as a cyclical thing, many economists – from Karl Marx to Joseph Stiglitz (in his 'efficiency wage' model) – have argued that unemployment is something that is inherent to capitalism.

This view starts from the obvious but important observation that, unlike machines, workers have minds of their own. This means that they can control how much effort they put in when they work. Naturally, capitalists have tried their best to minimize such control by introducing minute and easily observable tasks and/or introducing the conveyor belt, whose speed workers cannot control. Even so, there is some discretion left on the part of the worker over their **labour process**, and the capitalist somehow needs to make sure that the worker puts in the maximum amount of effort – or does not 'shirk', as some would put it.

The best way to impose such discipline on workers, according to this argument, is to make job loss costly to them by raising their wages above the market rate – if workers can get another job with equal pay easily, they will not be afraid of the threat of being fired. However, since all capitalists do the same, the result is that the overall wage rate is pushed above the 'market-clearing' level and unemployment is created.

It is on the basis of this reasoning that Marx called the unemployed workers the **reserve army of labour**, who can be called upon any time if the hired workers become too unwieldy. It is on this ground that Michal Kalecki (1899–1970), the Polish economist who invented Keynes's theory of effective demand before Keynes, argued that full employment is incompatible with capitalism. We might call this form of unemployment **systemic unemployment**.

---

* The Keynesian theory says that at that point the government should tighten its fiscal and monetary policies, lest the economy overheats and generates too much inflation.

*Different types of unemployment co-exist in different
combinations in different contexts*

All these different types of unemployment are real and can co-exist. Sometimes one type will be prominent while another may become so in other circumstances.

A lot of unemployment in the US and Europe in the 1980s was 'technological' in the sense that it was caused by the decline of a wide range of industries due to competition from East Asia. 'Systemic' unemployment, as its name suggests, has always been an integral part of capitalism, but it was virtually eliminated in Western Europe and Japan during the Golden Age. Today, a lot of countries are suffering from 'cyclical' unemployment due to demand deficiencies, while it was not significant in the boom years of the mid-2000s. 'Political' unemployment does exist, even though its extent is often exaggerated by the free-market orthodoxy.

*Who can work, who wants to work, and who works?:
defining and measuring unemployment*

How do we measure unemployment in practice? The most apparent method may be to count the number of people in a country's population who are not working. However, this is actually *not* how we define and measure unemployment in practice.

There are some people who are too young or too old to work. So we consider only the **working-age population** when we calculate unemployment. All countries exclude children from the working-age population, but the definition of children differs across countries; fifteen is the most frequently used threshold, but it could be as low as five (India and Nepal).[10] Some countries also exclude old people from the working-age population; the most frequently used threshold ages are sixty-four and seventy-four, but it could be as low as sixty-three or as high as seventy-nine.

Even among those who belong to the working-age population, not everyone who is not working is counted as unemployed. Some of them, such as students or those who are engaged in unpaid household work or care work for their family or friends, may not want a paid job. In order to be classified as unemployed, the person should have been 'actively seeking work', which is defined as having applied for paid jobs in the recent past – usually in the preceding four weeks. When you subtract those who are not actively seeking work from your working-age population, you get the **economically active population**. Only those who are economically active (that is, actively seeking paid jobs) but are not working are counted as unemployed.

This definition of unemployment, known as the ILO definition, is used by all countries (with minor modifications), but is not without serious problems. One is that 'working' is defined rather generously as doing more than an hour's paid work per week. Another is that, by requiring that people should have actively looked for work to be counted as unemployed, it excludes the so-called **discouraged workers** (people who have given up looking for work due to repeated failures in their job applications, even though they still want to work) from the unemployment statistics.[11]

REAL-LIFE NUMBERS

Unemployment rates in the rich countries have risen a lot since the Golden Age

During the Golden Age, unemployment rates in Japan and the Western European countries were 1–2 per cent, compared to 3–10 per cent typically found in the periods before that. In countries like Switzerland, West Germany and the Netherlands, it was often less than 1 per cent. The US, with 3–5 per cent unemployment rate, was then considered a high-unemployment country.

After the Golden Age, people in rich countries have become used to unemployment rates of 5–10 per cent, even though some countries, notably Japan, Switzerland, the Netherlands and Norway, have maintained low unemployment rates, at 2–4 per cent.

Following the 2008 global financial crisis, unemployment rates have risen in most rich countries. In the US, the UK and Sweden it rose quite substantially: from around 6 per cent to around 9–10 per cent. Five years after the crisis, their unemployment rates are still around 7–8 per cent. Some people claim that the 'real' rate of unemployment in the US could easily be 15 per cent, if we include the discouraged workers and those in time-related under-employment.

In the 'periphery' countries of the Eurozone, which were particularly hard hit by the 2008 crisis, the unemployment situation ranges from catastrophic to grim. In Greece and Spain the unemployment rate has risen from around 8 per cent before the crisis to 28 per cent and 26 per cent respectively, with youth (aged fifteen to twenty-four)unemployment rates over 55 per cent. The unemployment problem is also serious in Portugal (18 per cent) and Ireland (14 per cent).

Difficulty of defining unemployment in developing
countries: under-employment and low productivity

Unemployment rates in developing countries are much less straightforward to define and measure. The main source of the problem is that many people in developing countries are working according to the standard definition (one hour of paid work in one week) but may be 'under-employed' in the sense that they have a lot of idle periods during their work and/or are adding little to the economy's output.

In the poorest parts of the world, 50–60 per cent of people work in agriculture; the average for Sub-Saharan Africa is 62 per cent, and that for South Asia is 51 per cent. Most of them work on family farms, even though they may be adding little to output, as that is the only way they can lay claim to an income. It is debatable whether those people should be treated as employed, when removing them from their family farms would reduce the output by very little, if at all.

Outside the agricultural sector, there are a lot of people who are working too few hours (say, under thirty hours per week) *against their wishes*. They are in time-related under-employment. The ILO estimates that the proportion of the workforce in such a situation could be as high as 15–20 per cent in some developing countries. In these countries, the unemployment rate would easily rise by 5–6 percentage points if we converted those people to full-time equivalents.

Even when they work long hours, many people in poor countries are working in marginal jobs in the informal sector that add very little to the social output. It is because they cannot afford 'not to work'. Some of these jobs can only be described as 'invented'. These are people who catch doors for others entering an upmarket building, sell chewing gums that no one really wants and provide an unsolicited car-windscreen wash at a traffic junction – all in the hope that some kind souls may toss them some change. Whether to count all these people as employed or unemployed is a moot point.

Unemployment in developing countries

Bearing in mind that these figures need to be interpreted with utmost caution, let us look at the unemployment figures for developing countries.

Over the last decade or so, the highest-unemployment country in the developing world, according to the ILO, has been South Africa, with unemployment rates usually above 25 per cent and sometimes going over 30 per cent. It is closely followed by Botswana and Namibia (around 20 per cent). Other high-unemployment countries include Albania, the Dominican Republic, Ethiopia and Tunisia (15–20 per cent).

Medium-high unemployment is found in countries like Colombia, Jamaica, Morocco, Uruguay and Venezuela (10–15 per cent). We can classify countries like Brazil, El Salvador, Indonesia, Mauritius, Pakistan, Paraguay and Sri Lanka as medium-low-unemployment countries (5–10 per cent).

Some developing countries have very low unemployment according to the ILO data, ranging from 1 per cent to 5 per cent. These include Bangladesh, Bolivia, China, Guatemala, Malaysia, Mexico and Thailand.

Concluding Remarks: Taking Work Seriously

Work is the most dominant aspect of life for the majority of people. Even when they are officially classified as 'not working', such as homemakers, most adults work – often very long hours in hard conditions. In the poorer developing countries even a lot of children work. In those countries, people are so desperate that they often 'invent' jobs in order to survive.

Despite all this, in most economic discussions, people are mainly conceptualized as consumers, rather than workers. Especially in the dominant Neoclassical economic theory, we are seen as working ultimately to consume. Insofar as work is discussed, it ends at the factory gate, or shop entrance, so to speak. No intrinsic value of work is recognized, whether it is creative pleasure, sense of fulfilment or the feeling of dignity that comes from being 'useful' to society.

The reality is that what happens at work affects workers immeasurably, especially in the poorer countries, where many people are engaged in jobs that deprive them of their basic human rights, put them in physical danger and stunt their future developments (in the case of child labour). Even in the richer countries, what happens at work can make people fulfilled, bored, valued or stressed. At the deepest level work shapes who we are.

Work gets more attention when it is absent – that is, when there is unemployment. But even unemployment has not been taken seriously enough in the sense that it is accepted as something inevitable. Full employment – once the most important, and often achieved, policy goal in the advanced capitalist countries – is considered to be something unachievable and thus irrelevant. The human costs of unemployment – economic hardship, depression, humiliation and even suicide – are hardly recognized.

All of this has serious consequences for the way in which our economy and society is run. Work is seen as an inconvenience that we have to endure in order to get income, and we are seen as being purely driven by our desire to consume with that income. Especially in the rich countries, such consumerist mentality has led to waste, shopping addiction and unsustainable household debts, while making it more difficult to reduce carbon emission and fight climate change. The neglect of work means that deteriorating working conditions are accepted regardless of their impacts on workers' physical and mental well-being, as far as they are accompanied by rising wages. High unemployment is considered a relatively minor problem despite its enormous human costs, while a slight rise in inflation is treated as if it is a national disaster.

Work has become the embarrassing mad uncle of economics that we pretend does not exist. However, without taking work more seriously, we cannot build a more balanced economy and a more fulfilled society.

Further Reading

H. BRAVERMAN
Labour and Monopoly Capital: The Degradation of Work in the Twentieth Century (New York: Monthly Review Press, 1974).

B. EHRENREICH
Nickel and Dimed: On (Not) Getting By in America (London: Granta, 2002).

J. HUMPHRIES
Childhood and Child Labour in the British Industrial Revolution (Cambridge: Cambridge University Press, 2010).

S. LEE, D. MCCANN AND J. MESSENGER
Working Time Around the World: Trends in Working Hours, Laws and Policies in a Global Comparative Perspective (London: Routledge, 2007).

K. MARX
Capital (Harmondsworth: Penguin, 1976), vol. 1, chapter 15.

U. PAGANO
Work and Welfare in Economic Theory (Oxford: Blackwell, 1985).

G. STANDING
The Precariat: The New Dangerous Class (London: Bloomsbury Academic, 2011).

J. TREVITHICK
Involuntary Unemployment: Macroeconomics from a Keynesian Point of View (New York and London: Harvester Wheatsheaf, 1992).

CHAPTER 11

Leviathan or the Philosopher King?

THE ROLE OF THE STATE

'Government exists to protect us from each other. Where government has gone beyond its limits is in deciding to protect us from ourselves.'
RONALD REAGAN

'The proof that the state is a creation of nature and prior to the individual is that the individual, when isolated, is not self-sufficing; and therefore he is like a part in relation to the whole.'
ARISTOTLE

The State and Economics

Political economy: a more 'honest' name?

In the old days, no country had a Ministry of Defence. They all had a Ministry of War because, well, war is what it really does. Patents used to be called patent monopolies, as they were (and still are) artificially created monopolies, even though they may be socially useful. So there you have it. Sometimes, an old, forgotten name conveys the essence of the thing it is describing much better than the modern one does.

The same goes for the old name of economics – political economy, or the study of *political* management of the economy. In this day and age, when economics has become the 'science of everything', one can easily get the impression that government economic policy is really not particularly central to economics. However, much of economics is still about actions by the state, or the government – or recommendations against them.* And indeed even those economists who try to sell economics as a science of everything by showing that 'economic' (rational) decision is everywhere are – at least unwittingly – contributing to the debate on the role of the state in the economy. When they show that people behave rationally even in the most unlikely areas of life – family life, sumo wrestling and what not – they are saying that, in plain terms, people know what is good for them and how to achieve it. The implication is that they should be left alone: no paternalistic

---

* Many people use the term 'the state' as something broader than 'the government' and something akin to 'the country'. This distinction has good philosophical and political justifications. But, for the purpose of this book, the two terms can be used interchangeably.

government telling people what to do, believing that it knows what is good for them.

Of course, no serious economic theory says that the government should be abolished altogether. But there is a huge spectrum of opinion on the appropriate role of the state. At one end of the spectrum, we have the free-market view, which wants no more than the minimal state that provides military defence, protection of property rights and infrastructure (like roads and ports). At the other end, we have the Marxist view, which believes that markets should be marginalized – or even abolished altogether – and the whole economy coordinated through central planning by the state.

Once we depart from these two extreme views, the possible permutations of exactly what the government should or should not do become mind-bogglingly numerous. Indeed, even those who want the 'extreme' solutions of the minimal state or central planning cannot quite agree amongst themselves on, respectively, what exactly the minimal state should do or to what degree of detail the economy should be planned.

The Morality of State Intervention

The state cannot be above individuals: the contractarian view

A perennial theme in the debate on the role of the state is a moral one – whether the state has the right to tell individuals what to do.

Most economists these days believe in **individualism**, namely, the view that there can be no higher authority than individuals. In its purest form, this philosophical stance leads to the view that the government is a product of a **social contract** between sovereign individuals and thus cannot be *above* individuals. In this view, known as **contractarianism**, a state action can be justified only when every individual gives his/her consent.

'Nasty, brutish, and short': Thomas Hobbes and
the original contractarian argument

There are different theories of social contract, but the currently most influential version is based on the ideas of the seventeenth-century English political philosopher Thomas Hobbes. In his famous 1651 book, *Leviathan*, named after the biblical sea monster, Hobbes starts by presuming a 'state of nature', in which free individuals existed without a government. In that world, Hobbes argued, individuals were engaged in what he called the 'war of all against all', and as a result their lives were 'solitary, poor, nasty, brutish, and short'. In order to overcome this state of affairs, individuals voluntarily agreed to accept certain restrictions on their freedom imposed by a government so that they could have social peace.

Modern contractarian, or libertarian, argument on the role of the state

Hobbes himself actually used this theory to justify absolute monarchy. He advocated a total submission by individuals to the monarch's authority, which is justified by its ability to elevate humanity out of its state of nature. However, the philosopher Robert Nozick, the economist James Buchanan, the winner of the 1986 Nobel Prize in Economics, and other modern advocates of contractarianism have developed Hobbes's ideas in a different direction and advanced a political philosophy to justify the minimal state. In this pro-free-market version of contractarianism, more commonly known as **libertarianism** in the US, Leviathan came to depict the state as a potential monster that needs to be restrained (which is *not* what Hobbes intended). This view is best summed up in Ronald Reagan's comment that 'Government exists to protect us from each other. Where government has gone beyond its limits is in deciding to protect us from ourselves.'

According to the libertarians, any state intervention without the *unanimous* consent of all individuals in society is illegitimate. Therefore, the only justified actions of the government are things like provision of law and order (especially the protection of property rights), national defence and supply of infrastructure. These are services that are absolutely necessary for a functioning market economy to exist and thus whose provision by the state would be accepted by all individuals (were they to be asked). Anything beyond these minimal functions – whether it is minimum wage legislation, the welfare state or tariff protection – is seen as violating the sovereignty of individuals and thus the first step on 'the road to serfdom', as the title of Friedrich von Hayek's famous 1944 book goes.

The modern contractarian, or libertarian, philosophical position has to be taken seriously. Once you begin to believe that the state is 'above' its citizens, it becomes very easy to demand sacrifices by a minority for the 'greater good', arbitrarily defined by those who control the state. Indeed, the world has suffered from too many political rulers believing that they know what is good for everyone else – from Pol Pot and Stalin on the left to Pinochet and Hitler on the right – and imposing their views, often through violent means. Asserting that the state is not above its citizens is a very important defence of individuals against the abuse of power by the state, or, rather, by those who control the state machinery.

The contractarian argument exaggerates individuals' independence from society

Nevertheless, the contractarian position also has some important limitations. To begin with, it is based on a fictional, rather than real, history, as Buchanan and Nozick themselves readily admit. Human beings have never existed as free-contracting individuals in a 'state of nature' but have always lived as members of some society (for further discussions, see the section on the 'embedded individual' in Chapter 5). The very idea of the free-standing individual is a product of capitalism, which emerged well after the state.

Thus seen, by basing their theory on a fictitious history, the contractarians have vastly exaggerated individuals' independence from society and underestimated the legitimacy of collective entities, especially (but not exclusively) the state.

Market Failures

Markets may fail to produce socially optimal outcomes – this is known as market failure. I have already discussed the basic idea behind the concept in Chapter 4, using the case of externality. But here we investigate it in greater depth, as it gives us very important analytical tools to explore different roles that the state may play.

Some goods have to be collectively provided: public goods

Many goods (and services) are **private goods** in the sense that, once I pay for it – say, an apple or a holiday – only I can consume it. However, there are some goods whose use by non-payers cannot be prevented, once they are supplied. Such goods (and services) are known as **public goods**. The existence of public goods is arguably the most frequently cited type of market failure, even more than externality, the original market failure.

Classic examples of public goods include roads, bridges, lighthouses, flood defence systems and other infrastructure. If you can drive on a road without having paid for its construction, why should you, as a car owner, volunteer to pay up when someone is trying to raise money to build one? A lighthouse cannot selectively block its light from your ship because you have not contributed to its construction and upkeep, so you, as a ship owner, can let others pay for it and still enjoy its service.

In other words, if you can **free-ride** on other people to pay for a public good, you don't have the incentive to voluntarily pay for it. But if everyone thinks the same way, no one will pay for it, which means that the good is not going to be provided at all. At most, it may be provided in sub-optimal quantities by large consumers who would rather let some people free-ride on them than not have the good at all. A big company dominating an area may build a road and let other people use it for free, as the cost of not having a good road may be too high for its business. Even in this case, however, the road capacity will be determined by the company's needs, rather than by those of the society, and thus sub-optimal from the social point of view.

It is therefore widely accepted that public goods can be supplied in optimal quantities only if the government taxes all potential users (which often means all citizens and residents) and uses the proceeds either to provide them itself or to pay some supplier to provide them.

Most public goods are 'public' for political reasons:
relatively few goods have to be public goods

It is important to note that there are actually relatively few goods that *have to be* public goods. There are, of course, some goods from whose use it is impossible (or at least absurdly expensive) to exclude the non-payers. National defence is a classic example. It is impossible to fight a war in a way that only protects those who have paid for 'defence service'. Flood defence system is another example. You just cannot selectively flood the houses of those who have not paid for the construction of the system. But, in many cases, public goods are public goods only because we decide them to be so. Many 'public goods' that are financed by taxes and provided by the government can easily be turned into private goods. We can introduce tollbooths to roads and bridges, as many countries do. These days, it is even technically possible to replace lighthouses with radio signal services that can be provided only to the payers. Despite this, many governments provide a wide range of goods and services for (good and bad) political reasons.

Small numbers of suppliers lead to social inefficiency: imperfect competition

More controversially, many economists talk of market failure when there is monopoly or oligopoly – states of affairs collectively known as **imperfect competition** in Neoclassical economics.

In a market with a lot of competitors, producers do not have the freedom to set the price, as a rival can always undercut them until the point where lowering the price further will result in a loss. But a monopolistic or oligopolistic firm has the market power to decide – fully in the case of the former and partly in the case of the latter – the price it charges by varying the quantity it produces, as I explained in Chapter 2. In the case of oligopoly, the firms can form cartels and behave as if they are a monopoly, which allows them to charge the higher, monopoly, price.

However, according to Neoclassical economics, it is not the transfer of extra profit from consumers to the firms with market power that is considered to be a market failure. The failure is due to the social loss that even the firms with market power cannot appropriate – known as **allocative deadweight loss**.*

Break up, nationalize or regulate?: dealing with imperfect competition

If a market is dominated by firms with market power, it is argued, the government may try to reduce the deadweight loss by reducing their market power.

The most drastic of such measures is to break up the firm(s) with market power and thus increase competition in the market. The US government actually did this in 1984 with AT&T, the telephone service giant, which was divided into seven 'Baby Bells'. More usually, the government can ban

---

* When a firm has market power, the profit-maximizing level of output is lower than the socially optimal one, which is where the maximum price that a consumer is willing to pay is the same as the minimum price that the producer requires in order not to lose money. When the amount produced is less than the socially optimal quantity, it means *not* serving some consumers who are perfectly willing to pay more than the minimum price that the producer requires but who are unwilling to bear the price at which the firm can maximize its profit. The unfulfilled desire of those neglected consumers is the allocative deadweight loss, which is the social cost of monopoly and oligopoly.

oligopolistic firms from forming cartels and colluding in setting their prices. It can also keep the price in such a market down to a level as close as possible to what would have prevailed under perfect competition.

The case of **natural monopoly** – which is found in industries like electricity, water, gas and railways – poses a unique challenge. In these industries, having multiple suppliers each with their own networks of, say, water pipes or railways, increases the production cost so much that monopoly is the most cost-efficient arrangement. In such a case, the government may set up an SOE and run it as if it is *not* a monopoly. Alternatively, the government may allow monopoly by a private-sector firm but regulate its pricing behaviour, making it set its price equal to costs per unit (or **average costs**).*

*Compared to the cases of public goods or externality, the case of
market failure due to imperfect competition is more controversial*

Few economists would dispute that public goods and externalities cause market failure, although they may dispute the actual extents of those phenomena. When it comes to imperfect competition, however, the case is far more controversial.

As I discussed in Chapter 4, the Schumpeterians and the Austrians denounce the state of perfect competition, which the Neoclassical economists idealize, as a state of economic stasis, where there is no innovation. When the lure of (temporary) monopoly profit is exactly what motivates firms to innovate, clamping down on – or even breaking up – monopolies will reduce innovation and bring about technological stagnation. In what Schumpeter calls the 'gales of creative destruction', they argue, no monopoly is safe in the long run; General Motors, IBM, Xerox, Kodak, Microsoft, Sony, BlackBerry, Nokia and many other companies that once had near-monopoly of their respective markets and had been considered invincible have lost such positions and even disappeared into the dustbin of history, as in the case of Kodak.[1]

---

* Costs here include 'normal return', namely, the return that the firm's owners would have got from investing in other non-monopoly industries.

What constitutes a market failure depends on
your theory of how markets work

I have just shown that the same market dominated by a monopoly can be seen as a most successful one by one school of economics (the Schumpeterian school or the Austrian school) and as a case of most abject failure by another (the Neoclassical school). The case of monopoly may be the most extreme example, but throughout the book we have seen many cases in which some schools see a market success where others see a market failure. For example, I have pointed out that a Neoclassical economist might praise free trade for allowing all nations to maximize their incomes, *given* their resources and productive capabilities, but a developmentalist economist might criticize it for preventing more backward economies from *changing* their productive capabilities and thus maximizing their incomes in the long run.

The point is that what constitutes a market failure – and thus a justification for government action – depends on your theory of how markets work. Given this, if different economic theories have different views on how markets work or fail to work, we cannot make a balanced judgement on the role of the state without knowing a whole gamut of relevant economic theories. This point strengthens the case for a pluralistic approach to economics that I have made in Chapter 4.

Government Failure

The fact that a market is failing, some free-market economists rightly point out, does not necessarily mean that we will be better off with government intervention. These economists, such as Anne Krueger, James Buchanan and Alan Peacock and their followers, criticize the market failure argument for uncritically assuming that the state is a modern reincarnation of Plato's 'philosopher king' – benevolent, all knowing and all powerful. They point out that real-world governments are not like the ideal and may not be able to – or, worse, may not even want to – correct for market failures. According to this argument, known as the government failure argument or sometimes the public choice theory, the costs of government failure are usually higher than those of market failures. Thus, it is usually better to accept a failing market than to have the government intervene and mess things up even more.

Dictators, politicians, bureaucrats and interest groups: the government – or rather those who control it – may not even want to promote the greater good

The government failure argument cites a number of reasons as to why a government may not even *want to* implement the 'right' policies, even if it could.

In some cases, the government is controlled by a dictator who is interested not in citizens' welfare but in their own personal enrichment. Mobutu Sese Seko (Zaire, 1965–97) and Ferdinand Marcos (the Philippines, 1965–86) are the classic examples. These 'predatory states' or, rather, the strongmen who control them – are squeezing the economy through taxation and bribery, with disastrous long-term consequences.

In a democracy, the government is controlled by politicians whose primary goal is to gain and retain power, rather than promote public interests. They will consequently implement policies that maximize their chances in elections – increasing government spending without simultaneously increasing revenues, for example. In an electoral system based on constituencies rather than party lists, politicians will try to channel public finances to projects that develop their own constituencies, even when they create waste from the national point of view; this is why, for example, many countries have more airports and sports stadiums than they really need.

Even if politicians somehow choose the right policies, they may not be properly implemented because bureaucrats who run them have their own agendas. They will design policies in such a way that serves themselves rather than the electorate – inflating their departmental budgets, minimizing their efforts, reducing cooperation with other departments in order to defend their own 'turf' and so on. This theory is known as that of 'self-seeking bureaucrats'. If you want to see it in action, watch the BBC TV classic *Yes, Minister* and its sequel, *Yes, Prime Minister*, with the legendary South African actor Nigel Hawthorne (of *The Madness of King George* fame) playing the suave and devious mandarin Sir Humphrey Appleby.

Last but not least, there is lobbying from various interest groups – bankers lobbying for more lenient financial regulation, industrialists asking for increased trade protection, trade unions pushing for higher minimum wages, whatever the consequences, respectively, for national financial stability, consumer prices or unemployment. Sometimes those interest groups do not simply lobby but effectively take over the very government agencies that are supposed to regulate them – this is known as the theory of 'regulatory capture'. For example, reflecting the strength of the US financial industry, during the last thirty-two years (between Ronald Reagan's first presidency, 1981–5, and Barack Obama's first, 2009–13), six out of the ten holders of the US treasury secretary position (collectively in office for 21.5 years) had worked in the financial industry.[2] Two of them – Robert Rubin and Hank Paulson – had worked for one firm, Goldman Sachs.

The common point in all these theories is that the government is controlled and influenced by individuals who are like all other individuals – they are selfish. It is naive, if not exactly delusional, to expect them to put public interests before their own.

The government may not be able to correct for market failures, even if it wants to, due to asymmetric information and resource constraints

In addition to questioning the motives of the government – or, rather, of those who control the government – the government failure argument questions whether it is even capable of correcting for market failures, even in the unlikely case of it genuinely wanting to improve social welfare.

Government policies may fail due to asymmetric information. Asymmetric information, to remind you, means that a party in an interaction may know more about the activity that it is engaged in than does the other party. The government, for example, may continue infant industry protection for an industry because its lobbyists say that the industry has failed to 'grow up' due to bad luck, rather than a lack of effort to enhance productivity. Even when it has overcome the informational problem and somehow designed a good policy, the government, especially in poor countries, may simply lack the human and financial resources to properly implement it.

Depoliticization: rid the market of politics

When the intention and the ability of the government are suspect, the government failure argument emphasizes, letting the government intervene in the name of correcting for market failure may actually make things worse. Markets may fail, but governments almost always fail even more, is the conclusion.

The solution offered is to rid the market of politics – or, in fancier words, the **depoliticization of the economy**. To achieve this, the argument goes, the government should be shrunk to the minimum by cutting its spending (and thus taxes), deregulating markets and privatizing SOEs. In those few areas in which we still need the government, such as the provision of monetary stability or the regulation of natural monopolies, the policy process should be insulated from politics by granting political independence to the government agencies that actually do these things. An independent central bank and independent regulatory authorities of natural monopolies (e.g., gas, telecommunications) are the most frequently recommended examples.

Market and Politics

Government failures need to be taken seriously, but with a large pinch of salt

Government failures are real and need to be taken seriously. The government failure argument has done a service to our understanding of the economy by reminding us that real-life governments are not as perfect as the textbook government. Except for the 'predatory state', which is actually quite rare, all the examples of government failures raised by the argument are all around us. However, the government failure argument exaggerates the extent to which governments fail. When you think about it, if what it says is true, it would be a major miracle if there were any decent government at all in this world. In reality, many governments function quite well, while some do even excellently.

One reason is, of course, that politicians, bureaucrats and interest groups are not as selfish as the government failure argument depicts. There are many examples in real life of politicians striving to promote national interests rather than their chances of election, bureaucrats working in the spirit of public service rather than to have a cushy life and interest groups holding back their sectional interests for the greater good. On top of that, there are ways to control self-seeking behaviours of people in public life, ranging from the promotion of public service ethics to the introduction of rules on bribery and other corrupt practices (e.g., nepotism in hiring). True, these rules can be – and have been – circumvented or even perverted, as the government failure argument points out. But the fact that those rules are not perfect does not mean that they are totally ineffective. Imperfect they may be, but the fact is that we have the standards of public life that we have today in large part because of those rules.[3]

The proposal to depoliticize is anti-democratic

Given the possibility of government failure, it sounds like a great idea to depoliticize the economy by rolling back the state and giving political independence to essential agencies like the central bank. But what is this 'politics' whose influence we are recommended to curtail? In democratic countries, it is the influence of the people. Markets run according to the 'one-dollar-one-vote' rule, while democratic politics run on the principle of 'one-person-one-vote'. Thus, the proposal for greater depoliticization of the economy in a democracy is in the end an anti-democratic project that wants to give more power in the running of the society to those with more money.

There isn't a single 'scientific' way to draw the boundary between market and politics

The government failure argument asserts that economics, or the logic of the market, should trump politics – and indeed other domains of life, such as arts, academia and so on. This argument is these days so widely accepted that most people take it for granted. But it is a seriously flawed argument.

First of all – and this is a point that seems obvious to non-economists but that many economists find difficult to accept – there is no reason why the market logic should prevail over other domains of life. We do not live by bread alone.

Moreover, the argument is based on the implicit assumption that there is one correct, 'scientific' way of deciding what should belong in the domain of the market and what should belong in the domain of politics. For example, the proponents of the government failure argument say that things like minimum-wage legislation or tariff protection for infant industries are intrusions of 'political' logic into the sacrosanct sphere of the market logic. But there are economic theories that justify such policies. Given this, what these economists are doing is, in effect, labelling other economic theories as 'political', and therefore lesser, arguments while claiming that their own economic theory is somehow the right economic theory – or even 'the' economic theory.

The White Witch and the Deeper Magic: the
ultimate impossibility of depoliticization

Even if we accepted that the economic theory that the proponents of the government failure argument adopt is the 'correct' one, it is not possible to draw a clear boundary between economics and politics. This is because the very boundary of the market is in the end determined by politics and not by an economic theory – of whatever variety.

Before we even begin market transactions, we need (explicit and implicit) rules on what can be traded, who can trade them and how they can be traded in the market. All of these rules are restrictive in some ways, and therefore no market is genuinely 'free'.* And these ground rules cannot be determined by economic logic. There is no 'scientific' list of what should (or shouldn't) be bought and sold in the market. The decision is a political one.

All societies keep certain things off the market – human beings (slavery), human organs, child labour, firearms, public offices, health care, qualifications to practise medicine, human blood, educational certificates and so on. But there is no 'economic' reason why any of these should not be bought and sold in markets. Indeed, all of them are or were legal objects of market transactions in different times and places.

At the other end of the spectrum, we have made certain things into objects of market transaction that had not been so before. Before the introduction of the laws to protect patents, copyrights and trademarks in the eighteenth and the nineteenth centuries, 'ideas' (intellectual property) were not traded in markets. Today we buy and sell the rights to pollute ('carbon trading') or bets on notional economic variables (e.g., derivatives based on stock market index or on inflation rate), but these things did not even exist until one or two generations ago.

The government also sets the basic rules regarding what economic actors can and cannot do even within the domain of the market. False advertising, sales based on misleading information, insider trading† and other practices are all prohibited. Regulations regarding minimum wages, workplace health and safety and working hours set boundaries on how firms can treat

---

* This is what I meant when I declared that 'there is no such thing as a free market' in the first chapter (Thing 1) of my book, *23 Things They Don't Tell You about Capitalism*.

† This refers to the trading of shares of publicly listed corporations by individuals who have exclusive access to internal information about those corporations.

workers. Emission standards, carbon quotas and noise pollution controls regulate how firms may produce their outputs. And so on.

So politics is creating, shaping and reshaping markets before any transaction can begin. It is like the 'Deeper Magic' that had existed before the dawn of time, which is known to Aslan (the Lion) but not to the White Witch in *The Lion, The Witch, and The Wardrobe*, the children's classic by C. S. Lewis.

What Governments Do

These days, the government produces a huge range of goods and services – defence, law and order, infrastructure, education, research, health, pensions, unemployment benefits, childcare, care for the elderly, income support for poor people and cultural services (e.g., upkeep of museums and national monuments, subsidies to the national movie industry). The list is endless. Most governments also own SOEs that produce goods and services that private firms produce in other countries – electricity, oil, steel, semiconductors, banking, airline services and so on.

In order to do all this, the government hires a lot of people and spends a lot of money to purchase inputs, ranging from pencils to nuclear reactors. The salaries of government employees and the material inputs are paid for by taxes and other sources of government revenue. Taxes include personal income tax, corporate income tax (tax on incomes of companies), property tax, value added tax (or sales tax), tax on specified goods (e.g., alcohol, petrol) and so on. Other sources of revenue include dividends from SOEs, interest payments from financial assets that it owns and, in the case of developing countries, transfers from rich countries (foreign aid).

The government also transfers a lot of money from one part of the economy to another; it taxes some people and uses the proceeds to subsidize other people. Social welfare payments are the most important of government-mediated transfers. But they also include subsidies for particular types of production activities (e.g., agriculture, infant industries, declining industries) and investments (e.g., R&D by private-sector firms, energy-saving refurbishment of houses).

In addition to direct production, spending and transfers, the government sometimes uses its sheer weight to affect the level of activity in the economy. This is known as **fiscal policy**. Simply by spending more (or less) or taxing less (or more), regardless of the exact content of that spending and taxation, it can boost (or dampen) the economy. Using its monopoly over note issue, it conducts **monetary policy**, through the central bank, by varying interest rates or changing the amount of money in circulation, thus affecting the level of economic activity.

REAL-LIFE NUMBERS

The size of the government, measured by government expenditure as a proportion of GDP, has grown a lot in the last century and a half

Until the nineteenth century, governments were quite small everywhere, as they did relatively few things. In 1880, among countries for which the data are available, the biggest government was that of France, whose expenditure was equivalent to 15 per cent of national output. In the UK and the US, government expenditure was equivalent to 10 per cent of GDP. The Swedish one was only 6 per cent.[4]

Over the last century and a half, with the requirements of the modern economy, governments have grown a lot in size. Even in developing countries that tend to have a smaller government than do the rich countries, government expenditure typically is equivalent to 15–25 per cent of GDP.* The figure is 30–55 per cent for the rich countries, with an average of around 45 per cent (the OECD average in 2009). At the lower end of the distribution (30–40 per cent) are, in ascending order, Korea, Switzerland, Australia and Japan. At the other end (over 55 per cent) are, in descending order, Denmark, Finland, France, Sweden and Belgium. In the middle are the US and New Zealand (over 40 per cent), Germany and Norway (around 45 per cent) and the Netherlands and the UK (around 50 per cent).[5]

A lot of government expenditure is transfer, rather than own consumption or investment

Now, note that a lot of government expenditure is not consumed or invested by the government itself. It involves transfer of money from one part of the economy to another, especially social protection programmes,

---

* Exceptions include Myanmar (10 per cent) at the lower end and Mongolia and Burundi at the higher end (over 40 per cent).

such as income support for the poor and unemployment benefits. Therefore, when you calculate GDP you need to count the transfer elements out.

Transfer payments are equivalent to between 10 per cent and 25 per cent of GDP in the rich countries. So, for example, a government whose total expenditure is equivalent to 55 per cent of GDP may actually account for only 30 per cent of GDP, if the transfer payments it makes are equivalent to 25 per cent of GDP.

Transfer in the form of social spending is much lower in developing countries, so the gap between government expenditure as a proportion of GDP and the share of GDP produced by the government is much smaller in those countries. According to the World Bank data, social spending ranges from practically zero (e.g., Paraguay, the Philippines) to 4–5 per cent of GDP (e.g., Mauritius, Ethiopia) in most developing countries.

Despite the fact that it makes the government look bigger than it really is in GDP terms, most people still use the expenditure data (rather than value-added data) as the indicator of how important the government is in a country's economy. This may be justified on the grounds that something being a transfer does *not* mean that it has no effect. It is well known that, positively or negatively, social spending programmes affect people's attitudes and behaviours in terms of savings, retirement and work. They may even encourage people to take greater risk in terms of career choice, entrepreneurial activity and willingness to change jobs, by providing them with a 'safety net' – one famous slogan of the Swedish Social Democratic Party is 'secure people dare'.

The influence of the government cannot be fully captured by numbers

In no area of human life can numbers fully capture the reality. There are always aspects that are difficult to quantify, and, moreover, all numbers are constructed on the bases of particular theories, which by definition focus on some aspects of the reality while ignoring others, including quantifiable ones (recall the exclusion of household work in the construction of GDP).

But this problem is more serious in relation to the government because it is an actor that is uniquely endowed with the power to set rules that constrain and compel others. Regardless of the size of its budget or the number of SOEs it has, it can exert a strong influence on the rest of the economy if it sets a lot of rules and has the power to enforce them.

This is not an esoteric theoretical quibble. Until the 1980s, many people believed that the 'miracle' economies of East Asia, such as Japan, Taiwan or Korea, were paragons of free-market policies on the grounds that they had small governments (measured by their budget). However, being small did not mean that these governments were following a laissez-faire approach. During the 'miracle' years, they exercised a huge influence on the evolution of their economies through economic planning, regulation and other directive measures. By looking at only the budgetary numbers, people had come to seriously misunderstand the true nature and significance of the government in these countries.

Concluding Remarks: Economics Is a Political Argument

In the run-up to the US presidential election in 2000, there was an opinion poll, reported in the *Financial Times*, that asked people not just which candidate they supported but also why they didn't support the other candidate. Most frequently cited as the reason for not supporting 'the other guy', both by the Bush supporters and the Gore supporters, was that he was 'too political'.

Were those Americans seriously suggesting that they wanted to elect someone who wasn't good at politics for the biggest political office in the world? Of course not. They were saying those things because 'politics' had become a dirty word and therefore calling a politician 'political' has turned into a powerful way to discredit him or her.

Americans are actually not alone in this. There are some young democracies where politics arouses such passion that elections prompt riots and deaths. But in many other countries, we keep hearing about the lowest ever voter turnout in elections. Political parties are bleeding membership all around. From Imran Khan, the cricket player, in Pakistan to Beppo Grillo, the comedian, in Italy, many politicians come to prominence exactly because they are – how can I put it? – not politicians.

The growing mistrust in politics is partly the politicians' own doing. All around the world, they have done their best to discredit themselves, with Silvio Berlusconi in Italy being the master of the art. However, it has also been crucially promoted by free-market economics. Free-market economists, more specifically the proponents of the government failure argument, have persuaded the rest of the world, including many politicians and bureaucrats themselves, that we cannot trust those who run the government to act in public interests. Therefore, they have told us, the less a government does, the better it is. Even in areas where the government is a 'necessary evil', it should be constrained by rigid rules that politicians cannot mess around with. And this distrust in politics has in turn helped to popularize free-market economics, with its proposals to minimize the influence of politics on the economy.

But this view is based on very problematic theories, as I have explained in this chapter. It is not supported by evidence either. As I have shown throughout the book, virtually all economic success stories have been facilitated, if not necessarily orchestrated, by an active state.

Examples of successful state intervention do not, of course, mean that more government is always better. Real-life governments may not necessarily be the Leviathan of the libertarian discourse, but they are not the modern reincarnation of Plato's Philosopher King either. There are many governments that have harmed the economy, sometimes even disastrously. But the fact remains that the state still remains the most powerful organizational technology that humankind has invented and thus big economic (and social) changes are very difficult to achieve without it.

Further Reading

K. BASU
A Prelude to Political Economy (Oxford: Oxford University Press, 2000).

J. BUCHANAN
Limits of Liberty: Between Anarchy and Leviathan (Chicago: University of Chicago Press, 1975).

H.-J. CHANG AND R. ROWTHORN (EDS.)
The Role of the State in Economic Change (Oxford: Clarendon Press, 1995).

P. EVANS
Embedded Autonomy: States and Industrial Transformation (Princeton, NJ: Princeton University Press, 1995).

J. HARRISS
Depoliticizing Development: The World Bank and Social Capital (London: Anthem, 2002).

C. HAY
Why We Hate Politics (Cambridge: Polity, 2007).

F. VON HAYEK
The Road to Serfdom (London: G. Routledge and Sons, 1944).

P. LINDERT
Growing Public: Social Spending and Economic Growth since the Eighteenth Century (Cambridge: Cambridge University Press, 2004).

M. MAZZUCATO
The Entrepreneurial State: Debunking Public vs. Private Sector Myths (London: Anthem Press, 2013).

'All Things in Prolific Abundance'

THE INTERNATIONAL DIMENSION

International Trade

'Our Celestial Empire possesses all things in prolific
abundance'

In 1792, George III of Britain sent Earl Macartney to China as his special envoy. Macartney was to convince the Chinese emperor, Qianlong, to
allow Britain to freely conduct trade in all of China, not just through Canton
(Guangzhou), which was then the only port open to foreigners. At the time,
Britain was running a large trade deficit with China (so, what's new?) in
large part due to its new-found taste for tea. The British thought that they
might be able to reduce the gap if they could engage in freer trade.

The mission completely failed. Qianlong sent Macartney back with
a letter to George, telling him that the Celestial Empire saw no need to
have more trade with Britain. He reminded the British king that China had
allowed the European nations to trade in Canton only as a 'signal mark of
favour', as 'the tea, silk and porcelain which the Celestial Empire produces,
are absolute necessities to European nations'. Qianlong declared that 'our
Celestial Empire possesses all things in prolific abundance and lacks no
product within its own borders. There was therefore no need to import
the manufactures of outside barbarians in exchange for our own produce.'[1]

As it was not even allowed to *try* to persuade the Chinese customers to
buy more of its manufactured products, Britain resorted to stepping up its
opium exports from India. The resulting spread of opium addiction alarmed
the Chinese government into banning opium trade in 1799. That did not
work, so in 1838 the Daoguang Emperor, Qianlong's grandson, appointed a
new 'drug czar', Lin Zexu, to start a major crackdown on opium smuggling.

In response, the British started the Opium War in 1840, in which China was pulped. Victorious Britain forced China into free trade, including of opium, with the Nanjing Treaty in 1842. A century of external invasions, civil war and national humiliation followed.

David Ricardo challenges the Chinese Emperor – and Adam Smith: comparative vs. absolute advantages

Given China's eventual and ignominious adoption of free trade, people have made fun of Qianlong's view on international trade; this backward despot simply didn't understand that international trade is good. However, Qianlong's view on international trade was actually in line with the mainstream view among European economists, including Adam Smith himself, at the time. His view of trade is known as the theory of **absolute advantage**; the idea that a country does not need to trade with another if it can produce everything more cheaply than can its potential trading partner. Indeed – our common sense tells us – why should it?

But it should – according to the theory of comparative advantage, invented by David Ricardo (see Chapter 4). According to this theory, a country can benefit from international trade with another country, even when it can produce *everything* more cheaply than the other, like China could, compared to Britain, in the late eighteenth century – at least according to Qianlong's view. All that is needed is that it specializes in something in which its superiority is *the greatest*. Likewise, even if a country is rubbish at producing everything, it can benefit from trade if it specializes in things which it is *least* rubbish at. International trade benefits every country involved.

The logic behind the theory of comparative advantage is impeccable – given its assumptions

Since Ricardo invented it in the early nineteenth century, the theory of comparative advantage has provided a powerful argument in favour of free trade and **trade liberalization**, that is, reduction in government restrictions on trade.

The logic is impeccable – that is, insofar as we accept its underlying assumptions. Once we question those assumptions, its validity becomes much more limited. Let me explain this, focusing on two key assumptions behind the Heckscher-Ohlin-Samuelson version of the theory of comparative advantage (henceforth HOS), which we first encountered in Chapter 4 as lying at the heart of the modern argument for free trade.[2]

HOS structurally rules out the most important form of beneficial protectionism by assuming that all countries are equally capable

The most important assumption underlying HOS is that all countries have equal productive capabilities – that is, they can use any technology they want.[3] According to this assumption, the only reason why a country might specialize in one product rather than another is because that product happens to be produced using a technology that is in line with its relative factor endowment – that is, how much capital and labour it has. There is no possibility that the technology might be too difficult for the country (recall the BMW and Guatemala example from Chapter 4).

This totally unrealistic assumption rules out a priori the most important form of beneficial protectionism, namely, infant industry protection, whose key role in the historical development of today's rich countries we discussed in detail throughout the book.

HOS is overly positive about trade liberalization because it assumes that capital and labour can be remoulded for use in any sector at no cost

In HOS, not only is free trade good for the country but moving towards it in countries that have not practised it produces no casualties. When tariffs on, say, steel are reduced, consumers of steel (e.g., car-makers who use steel plates and final consumers of cars) immediately benefit because they can import cheaper steel. This will damage the producers (capitalists and workers) in the domestic steel industry in the short run, as companies lose money due to cheaper imports and workers lose their jobs. But, soon, even they benefit. It is because activities that are more in line with the country's comparative advantage – say, the production of micro-chips or investment banking – will now be relatively more profitable and thus expand. The expanding industries would absorb the capital as well as the labour formerly employed in the steel industry and, thanks to their higher productivities, pay them higher profits and wages. Everyone wins in the end.

But the reality is that most capitalists and workers in the industry that has lost protection remain hurt. Factors of production – capital and labour – are often fixed in their physical qualities; there are few 'general-use' machines or workers with a 'general skill' that can be employed across industries. Blast furnaces from a bankrupt steel mill simply cannot be remoulded into a machine that makes micro-chips and thus may have to be sold as scrap metal. When it comes to the workers, how many steel workers do you know who have retrained to work in the semi-conductor industry or, even more unlikely, in investment banking? (Recall the examples of *Roger and Me* and *The Full Monty* from Chapter 10).

HOS can present such a positive view of trade liberalization because it assumes that all capital and labour are the same ('homogeneous' is the technical term) and thus can be readily redeployed in any activity (technically this is known as the assumption of **perfect factor mobility**).[4]

Even the use of the compensation principle cannot quite hide the fact that a lot of people get hurt by trade liberalization

Even when they acknowledge that trade liberalization may produce losers, free-trade economists justify trade liberalization by invoking the 'compensation principle' (see Chapter 4). They argue that, as trade liberalization makes the whole country better off, the losers from the process can be fully compensated and the winners still have additional income left.

As I mentioned earlier, the trouble with this argument is that the compensation is usually not made. In the rich countries, there is partial – but only partial – compensation through the welfare state, which provides unemployment insurance and access to basic social services, such as education and (except in the US) health care. But in most developing countries the welfare state is very weak and has patchy coverage, so the resulting compensation is minimal, if not non-existent.

If the compensation is not made, invoking the compensation principle to justify a policy that hurts some people, such as trade liberalization, is tantamount to demanding that some people make a sacrifice for the 'greater good' – a demand that used to be made of people by the government in socialist countries, which free-trade economists so heavily criticize.

*International trade is essential, especially for developing
countries, but that is not to say that free trade is the best*

When they hear someone criticizing free trade, free-trade economists tend to accuse the critic of being 'anti-trade'. But criticizing free trade is *not* to oppose trade.

Apart from the benefits of specialization that the theory of comparative advantage extols, international trade can bring many benefits. By providing a bigger market, it allows producers to produce more cheaply, as producing a larger quantity usually lowers your costs (this is known as **economies of scale**). This aspect is especially important for smaller economies, as they will have to produce everything expensively, if they cannot trade and have a bigger market. By increasing competition, international trade can force producers to become more efficient – insofar as they are not developing-country firms that would get wiped out by vastly superior foreign firms. It might also produce innovation by exposing producers to new ideas (e.g., new technologies, new designs, new managerial practices).

International trade is particularly important for developing countries. In order to increase their productive capabilities and thus develop their economies, they need to acquire better technologies. They can in theory invent such technologies themselves, but how many new technologies can relatively backward economies really invent on their own? Perhaps one, such as North Korea's vinalon, which I mentioned in Chapter 7. Perhaps none. For these countries, therefore, it would be madness not to take advantage of all those technologies out there that they can import, whether in the form of machines or **technology licensing** (buying up the permit to use someone else's patented technology) or technical consultancy. But if a developing country wants to import technologies, it needs to export and earn 'hard currencies' (universally accepted currencies, such as the US dollar or the Euro), as no one will accept its money for payments. International trade is therefore essential for economic development.

The case for international trade is indisputable. However, this does *not* mean that free trade is the best form of trade, especially (but not exclusively) for developing countries. When they engage in free trade, developing countries have their chances of developing productive capabilities hampered, as I have pointed out in earlier chapters. The argument that international trade is essential should never be conflated with the argument that free trade is the best way to trade internationally.

How important international trade is for different countries
and how its importance has increased recently

In the early 1960s, international trade, defined as the average of exports and imports, in goods and services used to be equivalent to around 12 per cent of world GDP (average for 1960–64). Thanks to the fact that international trade has grown much faster than has world GDP, the ratio now stands at 29 per cent (average for 2007–11).[5]

Even though the share of trade in a country's GDP has risen in almost all the countries during the last half century, there are considerable international differences in their levels.

Listening to the American media over the last three decades, you might have got the impression that the US is a country that is uniquely suffering from the negative impacts of international trade – first with Japan and now with China. But imports accounted for only 17 per cent of US GDP (2007–11 average), while exports accounted for 13 per cent. Averaging the export/GDP and the import/GDP figures, you get a **trade dependence ratio** of 15 per cent. This is way below the world average of 29 per cent, cited above. Indeed, the US is one of the least trade-dependent countries in the world.

The only other major economy with a lower trade dependence ratio than that of the US is Brazil (12 per cent). Interestingly, Japan, which in popular imagery is the quintessential trade-driven economy, has the same trade dependence as that of the US (15 per cent). Other things (like economic policy) being equal, larger economies tend to be less dependent on trade because they can afford to have a more diversified production structure thanks to their size, which allows them to attain economies of scale in more industries.

At the other extreme, we have small trade-oriented economies like Hong Kong (206 per cent) and Singapore (198 per cent). Such economies not only trade a lot for their own needs because they are small. They also specialize in international trading itself, thus importing certain things only to sell on to others – this is known as 're-exporting'.

Many countries are far more trade-dependent than the
'world average', while only a handful of them are
significantly less so

Given that international trade is equivalent to 29 per cent of world GDP, you could say that countries with a trade dependence ratio close to it have 'average' trade dependence. These include some of the larger developed countries, such as France and Italy, and some very large developing countries, such as India, Indonesia and China.

Many countries have a trade dependence ratio that is well above average (say, above 60 per cent). This group includes some small rich countries (e.g., the Netherlands and Belgium), several oil-exporting countries (e.g., Angola and Saudi Arabia) and developing countries that have deliberately promoted manufactured exports through policy measures (e.g., Malaysia and Thailand).

Changing structure of international trade: the (exaggerated)
rise of services trade and the rise of manufacturing
trade, especially that from developing countries

Over the last half century, there have been a number of significant structural changes in international trade.

The first is the increase in the importance of services trade. Influenced by the recent media hype about new forms of trade in services – airline back offices, software, reading services for MRI results and what have you – most people have come to form the impression that services trade has been exploding in the recent period. However, the reality falls far short of this image. Services trade as a share of world trade did go up from 17 per cent in the early 1980s (1980–82) to around 20 per cent in the early 1990s. However, since then, it has been fluctuating around that level.[6]

Another, more important, trend has been the rise in the importance of manufacturing trade. According to an unofficial UN report, the share of manufacturing in world merchandise trade used to be 40–45 per cent in the first half of the twentieth century.[7] According to the official UN data (ComTrade database), it rose to 57–60 per cent by the 1960s and then to 61–4 per cent in the 1970s.[8] The dataset from the WTO, starting from 1980, shows the continuation of the trend, even though the exact figures differ from the UN data. In the early 1980s (1980–82 average), manufacturing accounted for 57 per cent of world merchandise trade. The ratio then rose and peaked at 78 per cent in the late 1990s (1998–2000 average). It has fallen since then and currently stands at 69 per cent (2009–11 average).[9]

What this means is that the rise in the importance of manufacturing trade has been far more significant – or even dramatic – than that of services trade. This is yet another piece of evidence that we are not (at least yet) living in a post-industrial knowledge economy (see Chapter 7).

The third notable structural change in international trade is the fact that developing countries have increased their shares in international manufacturing trade significantly from around 9 per cent in the mid-1980s to around 28 per cent today.[10] This rise has been in large part propelled by the rapid development of export-oriented manufacturing industries in China. China used to account for only 0.8 per cent of world manufacturing export in 1980, but by 2012 the share had risen to 16.8 per cent.

Balance of Payments

Balance of payments is a statement that shows how much a country is in debt or credit in which areas of its economic transactions with the rest of the world. As with any financial statement, it is boring stuff. But it is important that you know which items are in it, what they mean and what the numbers look like in reality, if you are to understand an economy's international position, so please bear with me for a few pages.

Trade balance (or balance of trade)

Trade involves not only the movements of goods and services but also the flows of money that go with them. When a country imports more goods and services than it exports, it is said to have a trade deficit, or a negative trade balance. When it exports more than it imports, it is said to have a trade surplus, or a positive trade balance.

Current account and capital-financial account balances

How do countries with trade deficits manage? Don't they have to find the money to pay for the import bills that are over and above their export earnings? Indeed they do. They can do this in two ways.

One is to earn money in ways other than through international trade (this is called 'income' in the technical language of balance of payments statistics) or to be given money by someone else (this is called 'current transfers').

Income includes compensation of employees and investment income. 'Compensation of employees' in this context is earnings of people working for foreign entities while being resident in the home country, such as Mexican workers commuting to their work in the US. 'Investment income' is income from financial investment abroad, such as dividends from shares of foreign companies owned by a country's residents.

Current transfers include **workers' remittances**, that is, money sent from workers resident abroad (more on this later) and **foreign aid**, namely, grants given by foreign governments.

Balances in trade, income and current transfers make up the **current account balance**. See the box on the following page to see how they add up.

Even after adding up trade, income and current transfers, a country may still have a current account deficit. In this case, it has to either borrow money (that is, run debts) or sell assets it has. The activities on this front are captured in the 'capital and financial account' (CFA), which is more often known simply as **capital account**. CFA is – surprise, surprise – made up of two main components – capital account and financial account.

The capital account is divided into 'capital transfers' (mainly debt forgiveness by foreign countries or, conversely, your country forgiving debts of other countries) and the 'acquisition/disposal of non-financial assets', such as selling and buying patents.

The financial account is mainly made up of portfolio investment, (foreign) direct investment, other investments and reserve assets. **Portfolio investment** refers to the acquisition of financial assets, such as equity (company shares) and debt (including bonds and derivatives). **Foreign direct investment** involves acquisition by a foreign entity of a significant (10 per cent is the convention) proportion of shares in a company, with a view to getting involved in its management.[11] 'Other investments' include trade credits (companies lending money to their buyers by letting them pay for their purchases later) and loans (especially bank loans). 'Reserve assets' include foreign currencies and gold that a country's central bank has. They are often referred to as **foreign exchange reserves**.

BALANCE OF PAYMENTS

(SELECTED MAIN COMPONENTS)

CURRENT ACCOUNT
Trade
 Goods
 Services
Income
 Compensation of employees
 Investment income
Current transfers
 Workers' remittances
 Foreign aid

CAPITAL AND FINANCIAL ACCOUNT
Capital account
 Capital transfers
 Acquisition / disposal of non-financial assets
Financial account
 Portfolio investment
  Equity
  Debt (including bonds and derivatives)
 (Foreign) direct investment
 Other investments (including trade credits and
  bank loans)
 Reserve assets

A country's current account balance and its capital and financial account balance, in theory, should add up to zero, but in practice there are always 'errors and omissions' that make the sum different from zero.

Different items can drive the balance of payments
dynamics in different situations

Changes in the trade account often drive the rest of the balance of payments. A rapidly increasing trade deficit due, say, to a major crop failure or to a sudden and large-scale trade liberalization can make a country accumulate foreign debts and sell its assets. The generation of a large trade surplus due to, say, a surge in the demand of its major mineral export may allow a country to buy assets from abroad, thus creating a deficit on the capital account. But there are also situations in which non-trade components are driving changes in the other components of the balance of payments.

Sometimes the increase in current transfers can drive the balance of payments dynamics. Workers' remittances into a country may suddenly increase because, for example, it has joined the EU and lots of its workers have gone to Germany to work. Or the country may see a sudden increase in foreign aid because, say, it has suddenly become important in the War on Terror – think Pakistan or Djibouti. The increase in the resulting availability of foreign exchange will allow the country to import more goods and services, resulting in the deterioration of its trade balance (that is, its trade surplus will shrink or its trade deficit will widen), even though its current account balance may improve.

On some occasions, it can be the capital account that drives the dynamics. A country may get a sudden surge in the inflows of portfolio investment because it has suddenly become a 'hot' investment destination thanks to, say, the recent election of a pro-business president who is promising a lot of reforms. Or it may experience a big increase in foreign direct investment because, for example, a large oil deposit has been found. But when these happen the demand for the country's currency rises, as people need it in order to be able to buy the country's assets. This will lead to the rise in the value of the country's currency, making their exports uncompetitive and thus increasing trade deficit. In this case, the changes in the capital account have driven the change in the trade account.

REAL-LIFE NUMBERS

Trade deficits and surpluses in some countries are
equivalent to around half of GDP

In most rich countries and middle-income countries, trade balances are likely to be equivalent to a few percentage points of GDP, either positive or negative. For example, in 2010, trade surpluses as a proportion of GDP were 1.2 per cent in Japan, 2.6 per cent in Korea, 3.9 per cent in China, 5.6 per cent in Germany and 6.5 per cent in Hungary. Trade deficits as a proportion of GDP were 1 per cent in Brazil, 2.1 per cent in the UK, 3.5 per cent in the US, 4 per cent in Ecuador and 4.4 per cent in India.

But quite a number of countries have trade balances that are very large as a proportion of their GDPs. In 2010, Brunei had a trade surplus equivalent to 49 per cent of its GDP, while Kuwait had 34 per cent and Luxembourg 32 per cent. Some poor countries with few natural resources to export have very large trade deficits – in 2010, Lesotho had a trade deficit equivalent to 67 per cent of GDP. Trade deficit as a proportion of GDP was also very large (over 40 per cent of GDP) in countries like Liberia, Haiti and Kosovo.[12]

Current account deficits (surpluses) are usually smaller
(bigger) than trade deficits (surpluses)

A country's current account deficit (surplus) is usually smaller (larger) than its trade deficit (surplus), as other items in the current account are likely to reduce (magnify) it.

For the rich countries, investment incomes are typically the items that reduce the deficits (or swell the surpluses) created by the trade component of the current account. In 2010, trade deficit was 3.5 per cent of GDP in the US, but its current account deficit was 3.1 per cent. In France, the figures were, respectively, 2.3 per cent and 1.6 per cent. The German trade surplus in the same year was 5.6 per cent of GDP but its current account surplus was 6.3 per cent.

For the developing countries, the main items that close the gap between trade deficit and current account deficit are foreign aid and, increasingly more importantly, workers' remittances, which these days are around three times foreign aid. In 2010, Haiti had a trade deficit equivalent to 50 per cent of GDP, but its current account deficit was only equivalent to 3 per cent of GDP. This was possible because there was a large amount of current transfers, such as foreign aid (equivalent to 27 per cent of GDP) and remittances (equivalent to 20 per cent of GDP).

Sudden surges in capital inflows and outflows can create serious problems

Sudden surges in capital inflows can lead to a significant increase in deficits on the current account, especially the trade component of it, as I mentioned above. As long as capital keeps flowing in, current account deficits equivalent to, say, several percentage points of GDP, or even higher, might not be a problem.

The trouble is that capital inflow can suddenly fall dramatically or even turn negative; foreigners might, for example, sell assets they own and take the proceeds out. This sudden change can push countries into a financial crisis, as their economic actors suddenly find that the assets they have are worth a lot less than their liabilities.

In the case of developing countries, whose currencies are not accepted in the world market, such a situation will also lead to a foreign exchange crisis, as they now have insufficient means to pay for their imports. The shortage in the supply of foreign exchanges leads to **devaluation** of the local currency, which makes the financial crisis even worse, as the repayment burden for the country's foreign loans would skyrocket in local currency terms.

This is what happened, for example, in Thailand and Malaysia during the 1990s. Between 1991 and 1997, the annual capital account surplus averaged 6.6 per cent and 5.8 per cent of GDP in Thailand and Malaysia respectively. This allowed them to maintain high current account deficits, equivalent to 6.0 per cent and 6.1 per cent of GDP respectively. When the capital flows were reversed – the capital account deficit suddenly surged to 10.2 per cent and 17.4 per cent of their respective GDP in 1998 – they experienced combined financial and foreign exchange crises.

Foreign Direct Investments and Transnational Corporations (TNCs)

Foreign direct investment has become the most dynamic
component in the balance of payments

In the last three decades, foreign direct investment (FDI) has emerged as the most dynamic element in the balance of payments. It has grown faster than international trade, albeit with a much greater fluctuation.

Between 1970 and the mid-1980s, annual global FDI flows (measured in terms of inflows) were equivalent to around 0.5 per cent of world GDP.[13] Since then, its growth accelerated relative to world GDP growth, until it went up to the equivalent of 1.5 per cent of world GDP in 1997. Then there was another acceleration in FDI flow, with the ratio reaching around 2.7 per cent of world GDP on average between 1998 and 2012, although with big fluctuations.[14]

What makes FDI particularly important is the fact that it is not a simple financial flow. It can also directly affect the host (receiving) country's productive capabilities.

FDI affects the productive capabilities of the recipient country

FDI is different from other forms of capital inflows in that it is not a pure financial investment. It being an investment with a view to influencing how a company is run, FDI by definition brings in new management practices. It frequently, although not always, also brings in new technologies. As a result, FDI affects the productive capabilities of the company that is receiving it, whether it is **greenfield** FDI, that is, a foreign company setting up a new subsidiary (like the Intel subsidiary established in Costa Rica in 1997) or it is **brownfield** FDI, that is, a foreign company taking over an existing company (like Daewoo, the Korean carmaker bought by GM in 2002).

The impact of FDI is not confined to the enterprise receiving it. Especially when the gap in productive capabilities between the investing country and the recipient country is large, FDI might have particularly strong indirect influences on the productive capabilities of the rest of the economy. This might happen in a number of ways.

To begin with, there would be 'demonstration effects', in which local producers watch TNC subsidiaries and learn new practices and ideas. Then there is the influence through the supply chain. When they buy from local suppliers, TNC subsidiaries will demand higher standards in product quality and delivery management than do their local counterparts. Local suppliers will have to upgrade themselves if they want to keep the custom of TNC subsidiaries. Then there are effects from the employees of TNC subsidiaries leaving them to join other firms or even to set up their own enterprises.

These workers can teach others how to use new technologies and how to manage the production process in a more efficient way. Collectively, these indirect positive effects of FDI are known as **spill-over effects**.

The evidence for positive effects of FDI is rather weak

Despite all these potentially positive (direct and indirect) effects of FDI, the evidence on whether FDI benefits the recipient economy is at best mixed.[15]

One reason for this is that the benefits I have discussed above are theoretical. Many TNC subsidiaries might actually buy very little from local producers and import most of their inputs – they are said to exist as **enclaves**. In these cases the benefits through supply chains will be non-existent. Workers can carry their knowledge from TNC subsidiaries to the rest of the economy only when there are already some local firms operating in relevant industries, whether as aspiring competitors or as suppliers. Frequently, this is not the case, especially when the TNC subsidiary in question has just come to exploit natural resources or cheap labour in your country rather than to establish a long-term production base.

But the more important reason why FDI has not unambiguously benefited the recipient economy is because it has negative, as well as positive, effects.

Some of the biggest companies don't make any
money – in the places they choose not to

In 2012, a public outrage broke out when it was revealed that Starbucks, Google and other big international companies have paid very little in corporation tax in Britain, Germany, France and other European countries over the years. This was *not* because they have not paid the taxes that they owe. It was because they never made much money and thus owed very little in tax. But if these companies are so incompetent, how is it possible that they have become some of the world's biggest and best-known – if not necessarily the most liked – companies?*

These companies minimized their tax obligations in countries like

---

* Some of you may remember that Dr Evil in *Austin Powers* movies plans his world takeover in the Starbucks Tower in Seattle.

Britain by inflating the costs for their British subsidiaries by having their subsidiaries in third countries 'over-charge' (that is, charge more than what they would have in open markets) the British subsidiaries for their services. These third countries were countries with a corporate tax rate that is lower than the UK rate (e.g., Ireland, Switzerland or the Netherlands) or even **tax havens**, namely, countries that attract foreign companies to set up 'paper companies' by charging very low, or even no, corporate taxes (e.g., Bermuda, the Bahamas).[16]

The age-old trick of transfer pricing

Taking advantage of the fact that they operate in countries with different tax rates, TNCs have their subsidiaries over-charge or under-charge each other – sometimes grossly – so that profits are highest in those subsidiaries operating in countries with the lowest corporate tax rates. In this way, their global post-tax profit is maximized.

A 2005 report by Christian Aid, the development charity, documents cases of under-priced exports like TV antennas from China at $0.40 apiece, rocket launchers from Bolivia at $40 and US bulldozers at $528 and over-priced imports such as German hacksaw blades at $5,485 each, Japanese tweezers at $4,896 and French wrenches at $1,089.[17] The Starbucks and Google cases were different from those examples only in that they mainly involved 'intangible assets', such as brand licensing fees, patent royalties, interest charges on loans and in-house consultancy (e.g., coffee quality testing, store design), but the principle involved was the same.

When TNCs evade taxes through transfer pricing, they use but do not pay for the collective productive inputs financed by tax revenue, such as infrastructure, education and R&D. This means that the host economy is effectively subsidizing TNCs.

There are also other potentially negative effects of FDI for the host economy

Transfer pricing is only one of the possible negative effects of FDI, especially when it comes to FDI into developing countries. Another one is that TNC subsidiaries may 'crowd out' local firms (in their own industry and in other industries) in the credit market. This might not necessarily be a bad thing if they are more attractive to lenders thanks to higher efficiency. But they might get easier access to credit, even when they are less efficient, because they are, well, TNC subsidiaries. They are seen, rightly, as being implicitly backed by their mother firms, which are far more creditworthy than any local firm in a developing country can aspire to be. If this is the case, TNC subsidiaries hogging the local credit market may mean loans going into less efficient uses.

Another reason is that TNC subsidiaries will be big firms in a monopolistic or oligopolistic position in the developing country market, even though they are small parts of the TNC that owns them. These subsidiaries can – and do – exploit such positions, which creates social costs, as discussed in Chapter 11.

Moreover, TNCs, having a lot of money and the political backing of their home countries, can change the policies of the host country in a way that is beneficial for them, rather than for the host economy. We are not simply talking about lobbying and bribing, as in the 2013 scandal involving GlaxoSmithKline and other global pharmaceutical TNCs in China. We are also talking about the **banana republic**.

The term is these days better known as a brand owned by Gap, the global clothing retail chain. But it has a dark origin. The term was coined during the time of the total economic and political domination of certain banana-growing countries in Latin America, such as Honduras, Guatemala and Colombia, by the United Fruit Company (UFC) in the early decades of the twentieth century. The most tragic episode in that history was the 1928 massacre of striking workers in a UFC banana plantation in Colombia; when it was threatened with an invasion by the US Marines to protect the interests of the UFC, the Colombian government sent in its army and killed possibly thousands of workers (the number has never been confirmed). The event was fictionalized in the masterpiece *One Hundred Years of Solitude* by the great Colombian writer Gabriel Garcia Márquez. American TNCs are said to have actively cooperated with right-wing military and the CIA to topple leftist regimes in Latin America in the 1960s and the 1970s.

In the long run, the most important negative effect of FDI is that it may make it more difficult for the host country to increase its own productive capabilities. Once you allow TNCs to establish themselves within your border, your local firms will struggle to survive. This is why many of today's rich countries – especially countries like Japan, Korea, Taiwan and Finland – strictly restricted FDI until their companies acquired the ability to compete in the world market. For example, had the Japanese government opened its automobile industry to FDI in the late 1950s, as was widely suggested following the debacle of Toyota's first car exports to the US,[18] Japanese car-makers would have been either wiped out or taken over by American or European TNCs, given the state of the industry at the time; back in 1955 General Motors alone produced 3.5 million cars whereas the whole of the Japanese automobile industry produced a mere 70,000.

Benefits of FDI can be only fully realized under appropriate regulations

FDI has complex effects that differ across industries and depending on country characteristics, making it difficult to generalize whether it is good or bad. Judgement on its desirability would also depend on the performance criteria (e.g., employment, export, productivity, long-term growth) and the time horizon you use, as their benefits tend to be more immediate while their costs may be of more long-term nature. Nevertheless, what seems certain is that countries, especially developing countries, can maximize the benefits from FDI only when they use appropriate regulations. And the list of regulations used for such a purpose is impressive.

Many countries have established rules on in which industries FDI may be made. They have demanded that TNCs have a local investment partner (known as **joint venture requirement**). They have had rules on how much of the joint venture a foreign investor can own; majority foreign ownership has typically been banned in important industries. Many governments have required that the TNC making the investment transfers their technologies to its local joint venture partner (**technology transfer requirement**) or that they train local workers. Countries have also demanded that TNC subsidiaries buy certain proportions of inputs locally (known as the **local contents requirement**).[19]

Japan, Korea, Taiwan and China have been particularly successful with these regulatory measures – they allowed, or even welcomed in some sectors, FDI but put in all those measures to ensure that the benefits were maximized while the costs were minimized. However, using the WTO agreement (known as the TRIMS agreement, or the Trade-related Investment Measures agreement), bilateral free-trade agreements (FTAs) and bilateral investment treaties (BITs), the rich countries (including Japan, which used to regulate FDI most severely in the world) have made a number of these regulations, such as the local contents requirement, 'illegal'.[20]

The success with all those regulations in countries such as Japan and China does not mean that 'stick' is the only way to manage FDI. Some other countries, such as Singapore and Ireland, have used 'carrot' in order to attract FDI into areas that they think are important for their national economic development.[21] Their 'carrots' included subsidies for TNCs making investment in 'priority' sectors, provision of custom-made infrastructure and production of engineers and skilled workers needed in particular industries.

REAL-LIFE NUMBERS

Growth in FDI flows

In the mid-1980s, when FDI started growing rapidly, total world FDI flow was around $75 billion per year (1983–7 average).[22] Today, at $1,519 billion (2008–12 average), it is over twenty times the mid-1980s figure, implying that it has grown at around 12.8 per cent per year. These figures look like huge sums and a very rapid growth rate, but they should be put into perspective.

In the mid-1980s, the world's total FDI was equivalent to 0.57 per cent of world GDP (1983–7 average of $13.5 trillion). The figure for the 2008–12 period, however large it may seem in absolute terms, is still equivalent only to 2.44 per cent of world GDP.

Most FDI happens between rich countries, but developing countries have recently become 'over-represented' in global FDI, largely thanks to China

Most FDI happens between the rich countries. In the mid-1980s (1983–7), 87 per cent of FDI went to the rich countries. Given that these countries accounted for 83 per cent of world GDP at the time, this meant that rich countries got slightly more than their 'fair' share of FDI. This ratio has fallen, although with ups and downs, to 66 per cent in the recent period (2008–12). Given that the rich countries still account for 70.8 per cent of world GDP in 2010, it is now the developing countries, rather than the rich countries, that are – once again, slightly – over-represented in global FDI.

The US has been by far the single largest recipient of FDI over the last three decades. Between 1980 and 2010, it received 18.7 per cent of world FDI inflows. It was followed by the UK, China, France and Germany.* Despite being by far the largest recipient of FDI in absolute terms, the US received much less than would have been expected from its weight in the world economy (it produced 26.9 per cent of world GDP during this period). In contrast, China and the UK received a lot more than would have been expected from their weight in the world economy.† Notable by its absence in this list is Japan. Despite producing 12 per cent of world GDP during this period, it received only 0.7 per cent of world FDI, thanks to its draconian regulation of FDI until recently.

Focusing on the more recent period, the top ten recipients of FDI (2007–11) are the US, China, the UK, Belgium, Hong Kong, Canada, France, Russia, Spain and Brazil. Of these, the US, France and Brazil got less than their 'fair' share, while all the others got more than their 'fair' share.[23]

The fact that developing countries as a group have become more important in the global FDI flows does not mean that all developing countries have been equally active participants in this game. Between 1980 and 2010, the top ten recipients of FDI flows into the developing world accounted for 75.7 per cent of total flows, despite accounting for only 71.4 per cent of developing world GDP.[24] In particular, China received 32.2 per cent of total FDI into the developing world during this period, despite accounting for only 22.8 per cent of developing world GDP.

The recent period has seen an increase in the share of brownfield investment in total FDI, changing the global industrial landscape

In the first seven years of the 1990s, brownfield FDI, that is, FDI in the form of cross-border M&A, was equivalent to 31.5 per cent of the world's FDI.[25] The number shot up to 57.7 per cent between 1998 and 2001 in the global cross-border M&A boom. After dipping back to 33.7 per cent for a few years between 2002 and 2004, it rose again to 44.7 per cent between 2005 and 2008. Even though the ratio has fallen to the lowest level in two decades (25.3 per cent between 2009 and 2012), following the 2008 global financial

---

* The figures were 9.4 per cent for the UK, 7.8 per cent for China, 4.7 per cent for France, 3.5 per cent for Germany.

† They both produced 4.4 per cent of world GDP during this period.

crisis, the general trend has been that brownfield FDI has risen relative to greenfield FDI.

This rise in brownfield investment is closely linked with what the Cambridge economist Peter Nolan calls the **global business revolution.**[26] In the last couple of decades, through an intense process of cross-border M&As, virtually all industries have become dominated by a small number of global players. The global aircraft industry is dominated by two firms, Boeing and Airbus, while industry observers are debating whether more than the top six mass-market automobile firms (Toyota, GM, Volkswagen, Renault-Nissan, Hyundai-Kia and Ford) can survive in the long run, which means that they are not even sure about such major companies as Peugeot-Citroën, Fiat-Chrysler and Honda.

Moreover, through what Nolan calls the 'cascade effect', even many of the supplier industries have become concentrated. For example, the global aircraft engine industry is now dominated by three firms (Rolls-Royce, Pratt & Whitney and Fairfield, a GE (General Electric) subsidiary).

Immigration and Remittances

Open borders – except for people?

Free-market economists wax lyrical about the benefits of open borders. They argue that open borders have allowed companies to source the cheapest things from across the globe and offer the best deals to consumers. Open borders, they point out, have increased competition among producers (of material goods and services), forcing them to cut their costs and/or improve their technologies. Any restriction on the cross-border movement of any potential object of economic transaction – goods, services, capital, you name it – would be harmful, they say.

But there is an economic transaction that they don't talk about in the same way – **immigration**, or cross-border movement of people. There are very few free-market economists who advocate free immigration in the way they advocate free trade.[27] Many free-market economists do not even seem to realize that they are being inconsistent when they advocate free movement of everything except for people. Others seem to instinctively keep away from the topic, deep down knowing that free immigration would be economically unfeasible and politically unacceptable.

Immigration reveals the political and the ethical nature of markets

What makes immigration – namely, the cross-border movement of people as providers of labour services – different from cross-border movements of other things (goods, financial services or capital) is that labour services cannot be imported without bringing their providers physically into the country as well.

When you buy an iPad from China or investment banking service from Britain, you don't need to have the Chinese assembly worker or the British banker come and live in your country. There are some cases in which workers commute across borders (say, between the US and Mexico), thus earning 'compensation of employees' in the income element of the current account (see above). In general, however, when people come to work in your country, they have to stay, at least for a while.

And when people stay and work within your borders, they have to be given certain minimum rights, at least in democratic countries.[28] You cannot say that a worker who has moved from, say, India to Sweden should still be paid an Indian wage and have only an Indian level of workplace rights because – well – he is an Indian.

But what rights should be given to the immigrants? Should they get the same freedom of choosing occupations, once admitted, or should they be tied to a particular industry or even a particular employer, as is the practice in many immigrant-receiving countries? Should immigrants be made to pay for certain social services that are free at point of access to citizens, such as basic education and healthcare?* Should we even make them conform to the cultural norms of the receiving country (say, a ban on the hijab)? These are all questions that have no easy answers – especially ones that standard Neoclassical economics can give. Answers to these questions require explicit political and ethical judgements, once again showing that economics cannot be a 'value-free science'.

Immigration usually benefits the recipient countries

There is a general agreement that immigrants themselves benefit from immigration – often greatly, especially if they are moving from a poor to a rich country. The opinion is more divided on whether the recipient

---

* But note that ultimately most citizens pay for parts of the costs of such services through taxes.

countries benefit, but the evidence suggests that they do, albeit to a limited extent.[29]

Immigrants usually come to fill labour shortages (though defining labour shortage is actually not a straightforward matter).[30] It could be general short-ages that they are filling, like the Turkish workers did in West Germany in the 1960s and the 1970s, when the *Wirtschaftswunder* (economic miracle) created all-round labour shortages. But more often they come to fill shortages in particular segments of the labour market – whether for '3D' jobs (not jobs in 3D cinemas, but dirty, dangerous and demeaning jobs) or for highly skilled jobs in Silicon Valley. In short, immigrants come because they are needed.

In some rich countries, especially in the UK (which actually doesn't have a particularly generous welfare state by European standards) there is a fear of 'welfare tourism' – immigrants from poor countries coming to live off the welfare state of the recipient country. But in most of these countries immigrants pay on average more taxes than they claim from the welfare state. This is because they tend to be younger (and thus don't use health care and other social services very much) and, thanks to immigration policy favouring skilled workers, tend to be more skilled (and thus earning more) than the average local person.[31]

Immigrants add to cultural diversity, which may stimulate both the natives and the immigrants into being more creative by bringing new ideas, new sensitivities and new ways of doing things. This is true of not just immigration-based countries, such as the US, but also the less immigration-driven countries of Europe.

Some native workers lose out but not by much and their woes are mostly created by 'wrong' corporate strategies and economic policies, not migrants

The fact that immigration benefits the recipient country does not mean that all citizens in that country benefit equally. Those at the lower end of the labour market with few prized skills, who have to fight for jobs with immi-grants, can lose out by being made to accept lower wages, poorer working conditions and higher chances of unemployment. But studies show that the extent of their losses is small.[32]

Especially in difficult economic times, such as the 1930s or today, disaf-fected native workers, manipulated by right-wing populist politicians, come to believe that their woes have largely been caused by immigrants. But much bigger causes of stagnant wages and declining working conditions are in the realm of corporate strategy and government economic policy: shareholder value maximization by corporations, which requires squeezing workers, poor macroeconomic policies that create unnecessary amounts of unemployment, inadequate systems for skills training that make local workers uncompetitive and so on. Unfortunately, the inability and the unwillingness of mainstream politicians to tackle those underlying structural issues have created the space for anti-immigrant parties in many rich countries.

'Brain drain' and 'brain gain': impacts on the sending countries

The immigrant-sending countries lose workers. This may be a good thing, if the country has high unemployment and it is unemployed unskilled workers who emigrate. However, those workers usually find it difficult to emigrate because immigrant-receiving countries want people with skills and because emigration costs money, which these workers don't have (e.g., search costs, application fees, air tickets). So very often it is the 'wrong' people who emigrate – skilled workers. This is known as **brain drain**.

Some of those skilled workers may learn even more skills in their destination countries and eventually come back home, teaching others new skills. This is known as **brain gain**, but the evidence for it is limited.

Remittances are the main channel through which
the immigrant-sending country is affected

The main channel through which the immigrant-sending country is affected is remittances. Remittances have complex impacts on the receiving country.[33]

A high proportion (60–85 per cent) of remittances is used for daily household expenses. This certainly improves the material living standards of the recipients. What is not consumed may be ploughed into small businesses run by families receiving remittances, generating further income. In countries like Mexico, remittances have also been channelled into public investments at the local level through the so-called 'hometown associations' (e.g., clinics, schools, irrigation).[34]

Having higher incomes, the members of recipient families do not have to work as much as before. This often means reduction in child labour. It also reduces infant mortality, as mothers with young children are given priority by the rest of the family to reduce outside work.

Last but not least, there are negative human costs to pay to get the remittances. Emigration often breaks up families and puts children in the care of others, often for the mothers to work as babysitters and housemaids elsewhere. The incalculable costs from such suffering may not be fully made up by remittances.

REAL-LIFE NUMBERS
Immigration into the rich countries has increased in the
last two decades but not as much as people think

Reading the popular press in the rich countries and observing the recent success of anti-immigrant parties in some European countries (especially France, the Netherlands, Sweden and Finland), you might get the impression that those countries have seen huge influxes of immigrants in the recent periods.

But immigration into the rich countries has not increased so dramatically. Between 1990 and 2010, the number of immigrants living in these countries increased from 88 million to 145 million. In proportional terms, this meant that the stock of immigrants in the rich countries rose from 7.8 per cent of the population in 1990 to 11.4 per cent in 2010.[35] This is a substantial rise, but hardly the seismic shift that it is sometimes made out to be.

One-third of immigrants live in developing countries

Immigration is not exclusively from developing countries into rich countries. There is a big flow of immigration between developing countries – usually from poorer to richer ones, but also between neighbouring countries due to natural disasters or armed conflicts.

As of 2010, there were 214 million immigrants worldwide; 145 million of them lived in the rich countries and the rest (69 million people) in developing countries, which means around a third of the world's immigrants live in developing countries.

Global immigrant stock as a share of world population
has risen very little in the last two decades

The share of immigrants in the population of the developing world has actually experienced a *fall* in the last two decades. It fell from 1.6 per cent of its population in 1990 to 1.2 per cent in 2010.

Since the population of the developing world is nearly 4.5 times that of the rich world (5.60 billion vs. 1.29 billion), this has nearly offset the rise in the immigrant stock of the rich world that I have discussed above. On the worldwide scale, immigrant stock has been basically stagnant – rising from 3.0 per cent in 1990 to 3.1 per cent in 2010.

Remittances have risen rather dramatically in the last decade

Remittances have dramatically increased since the early 2000s. As I mentioned earlier, it is, at over $300 billion, now around three times larger than foreign aid given to developing countries by rich countries (around $100 billion).

In absolute terms, the biggest recipient of remittances in 2010 was India ($54.0 billion).[36] It was closely followed by China ($52.3 billion). Mexico ($22.1 billion) and the Philippines ($21.4 billion) were distant third and fourth. Other developing countries with large remittances included Nigeria, Egypt and Bangladesh. Some developed countries – France, Germany, Spain and Belgium – also had high remittances.

The importance of remittances is seen more clearly when we see them in proportion to the country's GDP, rather than as absolute amounts. Even though they are the largest in the world in absolute terms, India's remittances are only about 3.2 per cent of its GDP. In some countries, remittances as a share of GDP could be gigantic as a proportion of GDP. In 2010, Tajikistan topped the world league table on this account, by having remittances equivalent to 41 per cent of GDP. Lesotho, with 28 per cent, came in a distant second. Kyrgyz Republic, Moldova, Lebanon and a few others had remittances equal to or bigger than 20 per cent of GDP.

High remittances can affect the recipient country
seriously, both positively and negatively

When remittances are this high, they can affect the recipient countries seriously, both positively and negatively.

On the positive side, an addition of financial resources equivalent to 20 per cent of GDP would raise a country's consumption and investment hugely. Large-scale remittances have also functioned as a shock absorber in many countries. After natural disasters (e.g., earthquake in Haiti), financial crises (e.g., South-east Asian countries in 1997) or civil wars (e.g., Sierra Leone, Lebanon), remittances are known to increase, partly because more people emigrate but also because existing workers send more money to help their families and friends in times of greater need.

On the negative side, however, high remittances have fed financial bubbles, as in the notorious case of the 1995–6 pyramid scheme of Albania, which collapsed in 1997. A sudden large inflow of foreign currencies in the form of remittances can also weaken the recipient country's export competitiveness by abruptly raising the value of its currency, thus making its exports relatively more expensive in terms of foreign currencies.

Concluding Remarks: Best of All Possible Worlds?

The rapidly changing international environment in the last three decades has significantly affected national economies in many ways. Greatly increased cross-border flows of goods, services, capital and technologies have changed the way in which countries organize their production, earn foreign currencies to import what they need and make and receive financial and physical investments. The increase in the cross-border movement of people has been far less than increases in other areas, but it has also significantly affected a large number of countries – by causing tensions between the immigrants and the 'natives' (in recipient countries) or by bringing in huge remittance flows that have significantly changed patterns of consumption, investment and production (in sending countries).

These changes, often summed up as the process of globalization, have been the defining feature of our time. In the last couple of decades, triumphant business elites, fashionable management gurus, politicians running powerful rich countries and clever economists who support them have declared the process to be an inevitable and unstoppable one. Claiming the process to be driven by technological progress, they have criticized anyone who is trying to reverse or modify any aspect of it as backward-looking. The 2008 global financial crisis has somewhat dented the confidence with which these people make their case, but the thinking behind it still dominates our world: protectionism is always bad; free capital flows will ensure that the best managed companies and countries get money; you have to welcome TNCs with open arms; and so on.

However, globalization is not an inevitable consequence of technological progress. During the Golden Age of capitalism (1945–73), the world economy was much *less* globalized than its counterpart in the Liberal Golden Age (1870–1913). And this was despite having much more advanced technologies of transportation and communications than the steamships and wired (not even wireless) telegraphy of the earlier period. The world has become globalized in the way it has in the last three decades only because the powerful governments and the business elite in the rich world decided that they wanted it that way.

Nor has globalization created 'the best of all possible worlds', to borrow a famous expression from the French writer and philosopher Voltaire's novella *Candide*, as its proponents have claimed. In the last three decades of hyper-globalization, economic growth has slowed down, inequality has increased, and financial crises have become far more frequent in most countries.

All of this is not to say that international economic integration is harmful in any form nor that countries should minimize their interaction with the outside world. On the contrary, they need to actively participate in the world economy, if they are to maintain a decent standard of living. When it comes to developing countries, interaction with the international economy is essential for their long-term development. Our prosperity absolutely depends on a serious degree of international economic integration.

However, this does not mean that all forms and degrees of international economic integration are desirable. Where and how much a country should be open, and thus how much overall international integration we should have in which areas and to what degrees, depends on its long-term goals and capabilities: protectionism may be good if it is done in the right way for the right industry; the same regulation of FDI may be good for some countries but harmful for others; some cross-border financial flows are essential while too many of them may be harmful; immigration may or may not benefit both the sending and the receiving countries, depending on how it is organized. Unless we recognize this critical point, we will not be able to reap the full benefits that international economic integration can bring us.

Further Reading

H.-J. CHANG
Bad Samaritans: Rich Nations, Poor Policies and the Threat to the Developing World (London: Random House, 2007).

P. HIRST, G. THOMPSON AND S. BROMLEY
Globalization in Question, 3rd edition (Cambridge: Polity, 2009).

R. KOZUL-WRIGHT AND P. RAYMENT
The Resistible Rise of Market Fundamentalism: Rethinking Development Policy in an Unbalanced World (London: Zed Books and Third World Network, 2007).

W. MILBERG AND D. WINKLER
Outsourcing Economics: Global Value Chains in Capitalist Development (Cambridge and New York: Cambridge University Press, 2013).

D. RODRIK
The Globalization Paradox (Oxford: Oxford University Press, 2011).

J. STIGLITZ
Making Globalization Work (London and New York: W. W. Norton and Co., 2006).

M. WOLF
Why Globalization Works (New Haven and London: Yale University Press, 2004).

What Now?

HOW CAN WE USE ECONOMICS TO MAKE OUR ECONOMY BETTER?

'It always seems impossible until it is done.'
NELSON MANDELA

How to 'Use' Economics?

My aim in this book has been to show the reader how to think, not what to think, about the economy. We have covered many topics, and I don't expect my readers to remember all – or even most – of them. But there are a few important things to keep in mind when you are 'using' economics (this is, after all, a User's Guide).

Cui bono?: economics is a political argument

Economics is a political argument. It is not – and can never be – a science; there are no objective truths in economics that can be established independently of political, and frequently moral, judgements. Therefore, when faced with an economic argument, you must ask the age-old question 'Cui bono?' (Who benefits?), first made famous by the Roman statesman and orator Marcus Tullius Cicero.

Sometimes it is easy to see the political nature of an economic argument because it is based on questionable assumptions that blatantly favour certain groups. The trickle-down argument, for example, crucially depends on the assumption that, when given a bigger slice of national output, the rich will use it to increase investments – an assumption that has not been borne out by reality.

In other situations, an argument may favour certain people unintentionally. For example, an argument using the Pareto criterion may seem not to favour anyone, as it says a change is a social improvement only when it makes some people better off without making anyone worse off and thus does not allow even a single person to be trampled on by the rest of society.

327

Yet it implicitly favours those who benefit more from the status quo, as the criterion allows them to prevent any change to the status quo that hurts them.

Political and ethical judgements are present even in ostensibly value-free exercises, such as defining the boundaries of the market. Deciding what belongs in the domain of the market is an intensely political exercise. Once you can drag something (say, water) into the domain of the market, you can apply the 'one-dollar-one-vote' rule to decisions surrounding it, making it easier for the rich to influence the outcome. Conversely, if you can take something (say, child labour) out of the domain of the market, it becomes impossible to influence its use with the power of money.

Saying that economics is a political argument does not mean that 'anything goes'. Some theories are better than others, depending on the situation at hand. But it does mean that you should never believe any economist who claims to offer 'scientific', value-free analysis.

Don't become a 'man with a hammer': there is more than one
way to 'do' economics, each with its strengths and weaknesses

As we have seen, there isn't just one right way of 'doing' economics, despite what most economists tell you. Though the Neoclassical approach has been the dominant one in recent decades, there are at least nine different schools of economics, each with its strengths and weaknesses.

The economic reality is complex and cannot be fully analysed with just one theory. The various economic theories conceptualize basic economic units differently (e.g., individuals vs. classes), focus on different things (e.g., macro-economy vs. micro-economy), ask different questions (e.g., how to maximize the efficiency with which we use given resources vs. how to increase our abilities to produce those resources in the long run) and try to answer them using different analytical tools (e.g., hyper-rationality vs. bounded rationality).

As the saying goes, 'he who has a hammer sees everything as a nail'. If you approach a problem from a particular theoretical point of view, you will end up asking only certain questions and answering them in particular ways. You might be lucky, and the problem you are facing might be a 'nail' for which your 'hammer' is the most appropriate tool. But, more often than not, you will need to have an array of tools available to you.

You are bound to have your favourite theory. There is nothing wrong with using one or two more than others – we all do. But please don't be a man (or a woman) with a hammer – still less someone unaware that there are other tools available. To extend the analogy, use a Swiss army knife instead, with different tools for different tasks.

'Everything factual is already a theory': facts, even numbers, are in the end not objective

Johann Wolfgang von Goethe, the German writer (*Faust*) and scientist (*Theory of Colours*), once said that 'everything factual is already a theory'.[1] This is something to bear in mind when looking at economic 'facts'.

Many people would assume that numbers are straightforward and objective, but each of them is constructed on the basis of a theory. I might not go as far as Benjamin Disraeli, the former British prime minister, who quipped that 'there are lies, damned lies, and statistics', but numbers in economics are invariably the results of attempts to measure concepts whose definitions are often extremely contentious or at least debatable.[2]

This is not just an academic quibble. The way we construct economic indicators has huge consequences for how we organize our economy, what kind of policies we implement and ultimately how we live our lives.

This applies to even the most basic figures that we take for granted, like GDP or the rate of unemployment. The exclusion of household work and unpaid care work from GDP has inevitably led to the under-valuation of those types of work. GDP's inability to take into account positional goods has directed consumption in the wrong direction and made it an unreliable measure of living standards for rich countries, where those goods are more important (see Chapter 6). The standard definition of unemployment underestimates the true extent of it by excluding discouraged workers in the rich countries and the under-employed in the developing countries (see Chapter 10). Naturally, these types of joblessness have been rather neglected by policy-makers.

All of this is not to say that numbers in economics are all useless or even necessarily misleading. We need numbers to be able to get the sense of magnitude of our economic world and monitor how it changes; we just shouldn't accept them unthinkingly.

The economy is much bigger than the market: the
need to think about production and work

Much of economics these days is about the market. Most economists today subscribe to the Neoclassical school, which conceptualizes the economy as a web of exchange relationships – individuals buy various things from many companies and sell their labour services to one of them, while companies buy and sell from many individuals and other companies. But the economy should not be equated with the market. The market is only one of many different ways of organizing the economy – indeed, it accounts for only a small part of the modern economy. Many economic activities are organized through internal directives within firms, while the government has influence over – and even commands – large sections of the economy. Governments – and increasingly international economic organizations like the WTO – also draw the boundaries of markets while setting rules of conduct in them. Herbert Simon, the founder of the Behaviouralist school, once estimated that only about 20 per cent of economic activities in the US are organized through the market.

The focus on the market has made most economists neglect vast areas of our economic life, with significant negative consequences for our well-being. The neglect of production at the expense of exchange has made policy-makers in some countries overly complacent about the decline of their manufacturing industries. The view of individuals as consumers, rather than producers, has led to the neglect of issues such as the quality of work (e.g., how interesting it is, how safe it is, how stressful it is and even how oppressive it is) and work–life balance. The disregard of these aspects of economic life partly explains why most people in the rich countries don't feel more fulfilled despite consuming the greatest ever quantities of material goods and services.

The economy is much bigger than the market. We will not be able to build a good economy – or a good society – unless we look at the vast expanse beyond the market.

So What?: The Economy Is Too Important to be Left to Professional Economists

All of this sounds fine, you may say, but so what? It would be entirely reasonable for you to say: I am only a consumer of information produced by professional economists, so what am I supposed to do with this new knowledge?

There is actually a great deal you can – and should – do with it. I will mention only the three most important things.

'An expert is someone who doesn't want to learn anything new': how not to be 'used' by economists

Harry S. Truman, in his typical no-nonsense style, once said that 'An expert is someone who doesn't want to learn anything new, because then he would not be an expert.'

Expert knowledge is absolutely necessary, but an expert by definition knows well only a narrow field and we cannot expect him or her to make a sound judgement on issues that involve more than one area of life (that is, most issues), balancing off different human needs, material constraints and ethical values. The possession of expert knowledge can sometimes give you a blinkered view. This dose of scepticism about expert knowledge should be applied to all areas of life, not just economics. But it is especially important in economics – a political argument often presented as a science.

You should be willing to challenge professional economists (and, yes, that includes me). They do not have a monopoly on the truth, even when it comes to economic matters (not to speak of 'everything'). To begin with, most of the time they cannot agree among themselves. Very often, their views can be narrow and distorted in particular ways – like all other professions, the economics profession is subject to what the French call *déformation professionelle*. It is entirely possible for people who are not professional economists to have sound judgements on economic issues, based on some knowledge of key economic theories and appreciation of underlying political and ethical, as well as economic, assumptions. Sometimes, their judgements may even be better than those of professional economists, since they may be more rooted in reality and less narrowly focused. The economy is too important to be left to the professional economists alone.

I would go one step further and say that the willingness to challenge professional economists – and other experts – should be a foundation of democracy. When you think about it, if all we have to do is to listen to the experts, what is the point of having a democracy at all? Unless we want our societies to be run by a body of self-elected experts, we all have to learn economics and challenge professional economists.

'Audite et alteram partem' (listen even to the other side): the need for humility and an open mind

On the walls of the city hall of Gouda in the Netherlands is written the Latin motto: 'Audite et alteram partem' (Listen even to the other side).[3] This is the attitude you should have in debating economic issues. Given the complexity of the world and given the necessarily partial nature of all economic theories, you should be humble about the validity of your favourite theory and should keep an open mind about it. This is not to say that you should have no opinion – you need to have your own – hopefully strong – view, but that is not the same as believing that it is right in some absolute sense.

I have argued that there is something to learn from all those different schools of economics – from the Marxist school on the left to the Austrian school on the right. Indeed, throughout history, too many lives have been ruined by people with excessive conviction in their own views – from the Khmer Rouge on the left to the neo-liberal market fundamentalist on the right.

'Pessimism of the intellect, optimism of the will': changes are difficult to make, but even big ones are possible, if you try hard enough and long enough

Throughout the book, we have seen how difficult it is to change economic reality – whether it is low wages in poor countries, tax havens that serve the super-rich, excessive corporate power or an overly complex financial system. Indeed, the difficulty of changing the status quo, even when most people agree that it is only serving a tiny minority, is manifested nowhere as clearly as in the limited reform that has been made to our current neo-liberal economic policies (and the economic theories that are behind them) even after the 2008 financial crisis has clearly shown their limitations.

Sometimes the difficulty is due to the active attempts by those who benefit from the current arrangements to defend their positions through lobbying, media propaganda, bribing or even violence. However, the status quo often gets defended even without some people actively 'being evil'. The 'one-dollar-one-vote' rule of the market drastically constrains the ability of those with less money to refuse undesirable options given to them by the underlying distribution of income and wealth (recall my criticism of Paul Krugman on low wages in Chapter 4). Moreover, we can be susceptible to beliefs that go against our own interests ('false consciousness' from Chapter 5). This tendency makes many losers from the current system defend it: some of you may have seen American pensioners protesting against 'Obamacare' with placards saying 'Government hands off my Medicare' when Medicare is – well, let me put it delicately – a government-funded and -run programme.

Acknowledging the difficulties involved in changing the economic status quo should not cause us to give up the fight to create an economy that is more dynamic, more stable, more equitable and more environmentally sustainable than what we have had for the last three decades. Yes, changes are difficult, but, in the long run, when enough people fight for them, many 'impossible' things happen. Just remember: 200 years ago, many Americans thought it was totally unrealistic to argue for the abolition of slavery; 100 years ago, the British government put women in prison for asking for votes; fifty years ago, most of the founding fathers of today's developing nations were being hunted down by the British and the French as 'terrorists'.

As the Italian Marxist Antonio Gramsci said, we need to have pessimism of the intellect and optimism of the will.

Final Thoughts: Easier Than You Think

The 2008 global financial crisis has been a brutal reminder that we cannot leave our economy to professional economists and other 'technocrats'. We should all get involved in its management – as active economic citizens.

Of course, there is 'should' and there is 'can'. Many of us are physically too exhausted by our daily struggle for existence and mentally occupied with our own personal and financial affairs. The prospect of making the investments necessary to become an active economic citizen – learning economics and paying attention to what is going on in the economy – may seem daunting.

However, these investments are much easier to make than you might think. Economics is far more accessible than many economists would have you believe. Once you have some basic understanding of how the economy works, monitoring what is going on becomes a lot less demanding in terms of your time and attention. Like many other things in life – learning to ride a bicycle, learning a new language or learning to use your new tablet computer – being an active economic citizen gets easier over time, once you overcome the initial difficulties and keep practising it.

Please give it a try.

Notes

PROLOGUE: WHY BOTHER?: WHY DO YOU NEED TO LEARN ECONOMICS?

1. These are the first sentences of his article 'The macroeconomist as scientist and engineer', *Journal of Economic Perspectives*, vol. 20, no. 4 (2006).
2. For a similar view, see the article, 'Is economics a science?' by Robert Shiller, one of the 2013 Nobel Economics laureates. The article can be downloaded at: http://www.theguardian.com/business/economics-blog/2013/nov/06/is-economics-a-science-robert-shiller.

CHAPTER 1: LIFE, THE UNIVERSE AND EVERYTHING: WHAT IS ECONOMICS?

1. R. Lucas, 'Macroeconomic priorities', *American Economic Review*, vol. 93, no. 1 (2003). This was his presidential address to the American Economic Association.
2. This is brilliantly explained by Felix Martin in his book *Money: The Unauthorised Biography* (London: The Bodley Head, 2013).
3. Many of these services also involve consumption of material things as well – for example, the food in a restaurant – but we are also purchasing the cooking and the serving services.

CHAPTER 2: FROM PIN TO PIN: CAPITALISM 1776 AND 2014

1. Before Smith, there were other economists, like the economic thinkers of Renaissance Italy, the Physiocrats of France, and the 'mercantilists', some of whom I discuss in Chapter 4.
2. Clifford Pratten, 'The manufacture of pins', *Journal of Economic Literature*, vol. 18 (March 1980), p. 94. Pratten says that the figure was for the more efficient of the two manufacturers then in existence. The less efficient one produced around 480,000 pins per worker per day.

3. Even in the most industrialized countries, like Britain and the Netherlands, over 40 per cent of people worked in agriculture. In the other Western European countries, the ratio was over 50 per cent and in some countries up to 80 per cent.

4. D. Defoe, *A Tour Through the Whole Island of Great Britain* (Harmondsworth: Penguin, 1978), p. 86.

5. Depending on the country, 60–80 per cent of those who work for capitalists work for **small and medium-sized enterprises** (SMEs), employing less than a few hundred people. SMEs are defined as enterprises employing less than 250 people in the European Union and less than 500 in the US.

6. At the time London was the biggest city in Europe and the second biggest in the world after Beijing, which had over 1.1 million people. Having just lost the American colonies, the British colonial territories at the time when *TWON* came out consisted of (parts of) India, Canada, Ireland and around a dozen and a half Caribbean islands.

7. The information in the rest of the section is from H.-J. Chang, *Kicking Away the Ladder: Development Strategy in Historical Perspective* (London: Anthem Press, 2002), pp. 93–9, unless otherwise specified.

8. All the information on the Bank of England banknotes is from the website of the Bank of England. See: http://www.bankofengland.co.uk/banknotes/Pages/about/history.aspx.

CHAPTER 3: HOW HAVE WE GOT HERE?: A BRIEF HISTORY OF CAPITALISM

1. A. Maddison, *Contours of the World Economy, 1–2030 AD* (Oxford: Oxford University Press, 2007), p. 71, table 2.2. The long-term historical growth figures in the next few paragraphs are also from the same source.

2. Britain's cotton textile output grew at 1.4 per cent per year during 1700–1760, but grew at 7.7 per cent per year during 1770–1801. Especially between 1780 and 1790, the growth rate was 12.8 per cent per year – high even by today's standards but astonishing at the time. The iron industry increased its output by 5 per cent per year between 1770 and 1801. These figures are calculated from N. Crafts, *British Economic Growth during the Industrial Revolution* (Oxford: Clarendon Press, 1995), p. 23, table 2.4.

3. See J. Hobson, *The Eastern Origins of Western Civilization* (Cambridge: Cambridge University Press, 2004) for evidence on how the early scientific and technological developments in the West drew extensively from the Arab, Indian and Chinese worlds.

4. An authoritative and balanced discussion on this is provided by P. Bairoch, *Economics and World History: Myths and Paradoxes* (New York and London: Harvester Wheatsheaf, 1993), Chapters 5–8.

5. B. Hartmann and J. Boyce, *Needless Hunger* (San Francisco: Institute for Food and Development Policy, 1982), p. 12.

6. Unlike political revolutions, such as the French Revolution or the Russian Revolution, economic revolutions do not have clear start and end dates. The Industrial Revolution has been defined as as long as 1750–1850 and as short as 1820–70.

7. R. Heilbroner and W. Milberg, *The Making of Economic Society*, 13th edition (Boston: Pearson, 2012), p. 62.

8. N. Crafts, 'Some dimensions of the "quality of life" during the British industrial revolution', *Economic History Review*, vol. 50, no. 4 (November 1997): table 1, p. 623, for the 1800 figure, and table 3, p. 628, for the 1860 figure.

9. See Chang, *Kicking Away the Ladder*, and H.-J. Chang, *Bad Samaritans: Rich Nations, Poor Policies and the Threat to the Developing World* (Random House, London, 2007), for further details.

10. Walpole's official job title was actually the chief minister, but we may be excused calling him the first prime minister. He was the first head of British government who controlled all ministries – before him, there had been two or even three joint heads of government. Walpole was also the first one who took up residence (in 1735) at 10 Downing Street, the famous official residence of the British prime minister.

11. Through the provision known as 'extra-territoriality', these treaties also deprived the weaker countries of the ability to try foreign citizens for crimes committed in their territories. Some other unequal treaties demanded that the weaker countries cede or 'lease' parts of their territories; China ceded to Britain Hong Kong Island in 1842 and Kowloon in 1860, while Britain 'leased' the so-called New Territories of Hong Kong for ninety-nine years in 1898. Unequal treaties often forced the weaker country to sell foreigners the rights to exploit natural resources (e.g., minerals, forestry) for minimal fees.

12. A. Smith, *An Inquiry into the Nature and Causes of the Wealth of Nations* (Oxford: Clarendon Press, 1976), p. 181.

13. Germany took Tanzania, Namibia, Rwanda, Burundi, Togo and so on, although many of these were given to the winners in the First World War. The US got Cuba and the Philippines, while Belgium took Congo.
Japan colonized Korea, Taiwan and Manchuria (the north-eastern part of China).

14. Between 1870 and 1913, per capita income growth in Latin America saw a massive acceleration, from -0.04 per cent during 1820–70 to 1.86 per cent at the end of this period, making the continent the fastest-growing region in the world (higher than that of the US, 1.82 per cent, in second place).

15. Calculated from A. Maddison, *The World Economy: Historical Statistics* (Paris: OECD, 2003), p. 100, table 3c.

16. These numbers and information in the rest of this paragraph are from C. Dow, *Major Recessions: Britain and the World, 1920–1995* (Oxford: Oxford University Press, 1998), p. 137, table 6.1 (for 1929–32) and p. 182 (for 1932–7).

17. This point is explained in an accessible way by Stephanie Flanders, the BBC economics journalist, at the following blog post: http://www.bbc.co.uk/blogs/thereporters /stephanieflanders/2009/02/04/index.html.

18. For example, it is estimated that the US government fiscal policy added a mere 0.3 per cent to the GDP between 1929 and 1933, against the 31.8 per cent fall during the same period (Dow, *Major Recessions*, p. 164, table 6.11), while UK fiscal policy added a mere 0.4 per cent, against the 5.1 per cent fall in GDP between 1929 and 1932 (ibid., p. 192, table 6.23).

19. Per capita income growth rate for the world fell from 1.31 per cent during 1870–1913 to 0.88 per cent during 1913–50. Maddison, *The World Economy*, p. 383, table A.8.

20. A. Glyn, A. Hughes, A. Lipietz and A. Singh, 'The rise and fall of the Golden Age', in S. Marglin and J. Schor (eds.), *The Golden Age of Capitalism* (Oxford: Oxford University Press, 1990), p. 45, table 2.4.

21. The average inflation for the ACCs during this period was around 4 per cent. Ibid., p. 45, table 2.4.

22. C. Reinhart and K. Rogoff, *This Time Is Different: Eight Centuries of Financial Folly* (Princeton: Princeton University Press, 2009), p. 252, figure 16.1.

23. Today, people think of the World Bank as the bank for poor countries, but its first clients

were the war-torn economies of Europe. This is reflected in its official name, which is the International Bank for *Reconstruction* and Development (IBRD). (Emphasis added.)

24. The ECSC coordinated efforts to upgrade the production facilities in the coal and steel industries. The 1957 Treaty of Rome created the European Atomic Energy Community (Euroatom) as well as the EEC. In 1967, these three communities were integrated to form the European Communities (EC).

25. Further details can be found in F. Block, 'Swimming against the current: the rise of a hidden developmental state in the United States', *Politics and Society*, vol. 36, no. 2 (2008), and in M. Mazzucato, *The Entrepreneurial State: Debunking Private vs. Public Sector Myths* (London: Anthem Press, 2013).

26. Glyn et al., 'The rise and fall of the Golden Age', p. 98.

27. The average inflation rate of Europe reached up to 15 per cent while the US rate also surged above 10 per cent. The UK suffered particularly, with the inflation rate reaching almost 25 per cent in 1975. From Dow, *Major Recessions*, p. 293, figure 8.5.

28. Growth rates in per capita income in the ACCs were 1.4 per cent during 1870–1913, 1.2 per cent during 1913–50, and 3.8 per cent during 1960–70. These figures are from Glyn et al., 'The rise and fall of the Golden Age', p. 42, table 2.1.

29. Ibid., p. 45, table 2.4.

30. It should, however, be noted that the Chilean government has had an important role in the economy even in the country's neo-liberal phase. CODELCO, the largest copper mining company in the world, which had been nationalized in 1971 by the left-wing Allende government, was kept under state ownership. A number of public and semi-public agencies (such as Fundación Chile) have provided its agricultural producers with subsidized technical consultancy and export marketing help.

31. S. Basu and D. Stuckler, *The Body Economic: Why Austerity Kills* (London: Basic Books, 2013), Chapter 2, for further details and analyses.

32. China's output in 1978 was around $219 billion. World output in that year was about $8,549 billion. Calculated from World Bank, *World Development Report 1980* (Washington, DC: World Bank, 1980), pp. 110–11, table 1.

33. Ibid., pp. 124–5, table 8.

34. China's GDP in 2007 was $3,280 billion. World GDP was $54,347 billion. World Bank, *World Development Report 2009* (New York: Oxford University Press, 2009), pp. 356–7, table 3. China's merchandise export was $1,218 billion, while that for the world was $13,899 billion (ibid., pp. 358–9, table 4).

CHAPTER 4: LET A HUNDRED FLOWERS BLOOM: HOW TO 'DO' ECONOMICS

1. Carl Menger is considered to be the founding father of the Austrian school, but some would rightly say that he was, together with Leon Walras and William Jevons, one of the founding fathers of the Neoclassical school. An even more complicated example is Frank Knight, the early twentieth-century economist, who taught at the University of Chicago. He is often thought of as an Austrian economist (no, not by his nationality – he was an American), but he had a lot of Institutionalist influences, and some of his ideas overlap with the Keynesian and the Behaviouralist ones.

2. Physicists have tried, and failed, to construct what they call the 'theory of everything'.

3. '. . . and in the darkness bind them', goes the rest of the sentence.

4. Joseph Schumpeter emphasized that all analysis in economics is preceded by a pre-analytical cognitive act, called vision, in which the analyst 'visualise[s] a distinct set of coherent phenomena as a worth-while object of [his] analytic efforts'. He pointed out that 'this vision is ideological almost by definition', as 'the way in which we see things can hardly be distinguished from the way in which we wish to see them'. The quote is from J. Schumpeter, *History of Economic Analysis* (New York: Oxford University Press, 1954), pp. 41–2. I thank William Milberg for pointing me to this quote.

5. The elevation of the individual by the Neoclassical school goes beyond the labelling of economic actors as individuals, rather than classes. Most members of the school believe in **methodological individualism** as well – namely, the view that a scientific explanation of any collective entity, such as the economy, should be based on its decomposition to the smallest possible unit – that is, the individual.

6. Another way to put it is to say that a society is in a state of Pareto optimality if no one can be made better off without making someone worse off.

7. In Akerlof's classic example of 'the market for lemons', given the difficulty of ascertaining the quality of used cars before purchase, prospective buyers will not be willing to stump up good money even for what is a truly good second-hand car. Given this, owners of good used cars will shun the market, lowering the average quality of cars further, leading, in the extreme case, to the disappearance of the market itself. See G. Akerlof, 'The market for "lemons": quality uncertainty and the market mechanism', *Quarterly Journal of Economics*, vol. 84, no. 4 (1970).

8. The remaining two volumes were edited by Engels and published after Marx's death.

9. For this history, see my books *Kicking Away the Ladder* (more academic and detailed) and *Bad Samaritans* (less detailed and more user-friendly).

10. Typically recommended were: promotion of new industries through tariffs, subsidies and preferential treatment in government procurement (that is, government buying things from the private sector); encouragement of domestic processing of raw materials through export taxes on raw materials or through a ban on their exports; discouragement of the imports of luxury goods through tariffs or prohibitions so that more resources can be channelled into investments; export promotion through marketing support and quality control; support for technological improvements through government-granted monopoly, patents and government-subsidized recruitment of skilled workers from economically more advanced countries; and, last but not least, public investment in infrastructure.

11. List started out as a free-trader, promoting the idea of a free-trade agreement between various German states, which was realized in 1834 as Zollverein (literally the customs union). However, during his political exile in the US during the 1820s, he came across Hamilton's ideas, through the works of Daniel Raymond and Henry Carey, and came to accept that free trade may be good between countries at similar levels of development (e.g., the German states then) but not so between economically more advanced countries, such as Britain, and backward countries, such as Germany and the US then. It may be added that, like most Europeans at the time, List was a racist and explicitly argued that his theory applied only to 'temperate' countries.

12. This contrasts with the predominantly (although not exclusively) one-way causality supposed by the Marxist school, from material production system – or the base – to institutions – or the superstructure.

13. Important names include, in alphabetical order, Alice Amsden, Martin Fransman, Jorge Katz, Sanjaya Lall and Larry Westphal.

14. On this debate, see D. Lavoie, *Rivalry and Central Planning: The Socialist Calculation Debate Reconsidered* (Cambridge: Cambridge University Press, 1985).

15. Herbert Simon, the founder of the Behaviouralist school, has pointed out that modern capitalism is better described as an 'organization' economy than as a market economy. These days, most economic actions happen within organizations – predominantly firms but also governments and other organizations – rather than through markets. See Chapter 5 for further discussion.

16. The idea that 'permits to pollute' can be bought and sold may still sound alien to many non-economists. But the market for these permits is already a thriving one, with an estimated value of trade in 2007 at $64 billion.

17. They are named, 'Marx the Prophet', 'Marx the Economist', 'Marx the Sociologist' and 'Marx the Teacher'.

18. Over time – in his grandchildren's generation, as Keynes put in a famous article titled 'Economic Possibilities for Our Grandchildren' (though he himself had no children) – living standards in countries like Britain will have risen sufficiently that not much new investment would be needed. At such a point, he envisaged, the focus of policy should be switched to reducing working hours and increasing consumption, mainly by redistributing income to poorer groups, which spend larger proportions of their incomes than the richer ones.

19. The history of financial speculation is beautifully documented in C. Kindleberger, *Manias, Panics, and Crashes: A History of Financial Crisis* (London: Macmillan, 1978).

20. He also earned large sums for King's College, Cambridge, whose investment portfolio he was in charge of as the bursar (financial manager) between 1924 and 1944.

21. Michal Kalecki (1899–1970), with his Marxist influence and interest in developing economies, and Nicholas Kaldor (1908–86), who had one foot in the Developmentalist tradition and who was, having been brought up in the Austro-Hungarian Empire, no stranger to the ideas of the Austrians and Schumpeter, were exceptions in this regard.

22. Veblen also tried to understand the changes in society in evolutionary terms, drawing inspiration from the then new theory of Charles Darwin.

23. Most members of the NIE accept the 'self-seeking' part of the 'rational self-seeking individual' assumption of the Neoclassical school, but most of them (not necessarily an overlapping set with the former 'most') reject the 'rational' part. Some of them, especially Williamson, even explicitly employ the Behaviouralist concept of bounded rationality, which sees human rationality as severely limited.

24. There is also an unacknowledged influence from the Marxist school (North was a Marxist in his young days), at least in terms of the subject matter, such as property relations (North and Coase) and the internal workings of the firm (Coase and Williamson).

25. Some Neoclassical economists have tried to reinterpret bounded rationality so that it fits into optimization models. Some argue that bounded rationality simply means that we need to see economic decision as the 'joint-optimization' of resource costs (a traditional Neoclassical concern) and the costs of decision-making. In another common reinterpretation, people are seen to optimize by choosing the best decision rules, rather than trying to make the right choice in every decision instance. Both these reinterpretations in the end do not work because they assume even more unrealistic levels of rationality than the standard Neoclassical model does. How can agents that are not even rational enough to optimize on one front (resource costs) optimize two (resource costs and decision costs)? How can agents that are not smart enough to make rational decisions on individual occasions design decision rules that will allow them to make optimal decisions on average?

26. H. Simon, *The Sciences of the Artificial*, 3rd edition (Cambridge, MA, The MIT Press 1996), p. 31.

CHAPTER 5: DRAMATIS PERSONAE: WHO ARE THE ECONOMIC ACTORS?

1. The data on intra-firm trade are hard to come by. Intra-firm trade is, at 20–25 per cent, estimated to be less important in services than in manufacturing. But in certain 'producer services', such as consulting and R&D, it is even more important than in manufacturing; in the case of US and Canadian firms, for which detailed data are available, it was in the region of 60–80 per cent. The data are from R. Lanz and S. Miroudot, 'Intra-firm trade patterns, determinants and policy implications', OECD Trade Policy Papers no. 114 (Paris: OECD, 2011).

2. MCC also has nearly 150 subsidiaries that are not cooperatives and over 10,000 workers who are not employee-partners. The sales revenue includes those of these subsidiaries.

3. Precisely for this reason, the first anti-trust law of the US (the Sherman Act of 1890) actually treated trade unions as anti-competitive 'trusts' – until the provision was dropped in the revised anti-trust law of 1914, called the Clayton Act.

4. The European Union (EU) derives its power from a mixture of money and rule-setting power. As seen in the recent 'rescue' packages for the 'periphery' countries, like Greece and Spain, some of its influence is through its financial power. But more important is its ability to set rules on all aspects of economic (and other) life in its member countries, including budget, competition among firms and working conditions. EU decisions are made on the basis of 'qualified majority voting' (QMV), in which votes held by each country reflect their population size but only up to a point, in a manner analogous to the distribution of electoral college votes for US presidential election among the fifty states of the US. In the Council of the European Union, Germany has ten times more votes than Malta (twenty-nine against three votes), but it has a population more than 200 times bigger (82 million v. 0.4 million).

5. The ILO is quite different from other UN organizations. While other UN bodies are inter-governmental organizations, the ILO is a tripartite body, made up of governments, trade unions and employers' associations, with 2:1:1 distribution of votes between the three groups.

6. There are a number of experiments that show that economics students are more selfish than others. Part of it may be the result of 'self-selection' – hearing that economics education today emphasizes the predominance of self-seeking, selfish people are more likely to feel that it is their kind of subject. But it may also be the result of education itself – being taught all the time that everyone is out to promote himself/herself, economics students may get to see the world more in that way.

CHAPTER 6: HOW MANY DO YOU WANT IT TO BE?:
OUTPUT, INCOME AND HAPPINESS

1. This is except for the very limited amount consumed by tourists.

2. This point is very clearly and carefully explained in J. Aldred, *The Skeptical Economist* (London: Earthscan, 2009), especially pp. 59–61.

3. Richard Layard, talking to Julian Baggini in 'The conversation: can happiness be measured?', *Guardian*, 20 July 2012.

CHAPTER 7: HOW DOES YOUR GARDEN GROW?: THE WORLD OF PRODUCTION

1. After the Gambia, Swaziland, Djibouti, Rwanda and Burundi.
2. Back in 1995, Equatorial Guinea's per capita GDP was a mere $371 a year, making it one of the thirty poorest countries in the world.
3. The information on the US mining industry provided below is from G. Wright and J. Czelusta, 'Exorcising the resource curse: mining as a knowledge industry, past and present', working paper, Stanford University, 2002.
4. These growth rates mean that Germany's 2010 per capita income was 11.5 per cent higher than its 2000 income, whereas the US's 2010 per capita income was only 7.2 per cent higher than its 2000 income.
5. The following R&D figures are from OECD, *Perspectives on Global Development 2013 – Shifting Up a Gear: Industrial Policies in a Changing World* (Paris: OECD, 2013), Chapter 3, figure 3-1.
6. In the poorer countries, with few corporations that are big enough to conduct their own R&D, the vast majority of R&D is financed by the government. The ratio could be nearly 100 per cent in some countries, but is typically 50–75 per cent. In the richer countries, the share of the government in R&D is lower, typically between 30 per cent and 40 per cent. It is considerably lower in Japan (23 per cent) and Korea (28 per cent), while Spain and Norway (both 50 per cent) make up the other end. In the US, the ratio is around 35 per cent these days, but used to be much higher (50–70 per cent) during the Cold War, when its federal government spent a huge amount in defence research (see Chapter 3).
7. Department for BERR (Business, Enterprise and Regulatory Reform), *Globalisation and the Changing UK Economy* (London: Her Majesty's Government, 2008).
8. Pierre Dreyfus, a former French minister of industry, as cited in P. Hall, *Governing the Economy* (Cambridge: Polity Press, 1987), p. 210.
9. The data in this paragraph and the next are from H.-J. Chang, 'Rethinking public policy in agriculture: lessons from history, distant and recent', *Journal of Peasant Studies*, vol. 36, no. 3 (2009), unless otherwise stated.
10. If we expand it to the industrial sector, the share in GDP was 30–40 per cent. Today, in none of them does it account for more than 25 per cent. The data are from O. Debande, 'De-industrialisation', *EIB Papers*, vol. 11, no. 1 (2006); downloadable at: http://www.eib.org/attachments/efs/eibpapers/eibpapers_2006_v11_n01_en.pdf.
11. In Germany, the share of manufacturing in GDP fell from 27 per cent to 22 per cent in current prices between 1991 and 2012. In constant prices, the fall was from 24 per cent to 22 per cent. Corresponding numbers in Italy were 22 per cent to 16 per cent in current prices and 19 per cent to 17 per cent in constant prices. In France (1991–2011), they were from 17 per cent to 10 per cent in current prices and from 13 per cent to 12 per cent in constant prices. The data are from Eurostats, issued by the European Union.
12. In the US, the share of manufacturing in GDP fell from 17 per cent to 12 per cent in current prices between 1987 and 2012. But, in constant prices, it actually rose a little, from 11.8 per cent to 12.4 per cent during this period. Between 1990 and 2012, the share of manufacturing in Switzerland's GDP fell from 20 per cent to 18 per cent in current prices. But when calculated in constant prices, it actually rose from 18 per cent to 19 per cent. The Swiss data are from Eurostats. The US data are from the US government's Bureau of Economic Analysis (BEA).
13. In Finland (1975–2012), the share in current prices fell from 25 per cent to 17 per cent but the share in constant prices rose from 14 per cent to 21 per cent. In Sweden (1993–2012), the corresponding figures were a fall from 18 per cent to 16 per cent and a rise from 12 per cent to 18 per cent. The data are from Eurostats.

14. Between 1990 and 2012, the share of manufacturing in the UK's GDP fell from 19 per cent to 11 per cent in current prices, representing a 42 per cent decline. It fell from 17 per cent to 11 per cent in constant prices, representing a 35 per cent decline. The data are from Eurostats, issued by the European Union.

15. All the data are from the World Bank.

16. For a more in-depth discussion, see G. Palma, 'Four sources of "de-industrialisation" and a new concept of the "Dutch Disease"', paper presented at the EGDI (Economic Growth and Development Initiative) Roundtable of the HSRC (Human Sciences Research Council) of South Africa, 21 May 2007, downloadable at: http://intranet.hsrc.ac.za/Document-2458.phtml.

17. The GDR framework identifies the share of burden for each country in reducing greenhouse gases to prevent the potentially catastrophic 'two-degree warming', considering both historical responsibility for global warming and capacity to bear the burden of adjustments.

18. See Aldred, *The Skeptical Economist*, Chapter 5, for further details.

19. Our perception of the risk of nuclear power stations is distorted by the fact that nuclear accidents have very high profiles in the news media, not least because they usually happen in rich countries. But, unbeknownst to the outside world, at least a few thousand coalminers die in accidents every year in China alone. We don't even know how many people have died from pollution from coal burning over the last couple of centuries all over the world. The 1952 Great Smog of London is said to have caused anything between 4,000 and 12,000 extra deaths, but that is just one – admittedly by far the worst – of dozens of years when Britain suffered from coal pollution. Today, many people in cities in China, India and elsewhere die prematurely from respiratory diseases caused by coal pollution. If we add all of these 'silent deaths' up, we can easily say that coal has 'killed' far more people than nuclear energy, even if we accept the most extreme – and highly disputed – estimates of one million extra deaths caused by the Chernobyl disaster (mostly through cancer due to increased radiation).

CHAPTER 8: TROUBLE AT THE FIDELITY FIDUCIARY BANK: FINANCE

1. Martin, *Money*, p. 242.

2. A lot of what I say about derivatives is derived from B. Scott, *The Heretic's Guide to Global Finance: Hacking the Future of Money* (London: Pluto Press, 2013), pp. 63–74 and my personal discussions with its author. J. Lanchester, *Whoops! Why Everyone Owes Everyone and No One Can Pay* (London: Allen Lane, 2010), Chapter 2, provides a less technical but an insightful explanation.

3. I thank Brett Scott for suggesting this example. In this sense, we can say that securitized debt products are derivatives in that they 'derive' their value from underlying assets. However, in the same vein, we can say that shares are also derivatives, as companies also have 'underlying' assets, such as physical equipment and other assets (like patents and other intellectual properties). Thus, all distinctions between different types of financial assets are in the end fuzzy.

4. Scott, *The Heretic's Guide to Global Finance*, p. 65.

5. Ibid., pp. 69–70.

6. On the history of the development of derivative markets and the role of the CBOT in the process, see Y. Millo, 'Safety in numbers: how exchanges and regulators shaped index-based derivatives', a paper presented at the Conference on the Social Studies of Finance, Center on Organizational Innovation (COI), Columbia University, 3–4 May 2002; downloadable at: http://www.coi.columbia.edu/ssf/papers/millo.rtf, and 'A Brief History of Options', downloadable at: http://www.optionsplaybook.com/options-introduction/stock-option-history/.

7. See Millo, 'Safety in numbers', and C. Lapavitsas, *Profiting without Producing: How Finance Exploits All* (London: Verso, 2013), p. 6.

8. H. Blommestein et al., 'Outlook for the securitisation market', *OECD Journal: Market Trends*, vol. 2011, issue 1 (2011), p. 6, figure 6, downloaded from: http://www.oecd.org/finance/financial-markets/48620405.pdf. According to the Eurostat, the EU's statistical agency, in 2010, GDP was €12.3 trillion in the European Union and €10.9 trillion in the US.

9. L. Lin and J. Sutri, 'Capital requirements for over-the-counter derivatives central counterparties', IMF Working Paper, WP/13/3, 2013, p. 7, figure 1, downloadable from: http://www.imf.org/external/pubs/ft/wp/2013/wp1303.pdf.

10. G. Palma, 'The revenge of the market on the rentiers: why neo-liberal reports of the end of history turned out to be premature', *Cambridge Journal of Economics*, vol. 33, no. 4 (2009).

11. Lapavitsas, *Profiting without Producing*, p. 206, figure 2.

12. J. Crotty, 'If financial market competition is so intense, why are financial firm profits so high?: Reflections on the current "golden age" of finance', Working Paper no. 134 (Amherst, MA: PERI (Political Economy Research Institute), University of Massachusetts, April 2007).

13. A. Haldane, 'Rethinking the financial network', Speech delivered at the Financial Student Association, Amsterdam, April 2009, pp. 16–17. The speech can be downloaded from: http://www.bankofengland.co.uk/publications/Documents/speeches/2009/speech386.pdf.

14. M. Blyth, *Austerity: The History of a Dangerous Idea* (Oxford: Oxford University Press, 2013), pp. 26–7.

15. The average shareholding periods for banks fell from about three years in 1998 to about three months in 2008. P. Sikka, 'Nick Clegg's plan for shareholders to tackle fat-cat pay won't work', *Guardian*, 6 December 2011, downloadable from: http://www.guardian.co.uk/commentisfree/2011/dec/06/nick-clegg-shareholders-fat-cat-pay?.

16. The financial sector has *not* always been more profitable than the non-financial sector. According to a study published in 2005, in the US, between the mid-1960s and the late 1970s, the rate of profit for financial firms was lower than that of the non-financial firms. But, following financial deregulation in the early 1980s, the profit rate of financial firms (on a rising trend, ranging between 4 per cent and 12 per cent) was significantly higher than that of non-financial firms (2–5 per cent) until the early 2000s (the data in the study ended there). In France, the profit rate of financial corporations was *negative* between the early 1970s and the mid-1980s (no data are available for the 1960s). With the financial deregulation of the late 1980s, it started rising and overtook that of non-financial firms in the early 1990s, when both were about 5 per cent, and rose to over 10 per cent by 2001. In contrast, the profit rate of French non-financial firms declined from the early 1990s, to reach around 3 per cent in 2001. See G. Duménil and D. Lévy, 'Costs and benefits of neoliberalism: a class analysis', in G. Epstein (ed.), *Financialisation and the World Economy* (Cheltenham: Edward Elgar, 2005).

17. Reinhart and Rogoff, *This Time Is Different*, p. 252, figure 16.1.

18. Palma, 'The revenge of the market on the rentiers', p. 851, figure 12.

19. W. Lazonick, 'Big payouts to shareholders are holding back prosperity', *Guardian*, 27 August 2012; downloadable from: http://www.theguardian.com/commentisfree/2012/aug/27/shareholder-payouts-holding-back-prosperity.

20. It remained at 99 per cent in 2011 and 2012. The data in this paragraph are from the Federal Reserve Board flow of funds data; downloadable from: http://www.federalreserve.gov/apps/fof/. Similar estimates up to the early 2000s can be found in Crotty, 'If financial market competition is so intense'. Another estimate comes up with lower numbers, but the trend is the same: just over 20 per cent in 1955, rising to around 30 per cent by the mid-1980s, rising to

50 per cent in the early 2000s, falling to around 45 per cent in the run-up to the 2008 crisis and rising back over 50 per cent by 2010. See W. Milberg and N. Shapiro, 'Implications of the recent financial crisis for innovation', New School for Social Research, mimeo, February 2013.

21. The information for GE is from R. Blackburn, 'Finance and the fourth dimension', *New Left Review*, May/June 2006, p. 44. J. Froud et al., *Financialisation and Strategy: Narrative and Numbers* (London: Routledge, 2006) estimates that the ratio could be as high as 50 per cent. The Ford number comes from the Froud et al. study and the GM number from the Blackburn study.

22. This point is very clearly and insightfully made by Andy Haldane of the Bank of England (see above) in 'The dog and the frisbee', speech delivered at the Federal Reserve Bank of Kansas City's 36th Economic Policy Symposium on 'The Changing Policy Landscape', Jackson Hole, Wyoming, 31 August 2012; downloadable from: http://www.bankofengland.co.uk/publications/Documents/speeches/2012/speech596.pdf.

CHAPTER 9: BORIS'S GOAT SHOULD DROP DEAD: INEQUALITY AND POVERTY

1. M. Friedman and R. Friedman, *Free to Choose* (Harmondsworth: Penguin Books, 1980), pp. 31–2.

2. For a more detailed argument along this line, see J. Stiglitz, *The Price of Inequality* (London: Allen Lane, 2012), Chapter 4.

3. Wilkinson's and Pickett's explanation is that lower-income individuals in more unequal societies are subject to greater stress than are their counterparts in more equal societies. This stress comes from what they call 'status anxiety', namely, the anxiety about one's low status and inability to overcome it, especially in early life. This stress, Wilkinson and Pickett argue, negatively affects the health of the individuals concerned and makes them more prone to antisocial behaviour, like crime.

4. Comprehensive and balanced reviews of the evidence can be found in F. Stewart, 'Income distribution and development', Queen Elizabeth House Working Paper, no. 37, University of Oxford, March 2000; downloadable from: http://www3.qeh.ox.ac.uk/pdf/qehwp/qehwps37.pdf, and in B. Milanovic, *The Haves and the Have-Nots* (New York: Basic Books, 2011).

5. Other indexes include the Theil Index, the Hoover Index and the Atkinson Index.

6. It is named after the early twentieth-century American economist Max Lorenz.

7. See G. Palma, 'Homogeneous middles vs. heterogeneous tails, and the end of the "Inverted-U": The share of the rich is what it's all about', Cambridge Working Papers in Economics (CWPE) 1111, Faculty of Economics, University of Cambridge, January 2011; downloadable from: http://www.dspace.cam.ac.uk/bitstream/1810/241870/1/cwpe1111.pdf).

8. For a detailed discussion of these points, see A. Cobham and A. Sumner, 'Putting the Gini back in the bottle?: "The Palma" as a policy-relevant measure of inequality', mimeo, King's International Development Institute, King's College London, March 2013; downloadable from: http://www.kcl.ac.uk/aboutkings/worldwide/initiatives/global/intdev/people/Sumner/Cobham-Sumner-15March2013.pdf. A user-friendly visual explanation can be found at: http://www.washingtonpost.com/blogs/worldviews/wp/2013/09/27/map-how-the-worlds-countries-compare-on-income-inequality-the-u-s-ranks-below-nigeria/.

9. See OECD, *Divided We Stand: Why Inequality Keeps Rising* (Paris: Organization for Economic Cooperation and Development, 2011), and ILO, *World of Work 2012* (Geneva: International Labour Organization, 2012).

10. The following Gini coefficients are for 2010 from ILO, *World of Work 2012*, p. 15, figure 1.9. Figures for Botswana and Namibia are from older sources.

11. Interestingly, the dividing line here is similar to what some of the friendly critics of *The Spirit Level* use when they say that inequality produces negative social outcomes in countries above a certain level of inequality.

12. UNCTAD, *Trade and Development Report 2012* (Geneva: United Nations Conference on Trade and Development, 2012), Chapter 3, p. 66, chart 3.6. The fifteen countries studied were Australia, Canada, Chile, China, Germany, India, Indonesia, Italy, Japan, (South) Korea, New Zealand, Norway, Thailand, the UK and the US. The data used ranged from 1988 for Korea to 2008 for the UK, showing the difficulty of getting information on wealth distribution.

13. Their income Ginis were below 0.3, but their wealth Ginis were over 0.7. Their wealth Ginis were higher than those of some countries with much higher income inequality, such as Thailand (just over 0.6 wealth Gini; income Gini over 0.5) or China (wealth Gini around 0.55; income Gini close to 0.5).

14. Detailed information is provided by ibid., especially Chapter 3.

15. A. Atkinson, T. Piketty and E. Saez, 'Top incomes in the long run of history', *Journal of Economic Literature*, vol. 49, no. 1 (2011), p. 7, figure 2.

16. Ibid., p. 8, figure 3.

17. F. Bourguignon and C. Morrisson, 'The size distribution of income among world citizens, 1820–1990', *American Economic Review*, vol. 92, no. 4 (2002).

18. UNCTAD, *Trade and Development Report 2012*. But see Milanovic, *The Haves and the Have-Nots*, Chapter 3, for a more cautious interpretation of the data.

CHAPTER 10: I'VE KNOWN A FEW PEOPLE WHO'VE WORKED: WORK AND UNEMPLOYMENT

1. J. Garraty and M. Carnes, *The American Nation: A History of the United States*, 10th edition (New York: Addison Wesley Longman, 2000), p. 607.

2. The ILO does not provide national breakdowns for forced labour due to the data quality problem.

3. There are different sources for working hours, but I use the ILO data because they are the most comprehensive. For the rich countries, I sometimes use the OECD data, when the ILO data are not available.

4. The hours are 1,382 hours for the Netherlands, 1,406 hours for Germany, 1,421 hours for Norway and 1,482 hours for France.

5. The hours are 2,090 hours for Korea, 2,039 hours for Greece, 1,787 hours for the US and 1,772 hours for Italy.

6. Korea actually had the longest working hours in the OECD (including Mexico) until 2007.

7. For further discussions, see Chang, *Bad Samaritans*, Chapter 9 ('Lazy Japanese and thieving Germans'), and H.-J. Chang, *23 Things They Don't Tell You about Capitalism* (London: Allen Lane, 2010), 'Thing 3' (Chapter 3).

8. According to the International Social Survey Programme, run by a consortium of research institutes in the US, the UK, Germany and Australia, workers from rich countries value security more highly than any other attribute of a job (e.g., wage, interestingness, usefulness for society).

9. The so-called active labour market programmes (ALMPs) in Sweden and Finland have vastly reduced such problems by retraining unemployed workers and helping them establish and follow through a re-employment strategy. See Basu and Stuckler, *The Body Economic*, Chapter 7.

10. In many poor countries, a lot of children below the threshold age work. Their employment is often not recognized in the official employment/unemployment statistics.

11. In order to deal with the difficulties created by discouraged workers, economists sometimes look at the **labour force participation rate**, which is the share of the economically active population (the employed *and* the officially unemployed) in the working-age population. A sudden fall in that rate is likely to indicate that there has been an increase in the number of discouraged workers, who are not counted as unemployed any more.

CHAPTER 11: LEVIATHAN OR THE PHILOSOPHER KING?: THE ROLE OF THE STATE

1. Some economists, including myself, go even further and argue that, in industries that require large capital investments for productivity growth (e.g., steel, automobile), 'anti-competitive' arrangements among oligopolistic firms – such as cartels – can be socially useful. In such industries, unfettered price competition reduces profit margins of the firms to the extent that it reduces their ability to invest, harming their long-term growth. When such competition leads to bankruptcy of certain firms, the machines and the workers deployed in them may be lost to the society, as they cannot be easily deployed in other industries. For example, see H.-J. Chang, *The Political Economy of Industrial Policy* (Basingstoke: Macmillan Press, 1994), Chapter 3, and A. Amsden and A. Singh, 'The optimal degree of competition and dynamic efficiency in Japan and Korea', *European Economic Review*, vol. 38, nos. 3/4 (1994).

2. The holders with a finance background were Donald Regan (January 1981–February 1985), Nicholas Brady (September 1988–January 1993), Lloyd Bentsen (January 1993–December 1994), Robert Rubin (January 1995–July 1999), Henry Paulson (July 2006–January 2009), Tim Geithner (January 2009–January 2013).

3. For information on corruption and other ills of public life in today's rich countries in the past, see Chang, *Kicking Away the Ladder*, Chapter 3, especially pp. 71–81, and Chang, *Bad Samaritans*, Chapter 8.

4. World Bank, *World Development Report 1991* (Washington, DC: The World Bank, 1991), p. 139, table 7.4.

5. The data are from OECD, *Government at a Glance, 2011* (Paris: OECD, 2011).

CHAPTER 12: 'ALL THINGS IN PROLIFIC ABUNDANCE': THE INTERNATIONAL DIMENSION

1. The full text of Emperor Qianlong's letter to George III can be found at: http://www.history .ucsb.edu/faculty/marcuse/classes/2c/texts/1792QianlongLetterGeorgeIII.htm.

2. There are other assumptions underlying HOS whose relaxation also undermines the 'free trade is the best' conclusion, even though I don't discuss them in this chapter. One of these is that of perfect competition (that is, the absence of market power), whose relaxation has generated the so-called 'New Trade Theory', represented by Paul Krugman. Another important assumption is that there are no externalities (see Chapter 4 for a definition of externalities).

3. The Ricardian version assumes that different countries have different productive capabilities but also assumes that these differences cannot be deliberately changed.

4. For a more detailed discussion, see H.-J. Chang and J. Lin, 'Should industrial policy in developing countries conform to comparative advantage or defy it?: A debate between Justin Lin and Ha-Joon Chang', *Development Policy Review*, vol. 27, no. 5 (2009).

5. Trade data in the next few paragraphs are from the World Bank data set, World Development Indicators 2013.

6. The data are from the WTO.

7. United Nations, *International Trade Statistics, 1900–1960* (New York: United Nations, 1962).

8. The number is based on export figures. For the period before the 1980s, there are quite significant gaps in export and import data, so the shares were 50–58 per cent in the 1960s and 54–61 per cent for the 1970s, if we use import figures.

9. As a proportion of overall trade (primary commodities, manufacturing, and services), manufacturing's share rose from 47 per cent in 1980–82 to 63 per cent in 1998–2000 and stood at 55 per cent in 2009–11.

10. The average for 1984–6 was 8.8 per cent. The average for 2009–11 was 27.8 per cent.

11. A more detailed definition is provided by the UNCTAD (United Nations Conference on Trade and Development) at: http://unctad.org/en/Pages/DIAE/Foreign-Direct-Investment-(FDI).aspx.

12. The figures were 63 per cent for Liberia, 50 per cent for Haiti and 42 per cent for Kosovo.

13. All the FDI flow figures cited below are inflow figures. In theory, inflows and outflows of FDI on the world scale should be the same, but the actual data always show discrepancies.

14. Calculation based on World Bank data.

15. See R. Kozul-Wright and P. Rayment, *The Resistible Rise of Market Fundamentalism: Rethinking Development Policy in an Unbalanced World* (London: Zed Books and Third World Network, 2007), Chapter 4, for an excellent review of the evidence.

16. On tax havens, see N. Shaxson, *Treasure Islands: Tax Havens and the Men Who Stole the World* (London: Vintage, 2012), and the website of Tax Justice Network, www.taxjustice.net. At the time of writing (autumn 2013), there has been a lot of talk of a clamp-down on tax havens, especially through the G20, but no concrete action has been taken.

17. Christian Aid, 'The shirts off their backs: how tax policies fleece the poor', September 2005, downloadable from: http://www.christianaid.org.uk/images/the_shirts_off_their_backs.pdf.

18. The story of this debacle is told in full in Chang, *Bad Samaritans*, Chapter 1 ('The Lexus and the Olive Tree revisited').

19. Further discussions of these measures can be found in N. Kumar, 'Performance requirement as tools of development policy: lessons from developed and developing countries', in K. Gallagher (ed.), *Putting Development First* (London: Zed Books, 2005). A more user-friendly discussion can be found in Chang, *Bad Samaritans*, Chapter 4 ('The Finn and the elephant').

20. For discussions on how these rules may be harmful for economic development, see H.-J. Chang and D. Green, *The Northern WTO Agenda on Investment: Do as We Say, Not as We Did* (Geneva: South Centre, and London: CAFOD (Catholic Agency for Overseas Development), 2003), and R. Thrasher and K. Gallagher, '21st century trade agreements: implications for development sovereignty', The Pardee Papers no. 2, The Frederick S. Pardee Center for the Study of the Longer-Range Future, Boston University, September 2008; downloadable from: http://www.ase.tufts.edu/gdae/Pubs/rp/KGPardeePolSpaceSep08.pdf.

21. See Chang and Green, *The Northern WTO Agenda*, for details on the Irish case.

22. The average over a period, rather than figures for particular years, has been used because FDI flows fluctuate a lot year by year.

23. The US got only 15.0 per cent of world FDI despite accounting for 23.1 per cent of world GDP during this period. In the case of France the corresponding numbers were 3.0 per cent against 4.3 per cent, while those for Brazil were 2.8 per cent and 3.0 per cent. In terms of over-represented countries, Belgium and Hong Kong stand out; they got respectively 6 per cent and 4.1 per cent of world FDI despite accounting for only 0.8 per cent and 0.4 per cent of world GDP. The UK (6.8 per cent vs. 4.0 per cent) was also strongly over-represented, followed by China (11.0 per cent vs. 8.5 per cent).

24. They were China, Brazil, Mexico, Russia, India, Hungary, Argentina, Chile, Thailand and Turkey.

25. The statistics available for brownfield FDI (that is, cross-border M&A) and for overall FDI flows are not directly comparable to each other. This is for a number of reasons. One reason is that part of cross-border M&A may be financed locally. Another reason is that payments for cross-border M&A may be made over a period, rather than in a single year.

26. See P. Nolan, J. Zhang and C. Liu, 'The global business revolution, the cascade effect, and the challenge for firms from developing countries', *Cambridge Journal of Economics*, vol. 32, no. 1 (2008).

27. Philippe Legrain, the author of *Immigrants: Your Country Needs Them*, is one of the few free-market economists who seriously advocate highly liberalized (although not completely free) immigration.

28. On the issue of worker rights in immigration, see M. Ruhs, *The Price of Rights: Regulating International Labour Migration* (Princeton: Princeton University Press, 2013).

29. Of course, this is excluding distress-driven immigration, namely, refugees from civil war or natural disaster in a neighbouring country.

30. On the debates surrounding the definition of labour shortage, see M. Ruhs and B. Anderson (eds.), *Who Needs Migrant Workers?: Labour Shortages, Immigration, and Public Policy* (Oxford: Oxford University Press, 2012), Chapter 1.

31. For example, see C. Dustmann and T. Frattini, 'The fiscal effects of immigration to the UK', Discussion Paper no. 22/13 (London: CReAM (Centre for Research and Analysis of Migration), University College London, 2013).

32. For example, see G. Ottaviano and G. Peri, 'Rethinking the gains of immigration on wages', NBER Working Paper no. 12497 (Cambridge, MA: NBER (National Bureau of Economic Research), 2006); downloadable from: http://www.nber.org/papers/w12497.

33. For a comprehensive discussion of the impacts of remittances, see I. Grabel, 'The political economy of remittances: What do we know? What do we need to know?', PERI Working Paper Series, no. 184 (Amherst, MA: PERI (Political Economy Research Institute), University of Massachusetts, 2008); downloadable from: http://www.peri.umass.edu/fileadmin/pdf /working_papers/working_papers_151–200/WP184.pdf).

34. In Mexico, the government used to match the sum of remittances used for those investments with public grants, but the scheme has been discontinued.

35. The data on immigrant stock in this and following paragraphs are from the World Bank's World Development Indicators database.

36. The remittances data in this and following paragraphs are based on the World Bank's Migration and Remittances Statistics.

EPILOGUE: WHAT NOW?: HOW CAN WE USE ECONOMICS TO MAKE OUR ECONOMY BETTER?

1. J. W. von Goethe, *Sämtliche Werke*, Part 1: *Maximen und Reflexionen, Schriften zur Naturwissenschaft*, Jubiläumsausgabe xxxix, 72, as cited in A. Gerschenkron, *Continuity in History and Other Essays* (Cambridge, MA: Harvard University Press, 1968), Chapter 2, p. 43.
2. Theodore Porter, the eminent historian of science, argues that even many scientific numbers are constructed in response to political and social pressures. See his book *Trust in Numbers: The Pursuit of Objectivity in Science and Public Life* (Princeton: Princeton University Press, 1995).
3. I thank Deirdre McCloskey for pointing me to this quote.

Index

T ────────────────

U ────────────────